And What Th

Born in Portsmouth, England in January 1923, Steve Masters joined the RAF in October 1941 at the age of 17½ and began training as a navigator qualifying in 1943. He eventually joined 7 Squadron, a Pathfinder Squadron at the time, based at RAF Oakington in Cambridgeshire. On the crew's 24th mission on the night of 15th/16th June 1944, their Lancaster Bomber was shot down over Arras in France. Following several days of evasion, Steve and Nat (Wireless Operator) were captured by the Germans and then interrogated by the Gestapo. After several weeks they began their journey to Stalag Luft VII POW camp in Upper Silesia (now part of Poland).

Steve's story details the rigours of life in Luft VII, which for him lasted around 5 months until the Russians began advancing. The camp was eventually abandoned to the Russians with the prisoners evacuated by the Germans. They set off on a gruelling 21 day forced march, which culminated in a squalid train journey in the depths of a European winter, arriving at Stalag IIIA at Luckenwalde, just south of Berlin. The conditions at this prison camp were far worse than he had previously endured. After several more tense and dangerous months, Steve was repatriated following the end of the war in Europe.

This is an aptly named page-turner of a book. Steve cleverly paints a clear picture of what happened to him and so many other prisoners of war. He remembers details which enrich and enhance the reader's experience, without ever being over-dramatic or sensationalist, whilst creating atmosphere from the start.

In memory of our father Steve Masters and the crew who served with him, some of whom made the ultimate sacrifice in the 1939 – 1945 World War II.

Pat Jones (nee Masters) and Alan Masters

All royalties from the sale of this book will be donated to the RAF Benevolent Fund.

First published in Kindle format 2nd May 2020

This edition published August 2020

Acknowledgements.

Many thanks to Pat Jones, Pete Masters and Phil Jones for their assistance with proof reading and to Roger Leboff for producing the front cover. Many thanks also to the rest of our relatives for their encouragement to get this book published which was my father's wish during his lifetime. Particular thanks go to Doug Masters, Steve's brother for his input to "About the author" section at the end of this book.

Alan Masters.

And What Happened Then?

A POW's story by Steve Masters

FOREWORD

This is not a story about war, rather a story of survival during a war. It is not intended to glamorise or over dramatise the situation, but simply report things as I saw them. It is the story of what happened to me after being shot down in Europe on the night of the 15th June 1944. It is also a story which belongs not only to me, but to thousands like me. In it I have tried to describe how I felt and what I did as an individual, but a large part of it involves several hundred others who shared my experience.

The original purpose of writing, was purely to keep my mind occupied, and it was never anticipated that anyone but myself would read it. Once having started however, I thought it would be a good idea to put down all I could remember, so that should I survive, I would be able to tell others what actually happened.

The first stage, which lasted a few weeks, was quite eventful and reported on in detail. When the situation developed into a dull routine, I stopped writing, as I was sure that I would have no problem in recalling it. By the time things began to happen again, it was too late and too difficult to do more than make simple notes of events.

There were many happenings which I did not record, as a result, they were not included in the story as they were either forgotten completely, or so hazy that it would be almost pure fiction.

It has been my aim to record only what I know to be fact from personal observation, or stories I was told which I believed to be true. Conversations which I was involved in have been described as I remember them. Some of these are very vivid in my memory, even to the exact wording used. Events which I have described, may not have occurred in the precise sequence as I have written them, as at times, things were chaotic and difficult to follow. These events did occur and even if they happened on another day, it makes little difference to the story and its outcome.

There were incidents which occurred that I would rather omit, as they were stories concerning others. Some of the tales are so painful that it would be unfair to remind those who were involved in such incidents. If they wish to tell the story, they will do so perhaps.

The crew who were with me on the day this story started, were my regular crew. We had first met at No 12 Operational Training Unit Chipping Warden, in August 1943 except for the Flight Engineer who joined us at Waterbeach Stirling Heavy Conversion Unit in October 1943. On completion of our training, we reported to 622 Squadron at Mildenhall, in late November 1943.

After ten operational sorties, we were selected for training as a Pathfinder crew. Following a short course at Warboys, we were then posted to No 7 Squadron (PFF) Oakington in April 1944. The sortie which proved to be our last, was our twenty-fourth operational flight, barely half way through our tour. The aircraft, for those who may be interested, was Lancaster MGF which finally crashed into Arras. The crew of which I was the Navigator were:-

Alan Grant	Pilot	Royal Australian Air Force
Steve Masters	Navigator	Royal Air Force
Richard Martin (Speed)	Bomb Aimer	Royal Canadian Air Force
Sydney Nathanson (Nat)	Wireless Operator	Royal Air Force
Ron Neills	Flight Engineer	Royal Air Force
Tom Barrett	Mid Upper Gunner	Royal Air Force
Bill Newton	Rear Gunner	Royal Air Force

It was fortunate that I met up with Nat the Wireless Operator shortly after our untimely arrival in France, but we didn't see Ron the Engineer for almost a month. At that stage, we had no knowledge of the fate of the rest of our crew and had to wait until the end of the war to find out.

There were many things which were to happen to us before that day came, a few anticipated, but many were not. Some of the situations we encountered were not always fully understood or appreciated at the time. It was only by referring to war histories written some time later, that things became apparent.

History books are of necessity, cold and factual, reporting

such things as tactics involved, numbers of men in the field or places captured. There is little written about the ordinary men and women, how they felt, as that of course is not history. The story I have presented, along with accounts written by contemporaries, may reveal a little of what was behind those official reports and the clinical analysis of historians. It was just one small part of the events in the 1939-45 World War.

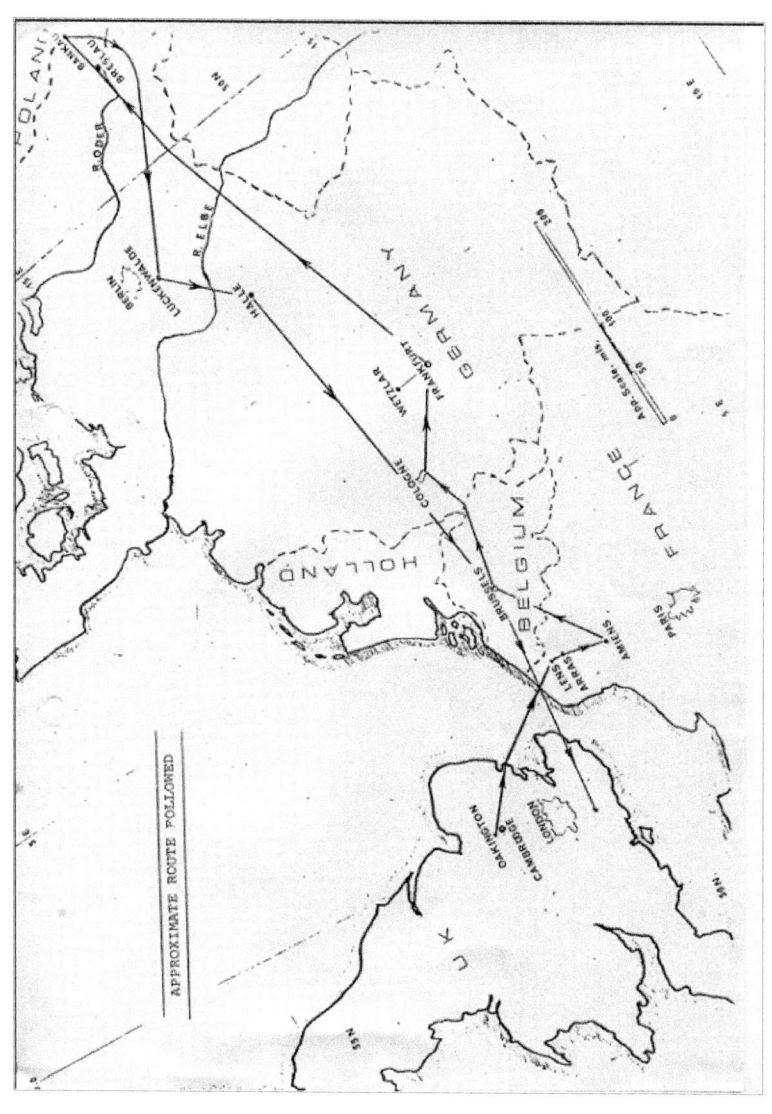

CHAPTER 1

The following is an attempt to record my experience from the time I was shot down until my return to England. The title I have used was inspired by comments made to me when people knowing this, would so often ask: 'and what happened then?'

The day prior to our fateful sortie was unusual in several ways and a departure from our normal routine. Dorothy who was on sick-leave had been with me for a fortnight and had just left on the mid-day train. By chance I remembered that I should inform the authorities that my next of kin (my wife) was now returning to her normal address in Portsmouth. The next unusual thing was the visit we made to a Bomber Squadron in Lincoln, to see if there was any news of our wireless Operator's brother missing on a Berlin raid nine weeks earlier. Unfortunately there was nothing to report and we were a slightly saddened crew as we flew back to base.

On our return, we were asked to assemble for a squadron photograph, which was most disturbing as many aircrew were very superstitious about this. It was claimed that the crew or crews photographed were likely to be shot down. This may have been on the skipper's mind when he said to me, 'I wonder who will be the first to go from this photograph?' little realising it would be us. During briefing later that day, no one mentioned the photograph or gave any indication of being more concerned than usual.

Some crews used to have premonitions about their fate, but if any of our crew members had such ideas, it did not become apparent. Our target that night of 15th June 1944 was a marshalling yard at Lens on the Belgian Border where, as I discovered later, a big stock of V1 flying bombs were being transported to the launching sites. This was our twenty-fourth operational flight and a short range one, so hopefully we would be home again soon.

As far as I can remember the Master Bomber had called us down from our original height to about eight thousand feet to assist in greater bombing accuracy. We had just dropped our bombs three minutes earlier and were heading away from the target. As was usual for the target area we were under some anti-aircraft fire with a few searchlights in our vicinity, if not actually on us. Suddenly there was a deafening bang and we dropped quite violently to port. Strangely enough I had the feeling that this was the end for us, as my mind instantly went back to a film I had seen a few weeks earlier where a bomber, when shot down, had responded in the same way.

We seemed to drop some distance before the aircraft was brought on to an even keel. Almost immediately the rear gunner called: 'Corkscrew port', and down we went again in a violent descent to port. By this time both gunners were firing almost continuously but when we should have rolled and climbed to starboard we seemed to wallow, then the skipper reported that it wouldn't respond to the flying controls. 'Down port', shouted the rear gunner again, continuing to fire. We did not know what type of fighter was after us, but we knew he was still there.

Suddenly the rear gunner called: 'Bale out, we have had it', and was immediately backed up by the mid upper gunner telling us we were on fire.

Despite my earlier feelings I didn't want to believe this was actually happening, so looked out of the astrodome to see what was going on. One quick glance was enough to convince me that we could not stay, as it seemed that both wings were on fire and the thought of two thousand gallons of petrol in our tanks, left no doubt in my mind. As I turned to go forward, I saw Ron come up from the bombing position to shut down No 3 engine as Alan the skipper had reported it on fire. When he reached up to do so, I saw Alan knock his hand down from the 'Fire Button'. He then gave the order to get out fast, at the same time closing all four throttles to reduce our speed. Determined now to get out, I moved from the astrodome, grabbed my parachute which I put on, climbed over my seat and moved forward.

As I approached the hatch, my intercom lead which was still plugged in, brought me to an abrupt halt. I tried to pull my helmet over my head but the new type I was wearing had the headphone leads at the back, which resulted in me being entangled with the lead. Pull as I might I could not free it and had to work my way back to my table to disconnect the plug. This was very difficult to do as the aircraft was starting to descend rapidly.

Subconsciously I noted the indicated speed, it was 320 knots and rising, so it was more important than ever to get out quickly. To reassure myself I checked that my parachute was on properly but to my horror, discovered that the rip-cord was on the left hand side. Stories came to mind of people who had done just this, then clawed through their parachutes with their right hand, looking for the rip-cord. I was determined not to make this error so grabbed it with my left hand, with no intention of letting go. It was probably still in my hand when I landed.

I realised we must be fairly close to the ground and I had visions of being seriously injured through the chute not opening properly. In that brief moment my thoughts were very active, should I bale out or should I stay with the plane and be killed instantly, it would save me so much trouble. I even considered pushing past the other crew members so that I could get right up in the nose to make sure I didn't survive. In less time than it takes to record, my mind was clear again and I realised I had to try to save my life.

Crouched as I was on the step behind Speed, our Bomb Aimer, I saw Ron struggling to get the hatch free. This was a very bad moment as it had jammed and every second the nose was dropping further and further. The speed was mounting rapidly and the scream of the diving plane was rising to a crescendo blotting out all other sounds except our guns which were still firing. This was becoming a nightmare as our chances of escaping from the plane were diminishing very rapidly indeed. Suddenly the hatch was gone, followed quickly by Ron and Speed, then it was my turn. My heart was in my mouth as I followed almost immediately, but not before I noticed the glow of fire outside the hatch. The last thing I remembered was tucking my head in and making a dive, but for some reason I lost consciousness and did not regain it until some time after I had landed.

As far as I can estimate I was out for about half an hour which I think was as well because I did not hear the other planes going home. I awoke to a feeling of loneliness and disappointment as I imagined that I could not have been very far from home when it happened and now I was absolutely cut off, for some time at least. My first real concern was for my bacon and eggs I was going to miss that night, which seemed of utmost importance to me at that moment. I could see it sitting on the mess table waiting for me, would someone else be eating it, if not what would become of it? Gradually the seriousness of the situation started to filter through to me as I began to realise that my back, head and legs were hurting; breathing was difficult also very painful. Despite these pains, I was satisfied that I had suffered no real injuries.

I was in no mood or condition to move at first, but just lay there trying to think, it was hard to do so, as my mind was completely dazed. I remembered I had baled out, but how where and when was beyond me for a while. As a result of this, I didn't know where I had landed, in fact I didn't even know which country I was in. I thought I was in France but wracked my brains trying to remember where our target had been, as this would have helped. I took out my pocket compass to try to orientate myself and determine where the coast should be but this only showed me its direction, I still had to determine my location.

All this time I had not even considered where I was lying, so it came as something of a shock to find myself on a roof with my parachute spread all over the place. More or less automatically I remembered instructions to hide my equipment and move away as quickly as possible if an attempt at escape were to be made.

I slowly gathered the parachute into my arms then realised I was all tangled up in my rigging lines and had to use my knife to cut myself free. Not until I had done this was I able to remove my harness and Mae West and look for a place to conceal it. Then came a bad moment, I heard what I imagined to be a patrol coming and looking down, saw some soldiers approaching with torches in their hands. They did not appear to be looking for me, but all the same I was worried as I was lying fairly close to the edge of the roof with yards and yards of white parachute in my arms. Quickly I covered it with my body, then lay still offering up a silent prayer that they would not see me. After twenty minutes I thought it safe to move, so wrapped the whole lot in my Mae West and stuffed it as flat as possible in a wide guttering. There was no other convenient place of concealment and I realised that if I was to leave the roof, I couldn't take it with me.

I estimated I was about thirty feet above ground and from what I could see there was no way down. To my left at a distance of about forty feet, I noticed a covered walkway which connected the building whose roof I was on, with another similar building the other side of some railway lines. I was apparently in a railway goods yard or industrial complex. Having made sure that my dumped kit was reasonably secure I started to crawl across the roof towards the walkway. Not an easy task, as even though it wasn't very steep it was constructed of corrugated asbestos or something similar.

I had lost one of my flying boots during the parachute descent and wished I had lost the other, because every time I moved, the zip on the front made a scraping noise which I was sure would alert the soldiers. I could stand it no longer and removed the boot, which presented another problem as now I had to crawl and maintain my balance with the boot in my hand. At last I reached the walkway where I thankfully stuffed the offending item, down behind a girder. I realised that it would only be a matter of time before my equipment was discovered, which I hoped wouldn't be too soon. My task now was to find a way to the ground and in doing so I scrambled over many roof tops as I crossed and re-crossed what must have been quite a large factory or warehouse. This developed into a depressing situation, as several times I thought I saw a way to the ground only to discover I was mistaken. It was raining hard, I was pretty well soaked to the skin and my socks were full of oozing mud as the gutters had not been cleared out for a long time.

Walking between two roofs I decided to travel right to the end and see what was there. I was surprised to find a tall chimney just across an alleyway and almost directly opposite where I was standing. There was a platform round the chimney which was only fifteen feet below me. From this platform was the very thing I was looking for, a ladder down to the ground. Could I jump this I wondered, as the gap was only about twenty feet across. Right on the moment of jumping, common sense prevailed as I realised what the consequences would be if I missed.

Reluctantly I retraced my steps across the roof tops only to discover what looked like a large shed. It was difficult to see exactly what it was in the dark but at the far end there was a faint glow which intrigued me. I now convinced myself that this was a station and I was on a high level platform similar to the one in Portsmouth Town station. The faint glow I could see at the end was the main exit. I edged forward into the darkened building and saw a handrail which I grabbed for support, then discovered a second rail on the other side of me, I was on a catwalk. If this was the case, then it was not a station, but as the light attracted me I had to keep going.

I was in for another surprise, part of the rail was missing but by inching forward carefully I found the rail again, only to discover that planks in the floor were missing. It was rather like a dream sequence, but this was no dream, this was real and rather dangerous. I had no idea what I would come across, or what was below me. I had no intention of turning back, even though it seemed a very long way to the light patch, I had to keep inching my way forward. It was obviously an exit I could see, but why the catwalk, which was proving to be in a very poor state of repair?

After what seemed an eternity I felt a solid floor beneath my feet, I had arrived. As I was now in danger of being caught in the open I decided that I would make my getaway as soon as possible. I stepped quietly to where the steps should be, ….. there were none, only railings, they were all round the platform and it was with a sick feeling I realised I was on a warehouse loading platform. I didn't need to look over the railings to confirm that I was a long way up, about sixty feet I estimated. It may not have been quite as high but whatever the case, there was no way down.

I could see no alternative, I had to risk that catwalk again without the benefit of the glow of light to guide me. At last I returned to my starting point in search of another way out and it was not until I came to a second open platform with railings, that I regained hope. Two vertical girders about four feet apart were within my reach and I knew that if I could wedge myself between them, I could work my way down in the manner used by mountain climbers. I got over the rail and hanging on to the top bar for safety, pressed my back against one girder with the intention of wedging myself between the two, by pressing my knees against the other. It was then I realised just how seriously my back was hurt as the pressure brought an excruciating pain. I knew I was defeated and had to get back over the rail again.

By this time I had really lost heart, I was trapped, so crawling in under the eaves of a skylight I settled down to wait for daylight and surrender. This gave little shelter from the rain, but it was too much effort to go back to a more comfortable spot I had seen earlier. There was one consolation, the cigarette I lit was kept dry by this small shelter and I was able to chew some spearmint from my escape pack. What puzzled me was the fact that I had made quite a noise on the roof, particularly when I accidentally dropped the plastic escape pack cover which had clattered quite a long way before it came to rest. Nobody had come to investigate even though people were working below, which was obvious as lights were showing through the glass roof panels near me, also I could hear voices and footsteps.

CHAPTER 2

About four in the morning as it began to get light, I took stock of my surroundings and what I thought was a road I had been looking down on, turned out to be a roof which was screening me from observation. When I realised how things had turned out, I decided to make another attempt at finding my way down to the ground, although I was rather doubtful about my chances of escape in daylight. I was faced with the prospect of descending into what was obviously a populated working area, at the same time avoiding detection.

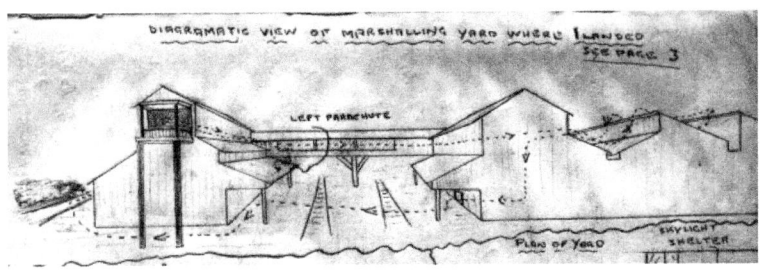

My chances were rather slim but action was better than simply waiting for capture and even though I was still very dazed and bemused, I was able to face the existing situation sensibly. I had no definite plan as to which direction to take, but decided to try to find my original starting place. This was a stroke of fortune as to my great relief, I found a ladder which I must have passed very close to in the dark. With extreme caution I descended, expecting to meet someone at any moment, but all I found were further ladders which eventually led me to the ground. This was a very tense moment as I knew people were about and I only hoped they were not working in that area. If I was going to get away I would have to break out of cover eventually. From where I stood, I could see a road and I felt that if only I could reach it I would be able to find a proper hiding place during daylight hours. My first task was to cross the railway lines, which would leave me exposed for longer than I would have liked, but I had to face it.

As quickly as possible I gained the shelter of a shed opposite, ripped off my tapes and brevet with my sheath knife then put them in my wallet. I was to regret this action later, but at the time it seemed to be a sensible thing to do. After I had covered up what I considered to be most conspicuous, I made for the road the other side of the building.

Once out on the road I not only felt very alone, I knew that I was likely to be instantly recognised as a stranger. There was a strong desire to approach the first house I might come to in the hope of getting help but on consideration, I wondered why anyone should offer me assistance, as not only was I dirty and unkempt, I was a stranger and a dangerous one at that.

Another factor to consider was the proximity of my parachute which was likely to be discovered at any time. It was still raining hard and I was walking shoeless, which in itself would have aroused suspicion, without considering the way I was dressed. Apart from being hatless and without shoes, I had no topcoat as protection from the rain. In addition I was wearing a fisherman's white jersey under RAF blue battledress, I might have been less noticeable in a fishing port but unfortunately I was a long way from one. I was dressed too well to be a tramp and I was unlikely to be mistaken for a Frenchman going about his lawful business. For the reason of my appearance alone, it was essential to get under cover as quickly as possible but it was also highly desirable to get away as far as I could from my original landing place.

Because of the early hour, it was not fully light and the road seemed to be deserted, which helped restore my confidence. I was feeling reasonably happy with my progress, until I reached a group of houses where I saw two people walking towards me. There was no place to hide and no way of avoiding them. I thought that this was the end for me until I noticed that they were working men, presumably just starting on an early shift.

I wasn't sure how they would treat me but decided to chance it and tell them who I was. They were surprised to say the least of it as our meeting was quite an unexpected event for them. After they had recovered from the initial shock, they seemed very pleased to have met me and gripped my hands in a way that appeared to be thanking me for something. Despite our language difficulties, we understood each other very well by using sign language. There was little they could do in the way of practical help, but pointed me in the direction I had already been taking, so I assumed that at least I was not walking into immediate danger. Thanking them, I walked on, hoping that I would not meet any Germans or antagonistic French people who would give me away.

Shortly after leaving them I heard a car coming so decided to take cover in a cornfield until it was well out of sight. My next problem was a house standing at a crossroads which was obviously occupied by Germans so wishing to avoid the risk of discovery I turned into the road which gave me the best cover available. This diversion from my intended route, proved to be the hand of providence taking control of my situation. It wasn't until I had walked down this road a little way, that I noticed a lonely house, which struck me as being a very suitable place to make for. Even if I could get no help, at least I might be able to hide during daylight hours.

Just about twenty yards from the house, my attention was drawn by someone hissing and waving violently, so before this should be noticed by anyone else, I sprinted for the porch of an outhouse. From this position of greater security, I worked my way round, until I got near to the person who was calling me.

I was feeling very dazed and my eyes would not focus properly, which I assumed was due to the knocking about I had received on landing. As a result, the first impression I gained of my would-be helper was a woman wearing a dust cap, but what I couldn't understand, she was wearing the uniform of a Flight Sergeant Wireless Operator and she knew my name. Gradually I got the idea that the face was familiar, in fact just like our own Wireless Operator, then it dawned on me that it was him.

This may not have been surprising at a distance but I was only ten feet from him. I hesitated for a few seconds before climbing the short ladder he pushed down to me. I could not help it as the thought crossed my mind that it was a trap and the person facing me was not Nat after all, with great insistence he urged me to climb up and join him, still calling me by name. This convinced me that somehow, he really knew me, then in a flash, my mind cleared enough to really recognise him. It was a tremendous relief to see him as at least one other crew member was alive.

Once up the ladder and the door closed behind me, we almost fell on each other in our welcome. The whole thing seemed like a bad dream but knowing that it was real, we had to settle down quickly to reality and decide on our future action. After a brief exchange of our recent experiences, we took stock of our situation. Fortunately neither of us had been injured in any way, only knocked about a bit, for which we were very thankful. Nat had gashed his head on landing but not seriously and now that the bleeding had stopped, he was able to remove the cloth he had used as a bandage. It was this which had made me think he had been wearing a dust cap. As he had spent a good part of the night in our present hiding place, he was now able to tell me something about it.

The building we were in was a small tool shed six feet off the ground and was in the garden of the house I had been making for when he saw me. It was now about half past five and people were beginning to stir in the house, so we discussed whether we should hide where we were, or approach the owners to see if they would give us help. This point was soon settled for us, as about ten minutes later, we looked through a gap in the wall and saw two German soldiers carrying a few pieces of equipment belonging to an aircraft. We did not attach very much importance to this at first, but when we saw Frenchmen examining a piece of engine about a hundred feet from our hiding place, we felt justified in assuming it came from our own crashed aircraft.

Obviously time for us to move, as the area was liable to be searched thoroughly. It was decided to go to the house as we were in need of food and a place to hide. The latter was perhaps of prime importance as we were in a very tight corner and liable to be discovered at any time.

We were about to leave, when Nat found some old discarded shoes under a pile of tools, so after a hurried search, I was equipped with footwear of a sort. One shoe was black the other brown and neither of them fitted very well, nor were they in their prime but at least I was better equipped for walking.

When we thought the coast was clear, we opened the door and lowered the ladder carefully, trying not to attract attention to ourselves by making any noise. As quickly as possible we got down the ladder and ran for the house, half expecting to be challenged by someone. We entered by the front door which was open and looked for signs of life. Moving through the house, we came upon a Frenchman sitting in his dining room and what a shock he had. This was not too surprising as he was being confronted by two dirty blood stained foreigners in his own house.

By the use of sign language, we told him who and what we were, also that we required assistance. This excited him no end as first he called his wife, then the rest of the family, who proceeded to argue violently. We were made to sit on the floor, to keep out of sight of German soldiers who were patrolling the railway line, just outside the house. It was apparent that they were very frightened and could do nothing for us, so we agreed to clear out.

To leave the house in broad daylight was a very tricky situation, as first we had to cross the railway by the level crossing just outside, but what was to be our next move? While we were contemplating this, we noticed that Germans were patrolling the line every few minutes and despite the increasing agitation of the family, we waited for our moment.

At last it was clear and rushing like maniacs we ran over the crossing and down the road into a cornfield. Urging Nat to follow my example, I dived as far as I could into the corn, clearing the edge so as not to break it down. Any broken corn would have really given us away. We laid still for a while but there was no sign of pursuit. It was this first close contact with the enemy, that turned them into real people. For years I had heard about them, read about them and seen their pictures but this was realism. It was rather like meeting a celebrity in person, but with sinister implications.

It was obvious to us that although there weren't many people about at that time, we would be discovered later in the day, so we struck straight across the cornfields, putting a good distance between ourselves and the railway, then commenced to look for a hideout. Without warning we came from behind a large building out on to a road, which ran through a small village. There was no retreat as we had been seen by some Frenchmen, so we put on a bold face and continued.

As we walked through the village, it seemed to me that there was an air of agitation present. People were standing in groups talking to each other as though something had just happened, or was about to happen. We received very strange looks and once or twice, I thought that someone was on the point of approaching us to maybe enquire who we were, as it was obvious we did not belong in that area. I don't know what they were discussing but whatever it was, we felt decidedly uneasy and concluded that we would not get the help we were hoping for.

We had not gone very far when a coach passed very close to us and to my horror, realised it was full of girls and Germans in uniform. Despite the fact that we were within feet of them and they were staring directly at us, not one seemed to regard us with suspicion. To me their looks were either, idle curiosity, disdainful, or just disinterested. The coach continued on its way, so preventing the occupants from having a better look at us, for which we were truly thankful.

We crossed the road with the intention of continuing in the same direction, when suddenly a German officer came out of a building only yards in front of us. There was little we could do except behave as though we had every right to be there. He gave us a momentary glance, turned on his heel, then walked away ahead of us. Fortunately we did not have to follow him for very long as we came to a narrow lane which we turned into. We didn't know where it would lead us neither did we care as we had felt very exposed walking down the road as we had been, now at least we had some cover.

After walking for a few minutes under cover of the bordering hedges, we once again came out into open country, which apart from a few isolated herds of cattle, seemed deserted.

We had no choice but to carry on, as if we turned back we were likely to meet trouble again. Pulling out my pocket compass I decided that the best heading would be South West as I wanted to keep approximately parallel to the coast but a few miles inland.

By now I had a rough idea of the area we were in and I only hoped I was right. I had often been told, but never realised until then, just how difficult it was to walk across open country in a straight line. Anyone watching us must have thought it strange as we followed a very erratic course in our progress across the fields.

After walking for some time, we came across a most unwelcome sight, as just off to our right was a flak tower which we would have to pass. Fortunately there was a large wood ahead of us that would give cover once we could get to it, but how to do so without arousing suspicion was a problem. We agreed that we should make a slight detour as this would reduce the time we were likely to be seen from the tower, even though it meant further to walk. I estimated we would be in full view for about five minutes and what a long five minutes that turned out to be. At any time I was expecting to hear rifle fire, or see soldiers approaching us, which tended to put us on edge.

Finally we passed out of sight of the tower and nobody had challenged us. We decided to skirt the woods rather than enter them although we were ready to dive in quickly if necessary. When we left the cover of the woods, it was with some relief that we saw another village not so very far away. This time, with a little more care, we could make our approach without being noticed. Our ideas had changed somewhat as we were now more anxious to find a place to sleep than we were to try to get help.

Creeping along a wall which bounded the local gardens and barnyards, we came to a big double steel door, which on closer inspection proved to be the very thing we had been looking for, the entrance to a hay loft. The problem now was to open the door quickly and get inside before we were spotted. This was managed by jamming a stick between the two doors and levering them open, wide enough for us to squeeze through. Every time we pushed the doors, which were on rusty rollers, they squeaked so loudly that it seemed we were bound to be discovered. Strangely no one heard us, or if they did, gave no indication of doing so.

Once inside, we created more havoc, as we disturbed the chickens which were running in and out of the yard. Finding a ladder propped against a wall, we climbed to the top of the rick which was about fifteen feet high, then prepared ourselves for sleep. As a precaution, we built a wall of straw around ourselves, so as to be hidden from view should anyone climb the ladder. Before I slept, I removed my socks which were still soaking wet from the roof escapade and buried them in the straw hoping they would dry.

Although I was desperately tired, I found it very difficult to sleep as my mind was quite active. In the past eight hours, a lot had happened, I had been shot down, found myself trapped on a roof, met my enemy face to face and walked for several miles across occupied territory. That was now in the past and I wondered what lay in the future.

I settled down in the hope that sleep would overtake me, as we expected to spend something like fourteen hours in the rick before we could move again. The time was about eight o' clock in the morning according to our watches, not that it mattered very much, as we were no longer governed by time, only our needs.

I had been asleep about three hours when we were roused by the sound of voices in the yard below, which I felt sure was going to lead to our discovery. It would have been a help to us to understand what they were saying as perhaps we had no cause for concern. Just as I was wondering what action to take should they climb the ladder, the local air raid sirens sounded. Almost immediately the group left our vicinity presumably to take cover.

Not long after the sirens sounded, we heard the bombers approaching and they seemed to be coming directly for us. Without doubt they were Flying Fortresses and when they started bombing we were of the opinion that the village or something close by was the target. None of the bombs came very close, but the whole place shook like a leaf and so did I. By the feel and noise of the raid it was a very large one, which didn't help my nerves very much as I was still shaken from our own recent event.

At last the bombers left which gave us a chance to settle down again in the hope we could sleep. As we were both feeling hungry, Nat produced a tube of condensed milk from his escape pack and we took just enough to give us a taste in our mouths. This must have helped us, as we soon fell asleep again.

CHAPTER 3

When darkness finally fell, we heard the farmer walking around closing up for the night, which made me think that we were locked in the barn. Our first concern though was getting to the ground again, which wasn't going to be as easy as it had been climbing up. Being very patient, we stayed where we were until we thought that the people in the farmhouse had settled down, while we waited, we found our socks and put them on. This was a most unpleasant experience, as not only were they as wet as ever, they were also very cold. This didn't bother us for very long, as we soon had more important things to think about.

After making a final check to ensure that nothing was left behind, we attempted the descent. It was now quite dark but fortunately the ladder was exactly where we had left it. Just to counteract this good fortune, we discovered that the ladder would not stay upright without support at the bottom. Jumping down was out of the question as we were unable to see what was below and the thought of landing on a pitchfork was a little daunting. While I was fooling about trying to balance the ladder, Nat crossed the rick looking for another way down, he found one, the quickest way, he fell off. Fortunately for him, he landed on a pile of straw, but I was not aware of this, all I knew he had disappeared. Suddenly I heard his voice from below which was quite a relief and while he held the ladder, I climbed down.

As we had suspected, the doors we had entered by were now firmly locked, which meant going through the farmyard, unless of course those doors were locked as well. Fortunately for us these opened easily but before we ventured out - we surveyed the situation. The yard itself was fairly large but directly opposite us was a gateway to the outside world. To our right, stood what we took to be a farmhouse and just outside the front door, we could just make out the shape of a water pump. This really was a blessing as we were very thirsty indeed, having had nothing to drink for several hours. We didn't care for its proximity to the house but we had to have water.

As quietly as possible, we crept up to the pump and started to fill our water bottles. No matter how careful we were, the pump groaned and rattled every time we operated the handle. Having filled our bottles, we turned to make for the gate and there alongside us was an ordinary tap, we could have kicked it. We consoled ourselves with the thought that it may not have been fit for drinking, which probably applied to the pump water as well. Just to make sure the water was safe to drink, we added some water purifying tablets obtained from our escape packs.

The gate was our next obstacle and when we first examined it, we thought we might have to risk climbing over, as it was so well barricaded. Looking at the height of the gate, we changed our minds and decided to remove the barrier, as it was our only way out. The gates had draw bolts which we expected, then in addition a very heavy bar had been placed across the gates, which on its own would have prevented an entry. Just to make sure, the farmer had propped a very heavy and long bar against the cross bar. It would have required someone with determination to effect an entry into this place and it was going to require an equally determined effort on our part to get out.

Removing the bars took a great deal of effort, as not only were they very heavy, we also had to make sure we didn't drop or bang them in any way. This meant we had to lower them very slowly to the ground. The easy part was drawing the bolts, as they moved without trouble and at last we were able to open up and step cautiously out into what proved to be a village street. If only that farmer had used a padlock as well, we would have been sunk.

I have often wondered since, what the farmer must have thought when he saw his carefully erected barrier equally carefully dismantled. As the gate was too high to climb easily, it must have been apparent to him that he had locked intruders inside. His next thoughts would be to wonder why the intruders were there as nothing had been stolen and apart from the ladder, everything was in its correct place, we had made fairly certain of that. Should the farmer ever chance to read this account, the mystery will be solved for him.

It was no trouble to go through the village as it was quite late at night, but all the same, we considered it advisable to leave the road and strike off across country. The thought of a curfew hadn't entered our heads at that time, but we knew that standing in the middle of a village street, was not the best thing to do. Our main aim was to carry on in a South Westerly direction for a few days, then turn towards Normandy. Referring to the compass, we decided that the best way was across an allotment to open fields which we could see beyond.

After trampling on a few cabbages, climbing over barbed wire fences and ditches, we came to a long straight road which was conveniently heading in the direction we wished to take. I think that road was the longest straight road I have ever been on. We walked for hours, turning neither left or right, except for the few occasions when we had to dive into ditches to hide from passing cars and lorries.

We never stopped to consider what might be in the ditches we dived into and quite often found bushes, brambles, muddy water and other unpleasant things. Strangely enough, despite our lack of caution, neither of us was hurt, at least if we were, we did not notice it. Thinking back, the pain which I had suffered on first landing was forgotten at such moments as these.

We were following the dead straight road for mile after mile wondering when it would change direction, or arrive at another village, or do something to change the monotonous aspect. I think perhaps we had even got a bit bored, as we seemed to be getting nowhere. Suddenly we pulled up with a jolt, as we saw a light shining on the road a few hundred yards ahead. It was impossible to tell what it was from that distance, but we believed it might be a road block which had been set up, possibly for our benefit. The Germans must have known that we were somewhere in the area.

They had found pieces of an aircraft and had not yet accounted for all of the crew members, so it was almost inevitable that they had started a search. Following a whispered consultation, we decided to take to the fields and make a large detour, then pick up the road again beyond the light. Nat volunteered to jump across the ditch and enter the field first to see if it was feasible to make the detour in the dark. Having done so, he indicated to me that it seemed to be alright and while he ventured further into the field, I followed a short distance behind. He had not gone very far, when with a cry of alarm he disappeared from view. As I dashed forward, I imagined that something serious had happened, but when I caught up with him, found that my fears were groundless. Walking through short corn stubble, he had fallen down a hole about three feet deep.

When we had made sure that no harm was done, we proceeded, taking care to avoid similar holes which seemed to be everywhere. The journey was quite hazardous, as in the dark it was difficult to see where we were going and what we might be walking into. We knew about the holes, but what else lay in wait for us? We assumed it was some kind of tank trap area or perhaps a defensive position, hardly the sort of place to wander about in at night. While we had been on the road, the bordering trees had helped us maintain direction, here in the open there was nothing to guide us, we had to press on and hope. When we estimated that we had passed the light, we struck back for the road.

This was easier said than done as by now we were in a cornfield and progress was becoming very difficult and tiring. I was a little bothered, as we should have been able to see the trees but it seemed very dark ahead and not as I expected. Without warning, we came up against an embankment about fifteen feet high and when we tried to climb it, discovered it was covered in loose earth.

Finally we reached the top where we received quite a shock, as in place of the road we had expected to see there was a double track railway. This came as a setback because now there was no telling where the road might be and in the darkness we could come up against a number of pit falls. We discussed this in whispers, lying flat on the ground with our heads below the sky line, praying that we would not be spotted by a railway patrol. At last a decision was made, so crouching low, we crossed the line at a run and dived for cover.

Descent was more of a problem than the climb had been but slipping and sliding for what seemed a long time, we at last found level ground. Here our problem of direction was solved, as by keeping low to the ground, we could see the outline of the trees which bordered the road we had been travelling on earlier. After crossing a large field of short scrub we were pleased to walk on the solid surface of the road once again.

Having overcome one problem, we were now faced with another as an air raid was taking place not so far away. There was no risk of being bombed, but we anticipated there might be increased military activity in the area, We continued our journey with utmost caution, ready to hide at the first sign of danger, but fortunately for us, we met no one, so after a while we were able to relax a little.

Within a few miles, we came to a fork in the road which was not shown on our map, one went to the South East and the other to the South, so we chose the latter. I very soon decided that we had made a mistake in choosing our road as it was in such a bad condition, full of ruts and holes. I was expecting it to terminate in a field and although it didn't actually do so, it almost seemed like it at times.

It was while we were trudging along that we saw a very strange type of aircraft flying overhead. It was difficult to see its shape but its engine note was unusual in that it made a popping noise and the exhaust flame was unguarded. We learned later that this was a V1 flying bomb which the Germans had just started using for the first time. We carried on, blissfully ignorant that it was on its way to England.

The more we walked, the more desolate the countryside seemed to become, which did nothing to cheer us up, as by now dawn was breaking and it was time to get under cover and rest for the day. Turning a corner, we discovered a village just ahead, which at that hour seemed deserted and silent. This suited us admirably as we were just about out on our feet.

The first house we came to seemed a likely place, as here again was another barn we might be able to hide in. It was while walking round the house looking for an entrance that our suspicions were aroused. For some reason or other we thought it might be occupied by Germans and we found out later, this was the case.

Proceeding along the village main street, we came to another building surrounded by barbed wire and high walls. It proved to be difficult to enter and the only place we could get to was an outhouse which was hardly suitable. As it was getting late, we decided to abandon that idea and look for another place quickly. Next door we found a house set back from the road. One which had several outhouses and stables, so we promptly climbed over the front gate. Once inside, we were hidden from the road, which enabled us to look round.

Leaving the gate, we crossed a cobbled yard to some stables, but these proved to be useless for our purposes, as in one we disturbed a horse which flew round in circles and in a second, dogs which started yapping their heads off. This was too much, we expected to be discovered any minute, so hurriedly we headed through an arch which led to a garden. We could not turn back as this would mean going out into the road again which would have been very dangerous.

We were now faced with a choice between going right through an orchard to fields beyond, or staying in a small shed full of farming tools. We chose the shed, hoping to get some sleep. No sooner were we in there, it began to pour with rain, some of which came through the roof - making us rather wet. We searched around for something to lie on and were lucky to find some clean sacks in a box. We piled these in a corner under a ploughing machine and lay down to sleep. This was not a very satisfactory arrangement as after two hours, we both woke up, cold, wet and pretty miserable, making further sleep out of the question.

Within a few minutes of our waking, a girl came from the house and walked down the garden. Due to the fact that we were uncomfortable, hungry and likely to be discovered anyway, we had made up our minds to approach her for help. Bearing in mind that she was probably going down to the toilet at the end of the garden, we agreed that it was best to wait for her return. I don't think I shall forget the look on her face when I stepped out and called to her, it was almost abject terror, she screamed and ran for the house.

This was something we had not anticipated and were rather worried at the turn of events. Sure enough, we saw some immediate action. First came the dogs we had disturbed earlier, then the man of the house. He was followed by his wife who was carrying a pitchfork, while close behind was the girl still looking very frightened. I think that she showed a great deal of courage in daring to approach the people that she was so frightened of.

The dogs reached us first, but instead of biting, they were licking us. We tried to ignore the farmer's wife who was intent on pinning us to the door with her pitchfork and continued to play with the dogs. The farmer was very puzzled by all this and dissuaded his wife from doing us a real mischief as he was rather anxious to find out who we were and what we were doing on his property. Rapidly using sign language and anything else we could think of, we told them who we were and that we meant then no harm. It was rather difficult to explain to them that we had been shot down and were hoping to walk to Normandy, but at last we made it sink in.

Producing my silk escape map, I asked them to show me where we were, as although I had a rough idea, it was nice to receive reassurance. They not only indicated our position, they also gave directions to help us in our further travels and in general seemed to be very sympathetic towards us. When we realised their attitude, we asked if they could give us shelter and perhaps a little food as we were so hungry. As soon as the woman learned of our plight, she hurried away, taking her pitchfork with her.

While she was in the house preparing something to eat, the farmer stayed talking to us, not that we could speak each other's language but we managed very well using signs. After five minutes or so, we were very pleased to see his wife appear, with coffee, bread, hard boiled eggs, sugar and enough butter for the bread. This must have strained their resources, as I am sure that they were rationed as we were at home. Pausing long enough to thank them, we piled in, while they stood and watched us. This was the first real food we had eaten since we had been shot down.

By the time we had finished eating, we were feeling so very much better and I am sure our benefactors realised our appreciation of what they had done for us. To put the finishing touch to our meal, we pulled out our cigarettes offered one to the Frenchman, then the three of us sat round and enjoyed a smoke. They were quite prepared to let us sleep there for a while and we were very pleased when they placed some fresh bundles of straw in a bran shed for us.

Eventually the farmer departed for the house, leaving us to our own devices, We entered the bran shed and crawled into the makeshift beds which we found were quite comfortable. Unfortunately we were feeling very cold, probably because our clothes were so damp and we found sleep rather difficult. Despite this, we were prepared to accept the discomfort as we were now in hiding and did not have to be constantly on our guard. Although the family must have been short of food, we received two more meals that day which helped considerably and made our situation more hopeful.

When the farmer came with the third meal of the day, we asked him if we could have an old jacket which was hanging in the shed and were very surprised when he refused our request. This gave us cause to believe we had made too many demands on him, but when he turned up later with two jackets in good condition, we realised that he was really doing his best for us.

At last it was approaching the time when we would have to leave and we were very pleased when the whole family came out to wish us good luck, at the same time give us advice on the direction we should take. This farewell took almost half an hour, by which time darkness had fallen and we were allowed out into the open. Making sure we had our jackets on, we pocketed some more food we had been given then said goodbye to the ladies.

The farmer acting as our guide in the dark, led us through his orchard, across a field until we reached a road. Wishing us God Speed he returned to his house, leaving us once again to our own resources, but in a much better state than we were before we had met him and his family.

CHAPTER 4

We had not gone far from the house, when we noticed two shadowy figures crossing the field just in front of us. Dropping to the grass and lying as flat as possible, we watched and waited to see who they were. It was now quite dark, so even though they passed within ten yards of us, we could not identify them. Something made us think that they were also downed airmen and considered attracting their attention. As this would serve no useful purpose, we waited until the coast was clear before moving on. Whoever they were, they gave the impression that their mission was more furtive than lawful.

This night's walking followed a similar pattern to the previous night and the thought that we were just a bit nearer Normandy spurred us on. We considered it amazing that although there was a curfew during the hours of darkness, we were never challenged while walking through the villages. I put this down to the fact that instead of trying to creep through the various places, we marched through, strictly in step. Anyone hearing us, might have made the mistake in thinking that we were a patrol, or that we had every right to do what we were doing. We had previously tried walking across fields in the dark and realised its difficulties and dangers, which is why we tried keeping to the roads whenever we could.

The first two or three villages we marched through, proved to be a bit nerve-racking as it seemed that every dog in the place, barked as we approached. On one occasion, I thought we had pushed our luck too far and were due for certain capture. The time was about two o'clock in the morning and as usual we were tramping through the village street making plenty of noise, suddenly, about ten yards in front of us a light from an open door flooded the road.

We stopped dead still, thinking of retreat as this could be a patrol coming out to investigate us; who else but Germans were likely to act in such a way at that hour of the morning? If we retreated, this would have been suspicious, but to carry on meant running the risk of meeting a real patrol. At last we decided to continue and hope for the best, which was as well, because directly we started forward again, the lights went out allowing us to continue as we hoped, safely. We could find no satisfactory explanation for this strange occurrence and it was very weird to pass close to the house. I wondered if we were walking into a trap, although there was nothing apparent and we heard no sound. I had the feeling that we were being very closely watched, but not by the Germans as they would have stopped us immediately. I wondered who it was behind those now closed doors and I felt extremely relieved when we left that village far behind.

One thing we had to do was fill our water bottles at every village pump we came to. As most of them squeaked pretty violently, we were scared of detection, even so, we had to have water. When I look back and realise what we got away with it amazes me, as several times we passed flak towers, military camps and German occupied houses, and never got challenged.

I remember the time we tried our hands at stealing. We were passing through a village whose main industry seemed to be dairy farming, when Nat noticed a milk churn outside a farm yard. Feeling rather thirsty, we thought we would like to try a drink of milk and the only thing preventing us was the padlocked lid. Adopting the air of an expert cracksman, Nat pulled out a nail file and set to work to pick the lock. After a very prolonged period of noisy clattering, the task was given up as hopeless, so just in case we had been heard, we made off as quickly as possible.

A system we adopted for night walking was to keep going for a defined period no matter how tired we felt, then rest for fifteen minutes. This was not very long considering our walking periods were of three hours duration. We were more or less obliged to adopt this rigid timing system, otherwise we would have spent too much time resting instead of pushing on. We considered it unwise to smoke while walking, so confined this activity until our rest periods. During these rests, we would hide in a hedge, take off our shoes, then lie down for a smoke followed perhaps by a vitamin tablet, a slice of bread, or whatever else we may have been given to eat.

There was a great temptation to extend our rest periods, as we were both becoming very tired through our exertions and lack of proper food. Our spur though was the desire to get to Normandy quickly. The alternative to this forced travel was to hide up somewhere which was impractical, as we needed food and in any case there was little purpose in hiding as we would get nowhere. We hoped our forces would eventually occupy the district, but it could take weeks or months and we were in a hurry. Our only possible chance was to be intercepted by the French Resistance group. This was a very slim chance indeed, as the Germans had taken very strong action against such activity in this particular area.

We realised that the longer we stayed at large, the greater the risk of capture and there was no telling what our fate might be should this happen. We were not exactly popular with the Germans and we knew that if we were captured, the treatment to expect would be imprisonment until the end of hostilities. We could receive a lot worse.

A big disadvantage we suffered from, was the unsuitability of our footwear. Nat was wearing flying boots which although comfortable enough while flying, were rather too large for prolonged walking. My shoes were those we had found in the shed on the first day and even then they had seen better times. Now the soles were broken and had holes in them, one heel had come off and nails were sticking into my feet. After any period of walking, our feet became swollen, hot and raw.

After leaving the village in which we had been disturbed by the light, we journeyed over miles of desolate wasteland. This was made even more unpleasant by a cold wind which had sprung up, bringing a fine drizzle with it. As dawn broke, we felt despair, there seemed nothing more than moorland all around us and the road we were on was virtually a cart track.

We were not too worried about being caught, as it was obvious that very few people ever visited the area, our concern was finding somewhere to sleep. Curling up in damp grass with nothing to cover us, would only be considered when we could no longer stand up. As we were not prepared to sleep in the open, we had little alternative except to keep going in the hope of finding a place to rest.

At last after three hours solid walking, we saw a small village in the distance, but what a distance, It seemed to take us for ever, but at last we made it. By this time we were becoming desperate for sleep and we had to find somewhere, but we were in for a great disappointment. I think we searched most of the buildings in the village and not one was suitable. Those that weren't bombed and in ruins, had no barns or outhouses we could crawl into, in fact the place was deserted.

I was sure this would be our last day of freedom, as it was daylight and we had nowhere to hide. We had walked in daylight before, on our first day, but then we were given little choice. Now it seemed that we were faced with the situation again. This time there was a difference, as by now we were very hungry, very tired and very wet. Before, there had been cornfields and hedges we could hide in, whereas now we were on open moorland.

After a short discussion we came to the conclusion that we had to risk it, so once again we pushed on out over the moorland feeling distinctly dispirited. Where previously we had struck so very lucky in finding food and shelter, now everything seemed to be set against us.

According to my watch, we had plodded on for a further hour when on reaching the top of a hill, we saw a small village in the valley below. This gave us fresh hope of finding shelter, so we headed towards the houses. Before we had gone very far, we noticed two girls and a fellow pushing bicycles up the hill. We waited to see who they were, being quite prepared to run should they seem to be unfriendly. The fellow was in the lead, so naturally we approached him first. He seemed very nervous, which I suppose was no wonder as we had neither washed or shaved for three days. It was early in the morning and the place was deserted except for the five of us. When the fact dawned on him that we were British aircrew on the run, he attempted to mount his bicycle and would have done so had we not forcibly prevented him.

By this time he was quite terrified and we were getting angry, we were determined to find out what we could concerning the location of the Germans. The girls had moved away and were waiting at a safe distance ready to flee, while we interrogated their companion. It became obvious that there was little to be gained by detaining him, so eventually let him go. Jumping on to his bicycle, he shouted the single word 'Deutsche' and rode off furiously after the girls. This was quite a different attitude to the others who had put themselves at risk to help us and I sometimes wonder what I would have done under similar circumstances.

It was no surprise to us that Germans were in the village in fact it would have been curious had they not been there. By the way the fellow had behaved, we got the distinct impression that the place was swarming with them. Bearing this in mind, we decided to be more cautious and make a detour through a small copse which would give us some cover on our approach to the village. From our vantage point on top of the hill, we were in an excellent position to survey the lie of the land. The village was roughly a mile ahead, but there was a stumbling block. Halfway to our goal was another of those dreaded flak towers which seemed to be dotted about all over the place. This particular tower had a commanding view of the surrounding countryside, including the road we were on. We were not too worried about the Germans in the village as we thought we could evade them easily enough, but we had no intention of walking down the road in full view of the tower.

Just to the left of the road, the fields sloped away for one hundred yards to a narrow cart track. If we could reach that without being discovered, we would be able to remain out of sight of the tower. As quickly as possible, we left the road, ducked behind the corn in a field then dashed for the cart track in the valley. We did not know it at the time, but this track was to lead us straight to the wood we had intended to make for,

As we headed down the lane, we saw a shed which we thought might give us some shelter, so taking care to remain hidden from the tower, we climbed the bank towards it. This was yet another disappointment to us, as apart from the fact that one side was missing and the floor covered in mud, there were two or three bulls wandering in and out of it. We didn't go any closer as I had no doubt they were bulls and no one was going to convince me otherwise.

Before going any further we decided to take a short rest in a small hollow against a haystack and at the same time have a snack. We still had some bread and eggs left which went down very well, then we attempted to sleep. We had been on our feet nine hours and were exhausted. Eating had been easy, sleeping was a different matter as although we were fully dressed and had pulled straw over ourselves, it was still too cold to sleep. This was not too surprising as the wind was blowing and the rain was still falling. I never realised that June could be so cold as this one seemed to be.

After half an hour, we had become too uncomfortable to stay where we were, so moved on to the village to find shelter. On arrival, we walked through an orchard and came to a small farmyard with some outbuildings. Making sure that no one was in the yard, we unlatched the gate and stepped inside, hoping to find a place of concealment. It was our intention to observe the people before approaching anybody. From our hiding place we saw an old man hobbling about on a stick and as he appeared to be very ancient, we thought that he would be of little use to us.

We waited for a while to see if anyone else would turn up and within about ten minutes a fellow of middle age appeared. We kept him under observation also, then decided he might be safe to approach. As he was about to leave the yard again, we got into a position near the exit, then stepped out in front of him. If we expected him to be surprised, we were let down as he accepted that we were hungry airmen as though it was quite commonplace, then muttering something in French, he left us. This action put us in a spot as we didn't know whether we should wait, or run for it. We were not left in doubt for long as he returned with a loaf, some cheese and a bottle of beer. Motioning for us to follow him, he walked down the lane a few yards ahead of us until he reached the road. With his hands behind him, he indicated which way he wanted us to go, then promptly left us to our own devices. It was quite obvious that he hoped never to see us again.

CHAPTER 5

The road we had been directed to take proved to be an unpleasant one as it was very steep with deep ruts and in our tired state it was extremely heavy going. Once we reached the top, we decided that we had travelled far enough for a while, so settled down by a haystack to rest our bodies and eat some of the food we had been given.

Pulling out the knife I had always taken on bombing raids, I cut off a slice or two of bread, placed cold bacon between the slices, then piled in, we were ravenous. I can't recall where the bacon had come from, but at that time we were not bothered, we had something to eat. Cheese was the next thing on the menu, at least that was our intention although I am afraid we did not expect it to be goat's milk cheese. This was not to our liking at all, so we had to throw it away.

The next question was what to do with the beer, as even though we were thirsty it was too much for either of us. It had a terrible taste and smelled even worse. We hated to waste it but it had to be poured away and the bottle disposed of. Just to make sure it would not be found for a while, I threw it as far as I could into a field of corn which was not due for cutting. I only hope that the Frenchman would have forgiven us for wasting the provisions which he could probably ill afford.

After this rest, we felt a lot better and it was with renewed vigour that we continued on our long journey to Normandy, which was still approximately one hundred and forty miles away. Through force of circumstance, we had been travelling East for a while which was rather disheartening, because it was my intention to go to the West as quickly as possible and every step towards the East meant two steps wasted. Now that we were clear of the village, we could resume our trend to the West which made us feel better.

Our journey took us along the ridge of a hill. parallel to the road we had been travelling along originally. Unfortunately after twenty minutes or so, the road turned East which meant we were forced to cross it if we intended to maintain our original heading. As we had no detailed maps, I was trying to navigate as I would in the air, in straight lines from point to point. This was the only way I could hope to reach our objective.

From our elevated position, we could see that once we had crossed the road, we would be compelled to move in open country. Dressed as we were, with civilian jackets over the top of our uniforms, we might be rather conspicuous but not to the extent we would have been without the jackets. However we were dressed, we still had to cross over.

We entered the trees bordering the road, preparatory to crossing when in the distance we saw a motorcycle combination approaching, occupied by two German soldiers. Before it reached us, a German staff car came from the opposite direction, leading us to believe that we were on a major highway constantly used by troops. Perhaps this was a hasty analysis, but we both agreed that it was not the sort of place to loiter in, especially as it was broad daylight, after waiting for a few minutes until the coast was clear, we dashed across the road to the shelter of the trees opposite.

Here another obstacle presented itself in the form of a barbed wire fence, just a few feet from the edge of the road. On the other side of the fence was a ditch six feet deep, so we really had a problem. It was obvious that we could not stay where we were, so it meant climbing the fence which in itself was no easy task. Not only was it fairly high, we were also quite close to the road and had to take care not to be seen by passing traffic, but we finally succeeded without damage to ourselves. The ditch we landed in, proved quite beneficial, as it allowed us to take stock of our surroundings and confirm our bearings without the risk of being Observed.

About a mile ahead in the direction we wished to take, was a large wood, which seemed to be an ideal place, as it was our desire to remain under cover as much as possible. The shortest route meant crossing cornfields and if we ruined any corn I am afraid that it was the least of our considerations at the time. We did spare some thought for the farmer and hoped he wasn't growing it for his own use.

Once in the wood, we realised our mistake, as instead of being able to walk easily, we were confronted by thick undergrowth. This disadvantage far outweighed the advantage that the cover of the trees gave us as we had great difficulty forcing our way through the shrubs and bracken. Our progress was extremely slow and to make matters worse, the ground sloped steeply upwards. We continued for quite some time as the wood was deeper than we imagined but there was no turning back. At last after a very tiring struggle, we emerged from the trees then sat down for a well earned rest.

It was while resting that it suddenly dawned on me that we were in the area of the Somme, a very familiar name and famous as a battlefield during the Great War of 1914-18. The ditch we had rested in earlier must have been one of the old trenches used during the fighting. To me there was a strange atmosphere about the place and I tried to imagine what it must have been like then. Now it was simply a peaceful scene, which, if our troops continued their advance, could quickly become a battlefield once more.

During this, our first real attempt at travelling in broad daylight, we were surprised to find so few people about. We were beginning to believe that the place was deserted except for Germans, until breasting a hill, we came upon a

French farmer ploughing his field. There was no point in trying to avoid him, as if he had been a collaborator we would be in trouble and if not, then maybe he could help us. He seemed quite friendly and not at all surprised when we disclosed who we were. Perhaps the French had become used to the members of the Royal Air Force wandering through their fields.

What was more than likely, the message had been passed around that we were in the region. Having almost run out of cigarettes, I asked if he had any to spare and I was very pleased when he gave me enough tobacco and paper to make several cigarettes. The only thing we could offer in exchange was an English cigarette which he accepted. It was apparent that he could do little for us, so we continued our journey.

Shortly after leaving the farmer, we picked up one or two propaganda leaflets dropped by the RAF more than two years previously. They seemed to be everywhere and I thought of the crews who had dropped them. Had theirs been a wasted effort as the leaflets were unlikely to have been read by many people in that area. We did consider keeping them as mementos, but eventually decided to throw them away as in the event of our capture, they could prove to be an embarrassment.

CHAPTER 6

We had travelled for a considerable distance that day before seeing any signs of habitation, so unlike our own country where it is difficult to avoid it. This had its advantages as the fewer people we met, the better, but there were disadvantages also, as we needed food and shelter. Normally these could only be found in the villages.

It was rather unfortunate that the village we eventually came across, had a flak tower very close to it and if we had attempted to stop there, we were in danger of being apprehended. Instead of entering the main street, we decided to by-pass it, using any cover we could to avoid being seen from the tower.

We succeeded in avoiding the tower and were walking down a lane which lead away from the village. It was a very quiet lane and we were not prepared for the large house which suddenly confronted us. It was occupied by Germans. If we had immediately doubled back, it would have looked suspicious, so we held our breath and kept walking. As soon as was reasonable, we left the lane and made for a nearby road where we had another shock, we were on a main thoroughfare. There was little else for us to do but be as bold as possible and walk until we saw a convenient place to strike off across country again.

Before we had gone very far, we were disturbed to see a German officer cycling towards us. There was no alternative except continue walking, as to run would really give the game away. We tried to appear as unconcerned with his presence as any local might have done although we were both very tense. As he drew level, he peered at us in an enquiring manner and it was obvious he wasn't too sure who we were. Thankfully he passed us, but then we made the mistake of looking back to see how far he had gone.

At that moment, he also turned to look at us. He was now riding quite slowly and appeared to be trying to make up his mind to turn back. He left it too late, as the instant he turned his head to see where he was going, we cleared the fence bordering the road and made off across the fields as fast as possible. I feel sure he must have been rather puzzled at our rapid disappearance as no normal person would have cause to leave a road in such a manner.

Once we had crossed the stream at the far side of the field, we felt we were safer, as we found a disused cart-track thickly covered by trees, which screened us from the road. There was no evidence of an immediate hue and cry, which meant that either the German had failed to report our presence or the authorities were unable to trace our movements.

After our unpleasant encounter, we walked for about an hour, until we came across a farmhouse. We needed to stop there as we had run out of food and were hungry. Drawing closer, we discovered that the place was surrounded by a barbed wire fence and the occupants of the house were gathered in the garden. We could not understand why they looked so scared, as it was nothing to do with our unexpected appearance, something else had frightened them. Disregarding their attitude we started to climb the fence when a middle aged fellow left the group and hurried over to us, indicating that we should stay outside. This seemed very strange treatment, but we waited for him to come to us.

It was no wonder he had stopped us, as for some reason which he did not explain, two German soldiers were patrolling the road outside his house. We begged for food, but he said he could not supply us with any, as unfortunately he had been bombed out of Amiens two weeks before. Because of this, he had a job to make ends meet for his family and himself which was understandable. Just before we left, he gave us instructions which allowed us to avoid the patrol and once again we found ourselves on our way, very weary, very hungry.

Owing to the possibility of road patrols, we walked across the fields parallel to the road, ready to hide if we heard transport coming. We were surprised to discover that we were being followed, not by Germans, but by a girl on a bicycle. When we saw her, we realised that she was beckoning us, so went over to see what she wanted. Without saying a word, she undid her coat, handed me a loaf, then cycled off. This struck us as being remarkably cool as she must have come out of the house under the very noses of the Germans.

It was now half past four in the afternoon which meant we had been on our feet for sixteen hours with hardly a break, so we thought it was time to look for a place to sleep. Approximately three miles ahead, was a fairly large wood, just what we had been looking for, but due to our weary condition, it took us over an hour to reach it. After the heavy going we had experienced with the last wood, we only went in far enough for cover. We finally lay down to rest, only to realise that it was much too cold to sleep. We had to find something to cover ourselves with, before there was any chance of sleep. At the time, we were right on the edge of a field which had bundles of grass hung out to dry, so while Nat built a wall of bracken to make a hiding place for us, I collected two or three armfuls of grass for a bed.

We should have been warm as it was the middle of June and we were dressed in full uniform, heavy flying jerseys and civilian jackets, but we were still cold. After sleeping from sheer exhaustion, we were awake again within an hour due to the discomfort we suffered. Sleep was impossible after this and even though we couldn't settle down again, we stayed where we were for a while to rest our aching feet.

By now, we were both feeling very uncomfortable and agreed that keeping on the move was preferable to staying around getting colder and colder, so we moved on. To add to our discomfort, we felt terribly thirsty and realised we would have to find water soon. It was Nat's idea that we obtained some from the next cow trough we came to, as treatment with our Halazone tablets would make it fit to drink. I was not at all anxious to do this for two reasons, the first was the risk of typhoid and the second concerned the cattle themselves as somehow we seem to have a mutual dislike for each other. At last I had to accept the fact that if we were to get water, it would have to be from a trough.

The very next one we saw was about twenty yards in from the edge of a field and separated from us by a barbed wire fence. There were several cows in the field, some very close to us, so hoping they would be sympathetic to our cause, we climbed the fence and approached the trough. We filled our water bottles as quickly as possible, trying to avoid the odd insects and things that were floating in the water, then beat a hasty retreat. I was very relieved to get back over the fence again as in such an exposed position, we had run the risk of being sighted. Two people seen collecting water from a cow trough would surely make even the most disinterested person a trifle curious. I often wonder how many times we may have been seen by French people who either wished they hadn't seen us, or pretended they hadn't, as we were a danger to them.

We wandered on for a while until we came to a main road where we were able to see a city in the valley some distance away. After consulting the escape map, we concluded that it was Amiens and the road we were on, lead straight to it. Having no other direction to take, we headed towards the city intending to strike off as soon as possible.

I was very anxious to leave this main road as we were now extremely vulnerable and I was desperately hoping to find a place where we could turn off. At last we saw a turning not too far down the road and increased our pace. We tried not to walk so fast as to arouse suspicion should anyone see us, which was a very difficult thing to do, as we really wanted to run but dare not.

It was as well that we were walking at a reasonable pace as to our dismay, we saw a person in khaki uniform coming towards us and he was German. I think he must have been drunk, as he was lurching along very unsteadily, but drunk or not, I didn't fancy an encounter with him. When he got closer, I noticed his red arm band with a black Swastika on it, denoting a member of the Nazi party. Not knowing quite what to do, I kept my eyes down, just giving him a surly glance as he passed. Nat, who was walking just behind me took a different attitude, as brightening up, he waved to the soldier and greeted him in French, which incidentally surprised both the German and myself. He gave us a bemused stare and staggered on.

Luckily for my peace of mind we were able to turn into the side road out of his sight, We were just congratulating ourselves that our drunken friend had not followed us, when a real threat presented itself. Just off to our left about one hundred yards away, we noticed a gun pit and as we were passing, three Germans rose up to take a look at us. This was serious, as we had the feeling that it was more than idle curiosity, especially when one of them produced binoculars. If we had wanted to run before, it was nothing compared to our desire to do so now. Appearing as unconcerned as possible, we walked on until a dip in the road hid us from their view. We feared they would follow us and although we stayed on the road for another half a mile or so, we saw no signs of pursuit. It is quite possible that they would not expect to find two enemy airmen walking past a defensive position in broad daylight. We could have been locals.

All this time, we had been walking towards a village where we were hoping to get food and possibly rest. If we had thought we were being followed, we would not have stopped in the village but continued until we found a hiding place. Satisfied that there was still no sign of being followed, we ventured into the village main street. Once there, we were at a bit of a loss as to what to do, as the place seemed deserted, so we wandered along in an aimless fashion.

Before very long, we saw three girls and a fellow coming towards us. It was apparent by their actions that we were arousing interest in them. They would have realised that we were not Germans and not locals either, which in such a small village, was bound to cause comment. As they passed us, we both gained the distinct impression that they wanted to speak and were not quite sure how to tackle us. Hurriedly I got Nat to agree that we should speak to them, in the hope that they were friendly.

Friendly or not, we were throwing ourselves on their mercy by appearing so openly in their village. By this time, they had virtually stopped and as I turned back to speak to them, one of the girls came to meet me. She did not seem very surprised when I asked if she could speak English. Fortunately, although she was unable to do so, her friend could and when called came to join us. The little group which now formed became embarrassing, as we were very conspicuous. As quickly as possible, we made them understand who we were and the position we were in. Indicating that we should follow, they led us to a farmhouse, where we were handed over to one of the many Frenchmen who had gathered out of curiosity.

Having done what was required of them, they left us. More or less taking us under his wing, the Frenchman led us into a small garden where he naturally started to question us in an attempt to establish our identity. Having satisfied himself that we were who we said we were, he went into the house, leaving us alone for a while. Shortly after this, the three girls reappeared to talk to us. They seemed quite excited at having met us, as this was a rare event in their lives, it certainly was in ours.

During a little chat, concerned mostly with exchange of names, home towns and the like, they asked for souvenirs. Nat gave one a twelve sided threepenny piece, which made me hunt for something to give away. This was when I parted with my navigator's brevet. I gave it to one of the girls, with the warning that she must make sure it remained hidden. The third girl was given a half crown piece, not quite so interesting perhaps, but still a souvenir of sorts.

We felt very much out of place, as we had neither washed, shaved or taken our clothes off for three days. In addition to this, we were filthy from crawling through ditches, fields and hedges, also we were suffering from lack of sleep. They in contrast, were dressed in their best clothes, which was a reminder to us that it was Sunday evening.

A Frenchman appeared from the house, carrying a bottle of wine which he presented us with, a very welcome gift indeed as we were so thirsty. It was not surprising that he questioned us also, as he was not prepared to give us help, unless he knew our background. It appeared that he was some sort of official on the French Railway and was very willing to help us. We sounded him regarding the possibility of arranging a lift in a railway truck towards Normandy. He decided that this would be fairly simple, which bucked us up no end.

I am afraid our elation was short lived, as presently his wife, daughter and one or two other members of the family, came out to look at us, which started a violent argument. Several times I heard the word 'Deutsche' used, while pointing towards the place we had seen the Germans earlier. It was quite apparent to us that we were worrying them, especially when one of the women started crying. The Frenchman who had befriended us was evidently backing us up, but he had to withdraw and admit defeat. Coming across to us, he said he was very sorry, but his women folk were very scared and wanted us to leave. Just about then someone came running in to say that Germans were approaching the village. We did not stop to ask where they were, but got ourselves ready to leave very quickly.

It was impossible to leave by the gate as we would be seen, so we were directed to crawl through the hedge into the next garden. This seemed simple enough, until we arrived there to find that it was surrounded by a very high barbed wire fence. The only way over, was to climb on top of a summer house conveniently placed, then leap out as far as possible so as to clear bracken and nettles growing the other side of the fence. Needless to say, it was quite a jar leaping from that height, and to make matters worse the ground was very uneven. Although our ankles and feet hurt us we didn't stop, as by now we were rather desperate to get away quickly.

Once clear of the buildings, we kept going fast, expecting to hear rifle shots or Germans calling on us to stop. Nothing happened and we continued for several hundred yards. We found it impossible to go too far as we were just about exhausted. Despite the fact that the Germans were not very far away, we stopped when we got to a haystack. This enabled us to get out of sight for a while as we had been so exposed running across the fields. Once having flopped on the ground, we agreed we could go no further and would have to rest. By pulling bundles of straw from the stack, we built a wind break and settled down to sleep. If the Germans found us then it was just too bad, we were almost past caring.

I suppose we had dozed off for about an hour when I was disturbed by Nat speaking to someone. I was certain that we had been caught at last, but it proved to be a man and a girl who had brought some food for us. They also told us that the Germans had left again, so we were relatively safe. We were disturbed twice more after this, by the railway official who wished us luck, then by the two who had visited us originally. They had come to tell us that it was now safe to leave and convey the good wishes of the people from the house. We thanked them all for what they had done and set off to find a road before it got too dark.

Knowing we were very close to the outskirts of Amiens we had to go very carefully, especially as the road we were on led into the city, that is if the milestones were to be believed. Approximately three miles from Amiens we struck off in a North Westerly direction, intending to give the city as wide a berth as possible. Presently the road turned on to South West and as we had been going in a Westerly direction for about four hours, I thought it would take us well clear of the city.

In the early hours of the morning, it started to rain in a fairly steady downpour and as there was no shelter, we could do little else but continue. After walking in the rain for a while, I noticed a strange blue glow in the distance. As we got closer, it became apparent that this was caused by several big blue flashes which rather looked like miniature lightening. By this time we could hear loud cracking noises which accompanied the flashes. Because of the heavy rain and the dark, it was not easy to see where it was coming from. Eventually we realised that we would pass right underneath the phenomenon. Then it dawned on me that the disturbance was caused by the rain falling on overhead power cables.

I was not too happy that the road now ran parallel to the cables and I cast many an anxious glance upwards at them. I was not prepared however for what came next. I saw what looked like a large building covered in blue flashing flames, a most eerie sight in the dark. I thought of secret weapons or something else equally as sinister and felt quite let down when we discovered that it was nothing more than a large transformer. This in itself was significant and should have told me we were heading into something larger than a village, but I was too tired to think of such things and we walked on.

CHAPTER 7

We had been travelling through a built-up area for something like ten minutes, when it struck me we must be in Amiens and not in an outlying village as I first thought. Almost coinciding with this idea, came the order to 'halt' uttered in German, followed by the chilling sound of rifles being loaded. We knew our wings had been clipped at last. Torches were switched on and turned to illuminate us, while two German soldiers approached with bayonets at the ready. They appeared to be extremely nervous, in fact more so than we were, until we had really convinced them we were aircrew who had been trying to evade capture.

Having realised this as fact, they relaxed in their attitude towards us, although we were still held at bayonet point. We had not been standing there very long, before the sound of booted feet heralded the arrival of a street patrol. Our captors who appeared to be on sentry duty, handed us over to the new arrivals with apparent relief.

I thought about this later and came to the conclusion that owing to the fact it was after curfew, they may have suspected that it was a French Resistance ambush, with us as the decoys.

Once we were handed over to the street patrol, it was indicated that we should march. We only travelled a short distance through the city and I for one was very thankful as I didn't trust our escort at all. They were hardly what I imagined a German military escort should be, as with rifles slung over their shoulders, one accompanied me, while the other followed a few yards behind with Nat. I became quite worried at one stage, as I got the distinct impression that my escort was wanting me to get ahead of him. He seemed to be very friendly, too friendly in fact, and I am almost sure that he invited me to escape.

I called to Nat to stick close to his guard, as I intended to do, because my guard was gradually dropping further behind me. I really think they wanted us to run, which if we had done, would have meant a bullet in the back not freedom.

I have spoken since to witnesses of such acts of treachery. It was surprising that we had not been searched, to see if we were carrying arms which we could have easily used on them. Their relaxed attitude was such, that I was able to remove a piece of bread from my pocket and drop it into the gutter. I considered that this might save some awkward questions later.

As we approached a large building, our guards smartened up and made us go ahead, while they stayed just behind with bayonets at the ready. It seemed that this was our destination, it had the impression of a barracks, or prison, quite solidly built. We stopped at a big wooden gateway under an arch then after much rattling of chains, pulling of bolts and creaking of hinges, we went through a big double door into an inner courtyard.

From there, we were guided into what seemed to be a guard room of sorts, as there were several soldiers lounging around, as if waiting to go on duty. Standing us against the wall, one of the soldiers went through our pockets, removing nothing except our matches, which he evidently wanted himself. Our civilian jackets were placed to one side.

Following this procedure, we were left alone for a few minutes until a German officer walked in, simply looked us over, rapped out orders, then left again. It all seemed rather strange until an armed escort marched us out across the courtyard, to a big wooden door. This was similarly bolted and barred as the main doors were.

Following a lengthy unlocking procedure, we were pushed forward, the doors locked behind us and we were left alone. By the aid of my petrol lighter, we made a survey of our surroundings. I imagine once that it had be either a stable perhaps or an old cell. There were no windows or any means of ventilation except for the cracks in the doors. The whole place was built of brick, floor included, which oozed moisture, and just above the floor iron rings were built into the wall.

Even if we were not as comfortable as we might wish, we had room to move as the cell was approximately ten feet square and twelve feet high. I was surprised to notice by my watch that it was now three o'clock in the morning. This meant we had been captured about half past two, although knowing that fact made no difference to our plight.

The first task was to sew on our badges of rank, as this might make things easier for us when we next faced our captors. To save petrol in my lighter, we tried to do our sewing in the dark and after working for ten minutes, Nat suggested that I lit up, so as to see what progress we had made. I considered this unnecessary as I knew by the feel that I was doing quite well with my tapes and was all for finishing off in the dark. Nat insisted on a light as his cotton was all in knots, his needles were on the floor and in general, his sewing kit was in a mess.

I had not suffered from such problems and was proud of my ability, so much so, that I pulled my tunic to the light to show Nat how good I was. What a shock I received, as though the tapes were in the right position, they were inside out. This struck us as very funny indeed and laughed our heads off. I don't know what the guards thought, hearing two prisoners convulsed with hilarity. They may have believed we were hysterical.

Once we had made ourselves as tidy as possible, we finished some hard boiled eggs and bread, then sat back to wait for morning, smoking the few remaining cigarettes we had. Sleep was next to impossible, but we dozed for short periods propped against the wall. It was a long uncomfortable night.

We waited until half past nine before there was any sign of activity. It sounded as though several people were approaching our place of confinement and we wondered what was happening. Eventually after the bolts were pulled and the doors opened, the Camp Commandant entered with two guards and two civilians. We were searched briefly and everything was removed from our pockets, then we were questioned regarding the food we had concealed in the cell.

Following our perfunctory examination, the officials went into conference, while we were kept against the wall by armed guards. It seemed to be quite a lengthy discussion and we would have liked to know what they were saying, as our fate depended on their decision.

Leaving the group, the only civilian who could speak English approached us for further questioning. His main idea was to find out where we had obtained the food, so I thought the best thing to do, was to tell him I had stolen it. This seemed to please him no end;
"So you stole it did you?"
This could be a trap, so I stuck to my story and confirmed the fact.
"Right" be said, "Then you will be sent to prison for it."

I couldn't help replying that I thought we were going there anyway as this statement of his seemed rather childish. His next action did cause me quite a lot of concern, as reaching out, he touched a piece of red cord which was tied to my neck band fastener. It was quite obvious to him that it was supporting something inside my battledress blouse. This

had either been overlooked in the earlier search, or had been left purposely for a moment of drama.
"What have we here?" he enquired.
"A knife!" I replied.
"How very interesting, we must have a look at it" and hooking his fingers under the cord, pulled it from inside my battledress. Removing it from its sheath, he studied it awhile, which I must admit, it did deserve more than just a passing glance. The handle was brass, inlaid with segments of pearl or shell, the blade was about six inches long and curved upwards to a point. My father had brought a pair of them back from Northern India and I understood that they were Afghan fighting knives.

At this point, I began to wish that I had been carrying a Boy Scout knife, or some such less evil looking thing.
"What do you carry this for?" I was asked and quite truthfully answered that it was for obtaining food and similar harmless activities.
"Have you killed anyone with it?' was his next question. I told him I hadn't.
Then; "Could it kill a man?" I agreed it could.
"Then it could kill you, couldn't it?"

This was getting a bit serious as despite his ham-ish acting, he was also a nasty piece of work enjoying what he was doing. He had an attentive audience, me, Nat and the two guards who were keeping us covered.

"Do you know what we do with your Commandos when we discover concealed knives, we run then straight through them". I told him that I didn't doubt it for one minute, but my knife was not concealed.
"I say it is," he replied and moving closer to me, he pressed the point of the knife against my heart.

I wondered what it was going to feel like being stabbed. The spell was broken when he said;

"What would you do if I pushed?"
Hoping he was just the boastful character I thought him to be, I looked him straight in the eyes, and said; "Drop dead".

An Englishman would have stabbed me for that, but perhaps he didn't understand, as removing the knife, he informed me that I would never see it again. Changing his attitude somewhat, he was pleased to inform us that due to the fact that we were picked up in civilian clothes and under unusual circumstances, we were refused entry into the military prison. We were to be taken to the Military Police Headquarters in the city for interrogation, where a decision would be made regarding our fate.

I took this to be bluff on his part, as I mistakenly imagined that we would be shipped off immediately to the RAF interrogation centre at Frankfurt. I was proved wrong, very wrong. We were hurriedly bundled across the yard, out through the gate then ordered into a private car which was waiting for us.

The German officer who was now in charge of us, seemed to be a very professional and efficient person, who I gathered was a Military Policeman. He told Nat to get into the front seat while I was to get into the back. I was then jammed in, with a soldier either side of me armed with sub-machine guns.

My original diary only mentions one, but I can recall my thoughts as I sat there. The barrels of the guns were resting on my thighs pointing at my stomach. If they had opened fire sitting as they were, they would not only have killed me, they would have chopped each other in two. I didn't think this was very sensible.

Just to make sure that neither of us caused any trouble, the officer, who was now sitting next to Nat, drew his revolver, draped his arm over the back of the seat, and placed the muzzle at the base of Nat's skull. We were then told that if either of us moved, Nat would have his brains blown out.

Apart from that threat, he seemed quite a reasonable type of person. He was not a bully who enjoyed uttering threats, but meant what he said. He explained that we had been refused entry into the military section of the prison, due to our civilian jackets and lack of badges of rank, when arrested, Because of this we were being taken to police headquarters to establish our identity. Strangely enough, despite our serious situation, we seemed to understand each other and I felt no animosity towards him.

After a ten minute drive through narrow cobbled streets, we came to a tall imposing building which the officer informed me was Police Headquarters. I did not worry too much as I was still thinking that we were following a routine, prior to despatch to Frankfurt.

We were ordered out of the car and taken into the building, carefully shepherded by our armed guards. Although there were several people about, no one appeared to take any notice of us, perhaps they were accustomed to seeing others being arrested.

Once inside, I was separated from Nat and shown into an office where all my personal belongings had been placed on a desk, then started a lengthy interrogation. The officer asked me where I had got my food and clothes, and if I could lead the Germans to the French who had helped us.

The authorities knew that we had received help in some way, as how else could we have obtained two identical jackets with all identifying marks and labels removed. If we had not been helped by the locals in any way then we had baled out wearing or carrying them, which put quite a different aspect on the whole situation.

I was threatened with shooting, civil prison, Gestapo and other equally fearful treatment, but what worried me most, he seemed to be totally disinterested in my service activities. He wanted proof that I was not a British Agent dropped by air. Repetition of my name, rank and number did nothing to satisfy him as he pointed out to me, that as a spy, I would most likely be given these sort of credentials which meant nothing to him.

After an hour of such treatment I was taken to another room, where I was handcuffed to a radiator and left to think for a while. This treatment was hardly what I had been expecting, so naturally I began to believe that things were going badly wrong.

My worries were not made any easier when I was taken back to the interrogation and found Nat sitting there with handcuffs on. Just before he was removed, we were both told that I was to be questioned again and if my answers did not agree with his, he would be treated very severely. Why it was to be him who was to receive the treatment, I don't know.

This time, my questioning mainly concerned the supply of the jackets. If it had been a Frenchman responsible, then they would find him and shoot him, if not then they would shoot me. My interrogator was quite insistent on this point and invited me to look out of the window. He then pointed to the wall I would be stood against to be shot.

Being a reasonable sort of man, he explained that shooting me on the spot, would be a lot easier for me than being handed over to the Gestapo. As an enemy agent, my fate would be the same, but it would take a lot longer, months in fact.

I really can't remember if I took the Gestapo threat seriously, although if I had known then, what I learned later about such prisons, I would have been very scared indeed. The intelligence lectures I received at home had not prepared me for this eventuality and I wasn't sure how to handle it.

The questioning continued always with the same theme, the origin of the jackets. At last he suggested that I would be taken in a car and driven round for several days if necessary until I recognised the places I had visited. I wondered how to counter this proposal, as I had no desire to be taken anywhere in one of their cars, except to a regular prison camp.

I explained that even if I wanted to, I would be of no help, as we entered and left villages at night, so had no real idea where we had been. It was probably quite true that I would not recognise the places by daylight, all the same, I hoped he didn't pursue the subject.

After this session, he thought it useless to question me any further, so left me with some French collaborators in another room. I supposed it was a plan to make me talk, as the people treated me very well. The radio was switched on to the BBC for me, then I was offered cigarettes and magazines. So that for a while, I was feeling quite comfortable. Despite this soft treatment, I didn't trust any of them.

I waited about an hour before being re-united with Nat, who by now was free of handcuffs. I was very pleased to see him as I had been having some doubts that I would ever do so again. He was no wiser than I regarding our next move, but we waited and hoped.

Before long, our original guards appeared to escort us, and we were informed that the military police had finished with us. We were to be returned to the military prison to see if we would be accepted now but this was not a certainty, as it rested entirely with the Commandant.

The alternative would be confinement in a civil prison. I never imagined that I would be pleased to be brought back and placed in that dark damp cell again, but I was, as at least we had avoided the firing squad.

Our life as Prisoners of War was just starting and we wondered what the future held for us, could it be any worse than what we had already experienced? We were to find that out.

CHAPTER 8

We stayed in the dark cell for three hours before guards brought us out into the light again. Without ceremony we were marched across the yard, up a flight of steps into the Commandant's office to be searched. The check we received was fairly thorough as we were stripped and our clothing searched for compasses, files, saws, or any other escape aids we might have concealed. I had to remove both my signet rings to make sure that nothing was hidden underneath, then my service and civilian watches were opened, but not harmed. Unfortunately my service issue watch had the Air Ministry stamp on the back, so it was confiscated in exchange for a receipt which was only worth the paper it was written on. Strangely enough, despite the legendary Teutonic thoroughness, they overlooked the silk map I was carrying.

Finally our name, rank, number and age was recorded, then we were subjected to having our fingerprints taken. This was done none too gently. When the formalities had been completed, we were taken up several flights of stairs to a small barely furnished room which was to be our home for a while. There were two iron beds, one with a thin mattress through which the iron frame beneath could be felt and the other so fat and round that it seemed impossible to lie on it. Under the only window was a deal table where two bowls and two spoons had been placed. This I think completed the furnishing, except for a dim electric light bulb, hanging from a very dirty ceiling. Before the guards left us, Nat was told that his bed was the one with the fat mattress and we were not to change.

Once we were on our own, we reviewed our situation. The room was at the end of a building on the top floor and overlooked a large square, surrounded on three sides by buildings. It had the appearance of being a barracks and as we were told later, it had been an old French Cavalry Barracks. The window was heavily barred with the addition of barbed wire entwined just below the window. Iron bars had been driven into the wall horizontally and four or five strands of barbed wire were stretched the whole length of the building. This was a sight which tended to discourage any ideas of escape from that place.

When we had looked from the window until we knew the view by heart, we both lay down without speaking a word, just thinking what was and what might have been. At that time, I think I felt the most deep despair I had ever experienced and there seemed to be no way out of it.

I must have dropped off to sleep for some time as it was seven o'clock in the evening when I was disturbed by a guard bringing our evening meal. He poured out two bowls of ersatz coffee and placed two pieces of bread on the table, with a small pat of butter for each, then left the room. We waited a while to see what else was coming, we waited in vain, there was nothing.

Feeling very thirsty, I made for the coffee and what a shock I received, it tasted vile. Not only was it without milk or sugar, the flavour was unrecognisable. The smell was unpleasant and the taste bitter. It was a taste that I am certain I will never completely forget. Simply by recalling that coffee I can re-create the atmosphere of those first days of imprisonment in Amiens. It was not until later that I was told it was made from toasted acorns.

I imagined the bread would be in the same class as the coffee and I was not wrong in my assessment. It was very dark muddy brown, far more solid and heavy than any English bread I have seen, also it was very sour. As hungry as I was it became a real struggle to swallow it and force back the feeling of nausea it caused me. Nat was unable to eat more than half of his so I took it away and hid it in my mattress as I was afraid that the guard, seeing we had left some, might cut our rations.

Eight o'clock next morning we heard our guard approaching with our breakfast, which made me think of more sour bread. I needn't have worried, as all we received was a bowl of coffee, which, with the bread retrieved from my mattress made a very meagre meal. Giving us time to digest our breakfast, our guard returned later to escort us to the wash room and toilet. The wash room was little help to us as we had no razor, soap, or towel and merely splashing water on our face did nothing for us. We were so filthy from our recent escapades we needed a long hot bath, but we were not going to get it. I was worried at the lack of soap as we had both received cuts about the head and face when we had baled out, which could turn septic if not cleaned properly.

It did not occur to me that if our minor injuries were going to turn septic, they would have done so long before this. After the brief freedom in the toilet, we were herded back to our room where we were left to sit and wait for our next meal, whatever it might be.

In between meals, there was absolutely nothing to do except look out of the window or talk. We had no books or cigarettes, no pens or pencils with which to write, in fact we had only what we stood up in. We patiently waited until two o' clock before our next meal was served, which turned out to be no more than a half pint of so called soup. This consisted of potato water which had a few grains of barley and a small potato added to it, hardly enough to keep us alive. This was typical of the meals we received while at Amiens. The rations did vary slightly, as sometimes we would have jam instead of butter, or boiled pea shucks in the soup in place of barley. The butter was white, unsalted and almost tasteless. Its consistency was more like face cream than anything else. The jam was of a nature completely unknown to us, its only resemblance to anything we knew was its red colour. It did contain something which represented strawberry jam pips, but we were convinced that they were genuine wood chips.

Just about four o'clock there came a diversion, as we were summoned from our room and taken downstairs. We wondered what was going to happen and were extremely pleased to discover that we were being allowed out for exercise. This was a most welcome break after the hole we were living in. Once out in the open, we were directed to fall in with a crowd of army fellows who had come from another part of the building. We had seen them previously up at their windows, while we were being searched. Having made sure that everyone was out, we were marched into a part of the square which had been divided into exercise compounds.

My first impression was a sense of the bizarre as to me it was rather like a film set, without lights or cameras. I had often seen such sights in the cinema, not dreaming that one day I would be taking part in a real life drama. There were forty five of us, four or five deep, walking in a circle round the compound, conversing quietly. Needless to say, we were very pleased to be in the company of our fellow men and had plenty to talk about. Nat and I were the only RAF aircrew there, the others were troops captured during the D-day invasion a few days previously. The group was a mixed one, and comprised of Paratroopers, Airborne troops, Commandos, Sailors and one or two Marines.

After half an hour of this circular walking, we were formed up and marched back to our different rooms, where once again we sat and waited for our next meal such as it was. It turned up at half past five this time and was no improvement on the previous evening's issue. Having little to do after this we retired early and brought to a close our first full day as Prisoners of War.

CHAPTER 9

In the morning, shortly after coffee, we were honoured by a visit from a German officer and wondered what he wanted. We then realised that he was accompanied by a guard and a Royal Marine. The officer who could speak a certain amount of English told me to collect my blankets, bowl and spoon, then follow him. I did as I was told, hoping it did not mean that we were about to be subjected to more unpleasant treatment. I did not feel very re-assured when, as we were leaving, the officer told Nat that he would never see me again. I had the feeling that Nat was to get priority in whatever they had in store for us and the thought entered my mind that perhaps the Royal Marine was not genuine. He was there for a purpose.

As I was being taken downstairs by the officer, I asked him what was the reason for telling Nat he would not see me again. He told me not to worry as I was going to join the other British prisoners and despite what Nat had been told, I would in fact see him. I didn't understand this mental torture, as there seemed to be no point to it, but kept my peace as I was not going to get a proper explanation from him.

We didn't go all the way downstairs, but stopped at a door on the first floor and on entering, discovered I was in the large room where the other prisoners were billeted. The officer now showed me to the bed I was to occupy which proved to be the bed the Marine had slept in. The officer, having completed his small task, departed, locking the door behind him.

The reason for my move was soon explained. The Marine who was suspected of a serious skin disease, had to be separated from the others to prevent it spreading and as ours was the only suitable room, I had been moved. Nat was not quite so fortunate as being Jewish, he had to risk the consequences.

Once the officer had left, the fellows all crowded round me clamouring for recent news. There was little I could tell them as they had only been captured two weeks before us and there had been little change. Despite their disappointment they made me welcome and I was accepted into their company immediately.

Naturally we asked questions of each other and exchanged experiences. I found their stories very fascinating indeed as they had all been involved with the actual D-day landings and in my eyes, they were something special. I had taken part in the initial softening up bombardment from the air which was a routine raid for us, these people had been engaged in the actual fighting. I was very thankful that I was aircrew.

A paratrooper who slept in the next bed to me had a most unfortunate time. Due to faulty navigation of his troop carrier, he had been dropped twenty miles from his correct position. When he landed he was on the North bank of the Seine, just outside Le Havre and very effectively cut off from the main party. Not knowing whether he was amongst friends or enemy, he buried his parachute and hid in a cornfield.

He had not been there very long before two soldiers approached him and thinking they belonged to his party, he gave the password. Instead of British soldiers, he had met the Germans who on hearing his voice had opened fire with revolvers. Seeing the necessity to silence them, he threw a hand grenade, which killed one and wounded the other.

As a result of this activity, the cornfield was swept by machine gunfire causing him to crawl to another field. He stayed there for ten days with no food and little water.

Eventually he became delirious and thinking he was approaching French women for help, he walked up to some German soldiers. That is how he finished up in Amiens as a prisoner of war.

I wondered how long it would be before I saw Nat again, as I thought that due to the infection he would not be allowed out for exercise, I need not have worried as he appeared as usual, the next afternoon. As it turned out, it was beneficial for Nat to have the marine with him as he, unlike ourselves, had his own billy can, This held much more soup than the standard bowl and as it was always filled, they both had more than the rest of us.

After two days, it was found that the Marine was quite fit so he was permitted to join the group again. I expected to be returned to the room with Nat, but unfortunately for him, he was left in solitary confinement, so causing him more misery.

Quite by chance I found a small stub of pencil in my pocket which both the Germans and I had overlooked. I knew that Nat had nothing to do in his cell, so managed to pass it to him on our next daily exercise. He was very pleased indeed as he was now able to amuse himself by writing down his thoughts and experiences. He had a fair supply of writing material as he was using the wallpaper which he tore off in strips.

This ability to talk to each other and pass things during our exercise periods, I found quite surprising, as I expected more rigid control to be used. It also amused me to think that although we were surrounded by barbed wire, the guards were posted at short intervals inside the compound armed not with rifles, but sub-machine guns. They must have thought we were extremely desperate.

Despite this armed vigilance during our daily exercise, we were able to supplement our diet from time to time. This was done by grabbing dog roses from a bush which was growing in the square. Chewing the rose petals may not have given us a great deal of nourishment but it did at least leave Some sort of taste in our mouths.

Another culinary delight was obtained from a carton of mint flavoured tooth powder. This had been obtained by a prisoner in a manner which did not concern us. Very generously he would share it out, by shaking a little into the palms of our hands, then we would sit quietly licking up the powder a little at a time, savouring the flavour as though it was nectar.

Although conditions were not all they might have been, we did have some amusements. The boys had pulled the blackout screens down and with the aid of scissors and a pencil made some packs of playing cards. This managed to keep us amused for hours. When not occupied doing this, we would often sit and look out of the window as there was nearly always something to see. The outside wall of the building we were in, faced South towards the town and the three windows overlooked the road which led to the main gate. We could always depend on seeing a party of Russian and Polish prisoners on their way to and from work.

We didn't know who they were as several classes of people were imprisoned in the building, the most numerous seemed to be political prisoners. In our opinion, this particular party was a forced labour gang, as when they moved about, their escorts were armed to the teeth with guns, rifles and a belt full of grenades. The treatment they received while within our sight was quite brutal, which made us wonder about the kind of treatment they received when alone.

On most days we would see civilians waiting outside, hoping to visit some of the inmates. Their waiting was often prolonged, but the duration of their visit short. They were more fortunate perhaps, than those civilians who would turn up under military escort, as these would disappear into the establishment and not return.

One time I saw a woman with a young child being escorted by a person in German uniform. He was urging them along with a sub-machine gun at their backs and being none too gentle. I felt very angry at this manner of treatment and even more so when I realised that this thing in German uniform was a Frenchman. I remembered him from my visit to Police Headquarters and he knew that I despised him.

Having been on German rations for several days, I became so weak that the daily half hour exercise was becoming too much for me, in fact even sitting up at the window or the card table was a strain. As a result of this, I spent most of my time just lying on my bed, simply talking or resting. It made me wonder how Nat was getting on by himself, as he had the added burden of loneliness to contend with.

Two or three days after he had lost the company of the Marine, the solitary confinement put him under severe stress, so he applied to the Commandant to be allowed to join us. This request was ignored for a while until a Staff Sergeant representing everyone, told the Commandant that he was not in order, keeping one of our members in solitary and we wanted him with us. Much to our surprise, our petition was effective and Nat was brought down to us the same day.

There was little to affect our monotonous life, except for an occasional night raid when we could see flares and anti-aircraft fire in the distance. These local raids rather worried an army sergeant who thought we could be in danger. He had the idea that bombs might be scattered far and wide, so hitting us. Eventually he confided his fears to me and asked me what the risks were. I explained that the aircraft approached on a set heading and bombs were aimed at flares on the ground. If there was a risk of cloud cover, marker flares supported by parachutes would be grouped over the aiming point. He then felt re-assured that bomb aimers did not simply drop their bombs where they wished. The next night raid in the district demonstrated my point and all was well.

One night having settled down to sleep, this same army sergeant came rushing up to my bed, and shook me until I woke up.
'Come quick and look at this' he said, 'I am sure we are the target.'
I couldn't hear anything at all and assured him that there was nothing in Amiens which would interest Bomber Command. He was very persistent and having got me out of bed, dragged me to the window saying,
'Look at that.'
My heart nearly stopped as hanging almost directly overhead, was a large group of target marking flares. I could hardly admit it to him that I also thought we were the target, but to pacify him I had to think quickly. I pretended to study the flares then told him we were quite safe, as due to the direction from which the bombers would approach, the bombs were unlikely to be anywhere near us.

I returned to my bed in a very anxious mood, whereas he returned to his quite happily. He must have thought I was a genius in tactics as strangely enough we heard nothing that night and I still don't understand why.

Day raids were continuous, so it was normal for us to see American bombers and fighters passing on their way to their targets. One particular day, we saw some American fighters much lower and closer than normal. A German convoy which was loading up in the nearby square suddenly stopped what they were doing and drove their trucks into the road which led to our building. Hurriedly they left the trucks and crouched against the wall. One of the fellows standing at the window with us, shouted 'Come on boys, they are down here, come and shoot them up'. It was almost as if they had been waiting for his order, as almost immediately the leader peeled off and came screaming down towards our barracks followed by four or five others.

Just in time we realised it was us they were after and not the convoy. In an instant we threw ourselves on the floor, as close to the wall as we could, hoping that it was thick enough to stop cannon shells, although we realised in a determined attack, our building offered little protection. Opening fire as they came, they swooped very low aiming straight at our building.

Suddenly above the noise of the guns we heard a short sharp eerie whine of bombs, so it was going to be curtains for us trapped as we were. The first explosions shook the building, blew some windows in and brought dust down from cracks in the ceiling. It was a miracle that no one was hurt although we were all quite shaken. As soon as things were quiet, we hurried to the windows that overlooked the inner courtyard. There we saw a line of four craters made by a stick of two hundred and fifty pound bombs. The nearest crater was only twenty yards from our building and we were told later that this particular bomb had bounced off our roof.

We were not sure what purpose the attack served, unless it was done to effect a breakout by political prisoners. If this had been the case, then as far as we were concerned in our little section, it hadn't worked. What had happened in other blocks, we had no means of finding out.

I suspect that a similar raid had taken place earlier, as the building next to us appeared to have had one end blown off and was now covered with tarpaulin.

It was apparent to us that we were unlikely to remain in this particular establishment for long as up to that time, we had not been interrogated properly and our food was virtually non existent. This was not what we had been led to believe by our own Intelligence officers.

Not knowing what was to happen made the days of waiting seem endless but after being locked up in the one big room for fourteen days, twelve of us were told we would be leaving that day. No indication of our destination but we were not worried, we would be leaving this dreadful hole. The day of waiting seemed interminable.

CHAPTER 10

Promptly at eight o'clock in the evening we were assembled ready for our departure. There was a strained air of uncertainty, at the same time, relief that we were leaving. We made our farewells to our recent companions, then were taken downstairs to the exercise yard where a coach was waiting. This seemed to be filled with civilians, RAF personnel and German soldiers, which left no room for us. It was not our fortune to ride in such style, as our transport was a canvas covered truck hitched on to the back.

Having suffered once again the inevitable head count, we were told to climb into the truck where we were joined by armed guards. It was not exactly designed for comfort as we had to sit on the floor, so we hoped it wouldn't be for too long. Finally when everyone was settled, the order was given to move off. Strangely, I almost felt happy that we were leaving, despite the fact we were heading for the unknown.

Turning a corner, we lost sight of the place which had been home for a short period and somehow I knew I would never feel homesick for it. Later however, there were times I would have willingly returned there in exchange for some of the situations we were to meet.

The feeling which surmounted even the doubtful pleasure of leaving Amiens was our hunger, heightened by seeing some of the guards eating. Noticing my envious eyes, one who was sitting next to me, offered Nat and myself a sandwich which we were very thankful to receive. Later the same guard offered us two and a half cigarettes, an almost forgotten pleasure as this was the first real smoke we had enjoyed in two weeks.

While in Amiens, we did not have the luxury of Red Cross parcels, therefore there were no cigarettes, unless a sympathetic guard smuggled some to us. It was a strange ritual, as the guard would pass the cigarettes through the door, then lock it again. Ensuring that he had not been seen, he would then open the door to give us a light. If several cigarettes were handed in, then we would split up into small groups, so that every group had one cigarette. This would then be passed around the group with each member taking only one puff and passing it on. As each took his turn, the others watched intently to make sure that the person smoking did not take more than one puff. This would continue until the cigarette was finished.

Now that we were clear of the Amiens prison, the smoking rules no longer applied, in any case, we had no need to share our cigarettes with anyone else. This was sheer luxury and we savoured them to the full. Now that we felt less hungry, our attention was turned to thoughts of the future. It was pointless to try to look too far ahead, so the main concern was our immediate destination. After questioning the guards, it was discovered that we were heading for Brussels where we expected to arrive early the following morning.

Things were proceeding fairly smoothly until about two o'clock in the morning when we ran into a very heavy thunderstorm. The rain which was the worst I had seen for a long time, began to form puddles on the roof of our trailer. After a while, there was so much water that the rear part of the roof gave way and showered on the guards sitting near the tailboard. We laughed inwardly at their discomfort but not for long as soon the wind and rain took its effect on our portion of the covering. In no time at all we were as wet as the guards, in fact, guards, prisoners and the inside of the trailer, were all as wet as the outside world. The people in the coach didn't care a bit as they were in the dry.

During the hours of darkness, we had been unable to see the places we were passing through, but as dawn broke we entered the town of Mons. To me this name was a legend connected to stories of the Great War and it had just become a reality. It may have been a nice place at one time, but what a depressing sight it now presented. The rain and grey skies gave an air of gloom to an already desolate scene. There was street after street of bombed and shelled buildings whose debris had spilled into the road. Bulldozers had cleared a lane just wide enough to let traffic through.

At seven o'clock in the morning, following a very wet and stormy journey, we entered Brussels, then after driving down a main road for quite a distance, we turned into a large courtyard. As soon as we had stopped, we were ordered out of our transport and told to fall in with the prisoners who had been in the coach. We were not allowed to stand around too long, but during the short period we did get, I tried to discover where we were and what our surroundings were like. As far as I can remember, the courtyard was surrounded on three sides by buildings, while the fourth side was enclosed by railings. Either inside, or just outside the courtyard was a clock, standing on a column possibly twenty feet in height. Beyond the railings was a main road and judging by the surrounding buildings we were in the centre of the city.

I gathered that the group we had joined were prisoners like ourselves, who had been collected from various assembly points. Surrounded by guards, we were shepherded towards a doorway which opened on to a flight of stairs. Mounting these, we came to another doorway and another flight of stairs, then yet another doorway followed by more stairs. Each door could only be opened from the lower set of stairs and in addition, a guard was permanently posted to lock or unlock the door as required.

Eventually we arrived in a large hall, where we were to be searched. We waited for an hour before the search even started, then one by one we were called forward. I became a bit concerned as I was still carrying my silk escape map which I had managed to smuggle through previous searches.

It was obvious that these people knew their job, so I had to rid myself of the map if possible. Failure to do so, might single me out for special treatment. The map was inside my shirt, spread out as flat as possible to avoid detection. I started to fidget a little, pretending to be uncomfortable and by doing this, managed to unbutton my jacket and shirt enough to drag the map out. After quite a long struggle, I was able to transfer it to my trouser pocket, but where to hide it was the next difficulty.

I was standing amongst a group of prisoners in a large hall, watched by guards. In front of us was a table where officers were recording prisoners' particulars and conducting searches. There didn't appear to be any hiding places for my map. If I dropped it on the floor, the action might draw attention, so it had to be a place where it would not become immediately obvious.

Just behind me, I noticed a radiator which seemed an ideal place of concealment if only I could reach it. Edging myself very slowly backwards, I managed to get there without any of the guards realising I had changed my position. I received some strange looks from other prisoners as they could see I was doing something unusual and were a little wary of me. Pretending I was resting against the wall, I gradually removed the map from my pocket and pushed it down the back of the radiator out of sight. There was no sudden challenge by guards, or anyone else, and it was almost a relief when I was called forward for my turn to be searched.

As prisoners completed the formalities, they were escorted away by a guard carrying a revolver. I noticed that prisoners were being taken in different directions which made me wonder why. I could understand the guards being armed, but to have drawn revolvers seemed quite unnecessary. It would have been impossible for a normal person to overpower a guard then make his getaway. To try to leave by the way we had entered, would have been suicidal and to find an alternative would require knowledge of the building.

From what I could see, I was the only one taken downstairs, the others were going along the corridor somewhere. Anything unusual tends to arouse suspicions for a person in these circumstances and I was no exception. I tried to think of what I might have done to deserve this special treatment, perhaps they had watched me conceal the map.

As we went downstairs, we stopped at each doorway, the guard gave the password and we were allowed through. On arrival at the ground floor I was now guided out into the courtyard and ordered to start walking. We crossed the square of the courtyard then passed through several alleyways, until we finished up at a building set apart from the rest. On entry, I discovered it was a cell block which contained ancient dungeons. Fourteen cells were arranged either side of a central passage, with one small room for a toilet. The light level inside was very poor, giving the whole place an atmosphere of gloom and despair. I felt no better when the guard opened a steel door four inches thick, ordered me inside a narrow cell, then closed and bolted the door behind me.

Through lack of sleep the previous night, I was feeling very tired, so stretched out on the lower half of a two tier bunk hoping to relax. The bunk was reasonably comfortable, but I think I had too many things on my mind to sleep easily.

With nothing else to do, I took stock of my surroundings. The cell itself which was brick built with a tiled floor, was approximately twelve feet by six feet. The furnishings consisted of the bunk I was lying on, a table, chair and an electric light bulb. The only light during the day came from a small iron grating set in the ceiling. The walls as far as I could estimate, matched the door for strength as they were about eighteen inches thick. The thing which made me appreciate that I was in a dungeon was the peephole in the door. This was an inch in diameter and had a small shutter on it operated from the outside. Fortunately, mine being broken, allowed me to look out into the passage.

Having discovered what little there was to discover about my cell, I lay back and simply stared at the bunk boards above my head. Nothing was really on my mind at that time, until my eyes suddenly focused on something written on one of the boards forming the base of the upper bunk. It was written in English and should have been a message of hope or something similar. As I deciphered it, I almost burst out laughing as an American comedian had written the statement: 'Buy US War Bonds'. For some reason, I decided that it was freshly written and quite illogically thought that he may have left something hidden in the cell for me to find.

I searched everywhere I could think of, under the beds, in them, and even behind them but there was nothing. It wasn't until I looked under the table that I discovered five or six crusts of black bread discarded in a corner. I dragged this treasure out, then sat on my bed and removed as much of the dirt and mildew as I could, without losing too much of the bread. Then with a feeling of pleasure, I chewed on the crusts to make them last as long as possible, I reflected on the fact that this was the first thing I had eaten since early the previous evening when the guard had shared his sandwiches with Nat and me.

The time by now must have been about mid-day. Shortly after this repast, I could hear cell doors being opened, some muttered phrases, then doors closed again. I wondered what was happening until my door was opened and a guard standing outside, handed me two slices of bread and honey with a bowl of coffee, I couldn't believe my luck, we were not being left to starve after all and I realised, I was not alone down there as I had thought. As soon as the guards had left, I shouted out to anyone that might hear me, what a relief when Nat answered, he was in the next cell.

After a few hours, I heard booted feet enter the dungeon block, a cell door open, a command in German followed by what sounded like prisoner and escort leaving. No telling where they were going, although as this seemed to be repeated at intervals, I hoped it was the start of the interrogation process. This may sound strange but I knew it had to be faced before being despatched to a prison camp and the sooner the better.

Naturally it was necessary to visit the toilet at times and what a performance that turned out to be. The first action was to alert the guard by means of a wooden signal arm operated from inside the cell. This was followed by considerable shuffling of feet in the corridor and the sound of a dog being brought into the cell block. When the door was opened, the prisoner would be escorted to the toilet, covered all the time by a rifle. Just to make sure that no one made a dash for the exit, another guard stood in the entrance door with a very large Alsatian dog. The return to the cell was quite straight forward as the prisoner made his own way back to it, then once inside he pushed the door closed. It was not until this time that the guard approached the cell, to slip the bolts across.

On one occasion when I requested to go to the toilet, the guard unbolted my door, then told me to wait until ordered to move. I was quite puzzled by this, especially as I heard another cell door open followed by the sound of a dog struggling. Eventually the guard gave me the order to proceed, and I stepped outside. I was surprised not to see him near my door, instead he had control of the Alsatian, I say control, it was anything but. The dog was only struggling a little at first, but when he saw me, he went berserk and attempted to come after me. With almost no prompting, I shot into the toilet and slammed the door after me. Things eventually calmed down outside and I was told to return to my cell. I stepped from the toilet and out into the corridor confident that everything was under control, the dog was still there. I am not normally worried by dogs, but this one scared me stiff. If there had been a world record for travelling from toilet to cell, I am certain I broke it that day.

Shortly after this incident, I heard two guards shouting at each other, the dog barking furiously, then the clang of a cell door. The impression I got from all this, was that the dog handler had left the cell block for a few minutes and had locked his dog in a cell. The remaining guard thought he was being clever by getting it out as protection while I went to the toilet. It was at this point that the guard discovered that the Alsatian to be a one man dog and he wasn't the man.

Just before mid-day next day, I heard the usual booted feet in the corridor outside and they had stopped at my door. It was not meal time, neither had I requested a visit to the toilet, therefore hopefully I was on my way to be interrogated. This assumption proved correct as I was taken back to the main building, upstairs to the place I had first been searched, then led into a small side room. This proved to be an ordinary office with the usual furniture, except that standing in the corner was a soldier who kept an automatic levelled at me all the time.

Bidding me 'Good Afternoon' a Luftwaffe officer entered, sat at the desk and indicated I should pull up a chair. No sooner was I seated than he flung at me;

'You are Flight Sergeant Masters, Navigator of a 'Lancaster', shot down over Arras at one thirty in the morning on the sixteenth of June'.

I must admit this sudden attack stunned me and I wondered where he had got his facts from. Apart from giving my personal particulars at Amiens, I had divulged nothing else but my name, rank and number. Neither confirming or denying the fact, I told him I could say nothing. He didn't seem very pleased at my reply and told me so. I was then asked about the letters on the side of the aircraft and this time I told him I had no idea, which was quite true. He stared at me in disbelief and standing up, said;

'Good God man, they paint them this big' and holding up his hands, indicated letters six feet high.

I suddenly realised what he wanted and apologized by telling him I thought he was referring to the serial number.

'Good,' he said 'I didn't think you were that stupid' and sitting down he prepared to record the letters.

'Now what are they?'

'I can't tell you! I replied. I thought he was going to have a fit, then suddenly calming down he said;

'You are being very stupid, Just look at me, I am a German officer in the Luftwaffe, now just turn round and tell me what you see'.

I told him, 'A soldier with a gun',

'Right,' he said 'You are not among friends now, you don't have the protection of your officers and colleagues, you are on your own in a foreign land. What is more you are a prisoner and one word from me, that guard will blow your head off'.

I appreciated the truth of his statement and felt terribly vulnerable, but still I would tell him nothing. His next threat was to leave me with the Gestapo for a week, after which time I would beg to see him. Only when I begged for mercy would he take my statement if he felt so inclined.

One thing that did impress me about my interrogator was not so much his tactics as his excellent command of English. This was so natural and without accent, he may well have been an Englishman.

His mood suddenly changed, no longer the arrogant bully, more the person resigned to carrying out his duties and in this manner, he floored me with a very casual off hand statement.
'It may interest you to know that both Sergeant Newton your Rear Gunner and Flight Sergeant Martin are dead.'
I felt the blood drain from my face, then I wanted to lean over and hit him hard for his callousness. Controlling myself, I simply remarked;
'Oh yes' trying to indicate it meant nothing to me.
Finally rising, he said that he was very sorry for me, but due to the fact I could not give satisfactory answers, I would be returned to a different cell. This change of cell meant that I would be waiting for transportation to a Gestapo prison.

Taking this as a dismissal, I prepared to go, but before I could move, he made an appeal on my behalf. 'For your own good tell me the letters on the side of your aircraft.'

Noting that I had nothing to say, he pulled out his watch and told me that I would have exactly one minute in which to answer, this was to be my very last chance. We both sat and watched the seconds ticking off, he on one side waiting for me to break, while I on the other side was wondering what his reaction would be like when I refused. Right on the minute he stood up, indicated to the guard to remove me, then strode out. I was very close behind him and was surprised when he suddenly stepped back and said;

'Have you changed your mind?'

When I said I hadn't, he told me that I was extremely stupid and I deserved what was coming to me, with this depressing message, he walked away down the corridor.

I hoped that the threat of a Gestapo prison was bluff, although it seemed as though my guard was not returning me to my original cell. The promise of a different cell was quite true as now I was taken along to a block of them in the main building. These were situated in a large hall which had been partitioned off to create several solitary cells.

The cell I was taken to was a vast improvement on the last place. True it was smaller, only measuring eight feet by six feet but it was on the outside wall of the building and had a double window which I could open. Naturally it was covered with barbed wire, which made little difference as I was too far above the ground to jump anyway. An added bonus was the view, as now I was able to look into the police offices on the other side of the alleyway and see things of interest. By squeezing up close to the window, it was also possible to look along the alleyway which enabled me to see a large canal, I believe that my cell was perhaps better situated than any other on that floor.

After I had been in my cell for a period, trying to imagine what it would be like with the Gestapo, I was ordered out and taken to a room I had not seen before. As I entered, I was greeted by an officer who informed me that he was the commanding officer of the unit. He wished to interview me as it had been reported to him that I was most troublesome. It appeared that I had failed to supply my last interrogator with certain information. Because of my lack of co-operation I was causing unnecessary delay to a party of prisoners due to be sent to a prison camp.

He could not have known that I had been threatened with the Gestapo, otherwise he would have played on that. At this news, my confidence returned, as I believed that nothing could have been as bad as the earlier threat. His interrogation was centred on the way in which I had been shot down and captured, also the names of the crew. He told me that I was the only one who had not written a report which was essential to my clearance.

He offered to show me reports written by others to prove his point, and I would be able to choose. I don't think he expected me to respond, but I asked to read the report written by a certain badly burned air gunner. I had already spoken to this man and had a rough idea of what had happened. If he had written one which I doubted, then I wanted to see how they may have doctored it. I don't know if the interrogator remembered our previous conversation but he replied;
'Sorry, he hasn't written his yet.'
I didn't like to mention that I was supposed to have been the last one, so kept my peace.

It was almost as though our earlier discussion had never taken place, as he now acted as if the interrogation was just starting. Handing me a form, he told me to enter my name, rank and number, which I did, then I was to write my account. I sat and stared at the paper for a while, then crossed out the space for the account and signed it. Suddenly be reached across the table, grabbed the paper, locked it in his drawer, then added;
'That was just what I was waiting for, you may go now.'

I had been returned to my cell and was sitting gazing from the window wondering what was to follow. It was while idly looking at the police offices, I realised that the solitary police occupant was waving to me in a form of greeting, and in need of a friend, I waved back. This started quite a long conversation in sign language and among other things, he asked if I needed cigarettes. If I could think of a way to collect them, he would give me some.

He had decided that throwing them across was much too difficult and might give the game away. Being a heavy smoker, I sat on my bed to find a means of doing so. As far as I could see, there was no obstruction beneath my window, so finally decided on a plan already half formed.

I started by unravelling the stitching from the end of my blankets, then tied them together to form a long line then fixed this to a piece of wood. The end of the line was weighed down with two trouser buttons. I would have liked something heavier, but nothing was available. I showed this to my friend and indicated I would lower it from my window. This started him off into a great pantomime. First he held up a piece of white paper, looked at his watch, then at the sky. Next it was a piece of carbon paper and a similar performance, this time with the addition of a whistled tune.

The message was quite plain. At eleven o' clock when it was dark, he would come beneath my window and whistle a tune. When I heard this, I was to lower my line, to which he would tie cigarettes and matches. Rather impatiently I waited until darkness fell, then opened the blackout covering the windows. This had to be done very carefully and slowly in order to prevent alerting the guard. Right on eleven o' clock, I heard the Belgian walking slowly up and down the alleyway beneath my window. He was whistling the tune to indicate that all was safe.

As quickly as possible I lowered the buttons, already anticipating the smoke I was going to enjoy. It was not to be, the line snagged just a few feet below the window. Try as I might I could get it neither up or down which almost broke my heart, I wanted those cigarettes desperately. Eventually I broke the line off short, closed the shutters and crawled into bed a very disappointed man. To make matters worse, I heard the Belgian outside my window for a good fifteen minutes and there was nothing I could do about it. I devised a means of letting him know what had gone wrong with the intention of communicating with him first thing in the morning.

I didn't get the chance, as at five thirty next morning I was removed from my cell for a reason I didn't care to contemplate. I was directed into a large room with thirty or forty other prisoners, which really made me wonder what was happening. I couldn't believe my luck, we were being assembled, preparatory to a train journey to Frankfurt interrogation centre. My relief was tremendous as it meant that I was not now destined for a Gestapo prison.

CHAPTER 11

If I had been pleased to leave Amiens, it was nothing, compared to the relief I felt at leaving Brussels. I didn't mind the transport to the station, even though it was rather unusual. We were locked in a cage, inside a van and to make absolutely sure we were secure, an armed guard was posted just outside the cage. The journey was only a short one and we were soon assembled on the platform at the station. It was natural that we should be eyed with great curiosity by the local population and I for one was pleased to board the train.

The level of comfort on the train was vastly superior to that of the van we had been delivered in, as we were put into First-class coaches supplied by French railways.

Despite our early departure from the prison, we did not leave Brussels until nine o'clock, which may have been due to disruption caused by the numerous attacks on the railways. If we needed proof of the effectiveness of our efforts it was here in Brussels marshalling yard. As far as I could see, out of a dozen or more lines, only one set was usable and that was a temporary affair. The rest of the yard seemed to be filled with wrecked engines, burned out coaches and smashed up rolling stock of all types.

As soon as the train started, we were made to sit very still and forbidden to speak, watched by guards patrolling the coaches carrying sub-machine guns. This enforced silence was too much for Nat who started talking as usual. Immediately a guard appeared, ordered him out of his seat then made him stand in the corner for nearly an hour. If we wished to go to the toilet, we had to call a guard who would accompany us until we returned to our seat. This immobility was very tiring indeed, particularly as we had to stay silent. I was able to study the damage of Liège fairly closely, as we stayed there for over an hour.

Unfortunately, the marshalling yard was hardly damaged but the built up areas either side were flattened. I was told later that the civilian population suffered very badly. When I asked the person who was telling me, how he knew this, he said that while escaping, he had been living in Liège.

Just outside the station, we had to cross a river which at one time had been spanned by a long stone bridge. Only one or two spans were left, the rest were smashed and in the river. To allow the trains to cross, huge bulks of timber had been rigged up on the wreckage, with the rails resting across them. It was certainly very precarious on that piece of track and I think we all breathed a sigh of relief when we were over.

Our journey continued East until we were approaching the German border. On arrival at the station of Herbesthal, we were taken from the train and told to enter some cellars under the railway. It was just starting to get dark at the time so I assumed that we were not allowed to travel at night. Conditions were very poor in the cellars as the air was cold and damp, a complete contrast to the hot oppressive air on the surface. The prospect of a night spent in this hole was far from attractive.

Shortly after our arrival, the guards brought us some soup, only enough for a cupful each, but it tasted excellent to us. We should have been issued with two slices of bread as well, but due to a distribution error, the prisoners in the next bay to us had eaten the lot. It was no surprise that there was no more forthcoming. Following the inadequate meal, there remained little else to do except try to sleep. This proved to be impossible due to the damp and cold, so instead we sat up all night talking.

Before we left next morning, we were given a cup of coffee which was particularly welcome after our very uncomfortable night. A few prisoners were then told to pick up the guards' kit bags as they were to be carried to the train. This was when the trouble started, one bag was left on the floor. It apparently belonged to the German Sergeant who was in charge of the party and he was determined that one of us would carry it. He looked around for anyone who was empty handed, which made me hope he wouldn't pick on me as I was feeling very weak indeed. Walking down the line of prisoners, he came to one dressed in civilian clothes and ordered him to pick the bag up.

The prisoner had no intention of doing so, as pulling himself to attention he announced;
'I am an American officer and have no intention of working for the Germans in any way'.
I don't think I shall forget that moment, as pulling out his revolver the guard addressed the American;
"As far as I am concerned you are a civilian, as if you were a soldier as you claim to be, you would be dressed as one. I am your superior and have given you an order, if it is not obeyed within the count of ten, I will shoot you.'

An immediate deathly silence fell, except for the steady counting of the guard. Everyone was dumbfounded by the statement, as it was quite obvious the threat would be carried out without the slightest hesitation. Isolated as we were in an underground shelter, no one outside would know of the drama

I was particularly worried, as I was standing immediately behind the American. The revolver was the biggest I have ever seen and I knew that if he fired, the bullet would go right through him, then kill or injure me. I felt my flesh creeping as I stood there looking down that tremendous muzzle. It was my intention to wait until the count of nine, then dive sideways. Any movement before that, might have caused the guard to react immediately.

After two or three seconds had elapsed, we recovered from our initial surprise and appealed to the American to carry out the order he had been given. It was apparent from the guard's attitude that he really meant what he had said. At last, very reluctantly, the American did as he was told and picked up the bag. It was a great relief to us, particularly when the revolver was returned to its holster.

I had a strong feeling that the guard would have enjoyed shooting the American, which was a chilling thought. I am pleased to say that we did not come across this attitude very often, as killing for pleasure is no part of war.

When the tension was relieved, bags and packages were all picked up, then once again we returned to the open air and the warm July sun. After the cold of the underground cellar, the warmth was very welcome, and in no time at all we had thawed out.

The train was standing in the station already waiting for us so we were soon loaded into specially reserved coaches. It was not soon enough I am afraid, as we were able to see boxes of cherries being off loaded from the train. This was a real torture to us in our hungry state, but it was soon forgotten as we quickly fell asleep in the comfortable coaches.

Passing through Aachen, we arrived at Cologne, the first of the big cities in the Ruhr, one which gave us so much trouble with its anti-aircraft guns and searchlights. I have never seen such devastation as I witnessed then. True I had seen a lot of bomb damage at home, but nothing to compare with this. The streets were piled with rubble, except for a narrow track sufficient only for single line traffic. As far as I knew, it had not been bombed for two or three months. The cathedral stood out from all this destruction, and from what I could see, was untouched.

We remained in Cologne central station for such a long time, I thought we might be getting out there. It was rather a daunting prospect as the civilians did not appear too kindly disposed towards us. When we eventually did move, we crossed the Rhine to the marshalling yard on the East side of the city, which gave us a better view than before. We were able to see more of the cathedral, which even at a distance appeared very beautiful.

It was probably here that the anti-aircraft gun was unhitched from the rear of the train. It had been necessary while travelling through Belgium, but now we were in Germany it seemed it could be dispensed with. Perhaps our 'Train Busters' hadn't come this far yet.

After leaving Cologne, we headed South, keeping to the West bank of the Rhine. We passed through Bonn, Koblenz and Mainz, all places that had only been names to me. Until I had parachuted into France, I had not set foot on European soil before, so everything was new and fascinating.

The journey itself was very interesting and the scenery beautiful, but I would have appreciated it a great deal more had I not been a prisoner. For most of the way, the banks which in parts were thickly wooded, rose to a height of two to three hundred feet above the river. There were houses and castles built on isolated mounds, which reminded me of stories and pictures I had known as a child. They were 'Grimm's Fairy Tales' come to life and gave me the same uneasy feelings that the stories and pictures had given me when I was young.

Not all of the castles gave me that feeling and despite my situation, I really enjoyed the scenery. There were white stone buildings with tiled conical roofs, turret rooms with battlements and in some cases there were moats crossed by drawbridges. This had nothing to do with the present conflict and the violence that was taking place, this was an escape into the past.

At last we pulled into Frankfurt, at one time the chief interrogation centre for the RAF. Naturally we expected to detrain there, so it was quite a surprise when the train left again for another destination. We were moved a distance of twenty miles North of the city to a place which turned out to be a Dulag Luft. It was a pleasant change to get out of the train and stretch our legs for a while, although before I was finished, I had a trifle too much leg stretching.

When we formed up outside the station preparatory to marching to the camp, several civilians gathered around us in an ominous manner. Things looked nasty when one or two people spat at us and one woman tried to hit a prisoner with her umbrella. Fortunately, the guards did not intend to let us be attacked, as loading their weapons, they told the crowd they would open fire if they didn't back off.

I have heard since that some American aircrew had been lynched by the crowd there and had finished up hung on the lampposts. It is as well I didn't know it at the time otherwise I might have been even more worried.

It was only a matter of a two mile march to Dulag Luft, but to me it was a nightmare. For a reason I don't understand, I was in a state of near collapse, and often wondered why I hadn't. It was true that we had been on a starvation diet for a while, but I expected to last longer than I seemed to be doing. Finally we arrived at our new place of imprisonment, my third, how many more were there to be and how long was it all going to last?

CHAPTER 12

Having arrived at our camp, we were crowded into a small room and the door locked behind us. I feel sure it was designed to make people talk among themselves, as apart from being packed in tight, there were no guards visible. In addition to this, the room was very hot and airless, partly caused by the sun shining through a sealed window. We were all perspiring very freely and feeling extremely thirsty. This had the effect of getting us to talk, even if only to comment on the heat and our discomfort.

It was suggested we say nothing, as the room was most probably fitted out with listening devices, so our conversation centred mainly on our thirst. After a while, a big jug of water and glasses were brought into the room, which we consumed very quickly, causing us to perspire even more.

One by one, we were taken to a small room, stripped and searched. Having completed this formality a slip of paper with cell block and cell number was handed out. This we had to give to a guard whose duty it was to escort us to the designated place.

I remember that when I had been searched, I simply slipped my trousers and singlet on, then walked to the cell with my other clothes under my arm. Once inside, I sat on the bed, pulled on one of my socks, then dropped right off to sleep. When I awoke at half past three I felt cold, so got into bed properly and did not waken again until nine o'clock.

Looking round my cell, I discovered that in common with other places, there was a system of alerting the guard by means of a wooden signal arm. Several times I rattled it about, but no one came which was serious as by now I was getting anxious to visit the toilet. I began to think that perhaps we were not allowed out and that some form of bucket or portable latrine was placed in the cell. It was fairly obvious that no such thing existed as the bed was the only piece of furniture visible. Then it struck me, I hadn't looked in the obvious place and there sure enough was a large glass container rather like a wine decanter.

I was surprised to see that it had not been emptied which meant that the cells were not visited very frequently. When I dragged the bottle out into the light, I was even more surprised than ever to notice that not only had it not been emptied, it also contained small pieces of greenery and tiny blue flowers. I came to the conclusion that the previous occupant had either been afflicted with some strange disease, or was a practical joker.

I was just about to use the bottle, when a commotion outside my door heralded the arrival of a guard. When the door was open, I could see he had two buckets, so I was right, the bottles were emptied infrequently. He pointed to the bottle in my hand and demanded that I gave it to him, I just as firmly refused and by sign language indicated that I hadn't used it yet.

He looked at me as though I was demented and snatching the bottle from me, emptied it into one of his buckets. To my utter amazement, he dipped a ladle into a full bucket and filled my bottle with more liquid containing greenery and flowers. This time, the liquid was exceedingly hot, then before I got over this, he handed me two slices of bread and locked me in again.

It suddenly dawned on me, this was breakfast and also my first experience of German tea. Eventually the guard did allow me to go down the corridor, then when I returned, I tried this so called tea. I discovered why it was left in the bottle, it was absolutely vile and no matter how many pretty flowers they put in it, I couldn't possibly drink it.

Midday I was taken from my cell and paraded with several others in the corridor. We were told that it was no longer necessary for us to remain in our solitary cells, therefore we were to be sent across the road to some huts where we would stay the night. The following day, we were to be sent by train to a transit camp at Wetzlar.

It was a marvellous feeling to live more or less normally again, instead of being locked up in a lonely cell. Not only could we mix with others, we were also able to walk about in the open. True we still had barbed wire round us but we now had greater freedom than at any time since our capture.

I was not the only one who felt this way as I soon found out from my room mates, we all wanted to talk each other's heads off. There were seven in the room beside myself and quite a mixed bunch we proved to be. There were three RAF NCO's, four American NCO's and one American officer. I had several long talks with the last mentioned as he was also a navigator and we discovered our techniques were quite different. I didn't realise until later that he might have been a plant, although even if he had been, he would not have heard anything that wasn't common knowledge. I am quite satisfied that I didn't mention anything about my secret equipment as I wouldn't even talk to my own crew about that.

While walking round the compound, one of the fellows noticed some plants which he claimed were cabbages. I doubted this, but I was hungry enough to eat anything. We collected a big bunch, chopped them up with a few strange looking roots and put them in a bowl of water, Entering a boiler room, we placed our prize on the fire, hoping it would soon boil. We could hardly stand there waiting, so we wandered round the compound until we were sure our 'vegetable soup' was ready.

What a blow, when we returned, the boiler house was locked and we had lost our meal. Maybe fate had taken a hand in this as we could well have been poisoned by our unknown vegetables. We didn't fret too much about this loss as very soon we had something else of interest to think about. Someone who had been searching around, discovered a shower and what was more important a boiler which heated the water for it.

All that remained for us to do was find wood for the fire. By scouting around for a while, we collected quite a reasonable amount, enough to give sufficient hot water for the small group who had gathered for the purpose.

What a pleasure that proved to be, as it was the first proper wash I had been able to have in over three weeks. It was also the first time I had completely removed my clothes without being searched. Just as we had finished our showers, somebody found some old razor blades. This inspired one of the officers who had joined our group, as he went off in search of a razor and surprised us when he returned with three. The blades had to be sharpened on a piece of stone before they could be used and even then they weren't brilliant.

It was agreed that those with the toughest beards would go first. As I was one of the youngest, I came near the end, but even so it was a relief to be able to shave again. The shave itself was very hard going, but we were all determined to make ourselves look presentable. One American proved to be extremely generous, as he had some cigarettes which he offered to share around. This meant we could have two cigarettes each, a real bonus for us, as not only did we enjoy the cigarettes, it helped to dull the pangs of hunger a little.

Later on, Chris Columbus, one of my room mates, persuaded a guard to part with some French tobacco, then proceeded to show me how to roll economy cigarettes. He claimed it was a cowboy style which used about half the normal amount of tobacco and lasted about twenty minutes. I am not sure about the cowboy part of the story, but the rest lived up to his promises.

As expected, we were woken up at five in the morning after a very good night's sleep and prepared for our departure to Wetzlar. We were asked to sign a parole for our journey to the station, which caused us some misgivings as we felt we had no right to do so. It was pointed out to us that we could go easily in comfort, or suffer very severe restrictions.

I think the thing that made us all sign, was our reluctance to escape anyway, as this was such a hostile area, already demonstrated to us on our journey up from the station. Having received our signatures, the Germans formed us up and marched us away from the camp we had occupied for less than forty eight hours. Fortunately for us, we arrived at the station without incident and boarded the train for this unknown place of Wetzlar. None of us had ever heard of it before, let alone knew where it was, so we were off on a mystery tour.

The whole thing was in fact a mystery and there was quite a lot of speculation as to what the new place might be, or why we were going there. Our Intelligence officers had prepared us for a Dulag Luft at Frankfurt followed by a permanent Stalag, but certainly not Wetzlar, neither had we expected the Brussels interrogation centre.

We were not left in doubt long as the journey lasted four hours, which was really longer than it should have been as we only travelled about twenty miles. When we finally arrived, we were assembled in a large room and addressed by the Camp Leader, an American officer. He informed us that we would be given sufficient kit for our needs, followed by a hot shower and a good meal, in preparation for our posting to permanent Stalags. It seemed that this was not an interrogation centre, purely a kitting out and cleaning station. A very necessary establishment I should say, as most of us had been living rough for a long time and were beginning to look like tramps.

Following this short briefing, we filed into what proved to be an equipment store. Here we were given such items as underclothes, shirts, topcoats, boots, socks, in fact anything which we were either short of, or needed to replace. Up to this time, our sole possessions were what we stood up in, which in some cases was very little.

It was a marvellous feeling to emerge from the showers feeling really clean, then to put on new clothes was a pleasure indeed. My greatest personal relief was to be able to discard my worn out odd shoes, which I had been wearing since I found them on my very first day in France. Now I was able to wear a good strong pair of boots, which really felt very comfortable. In addition to this I had some decent trousers and a warm shirt of American origin.

At this point, it was revealed to us why we had not gone to Frankfurt as expected. During a night raid a few weeks before, a four thousand pound bomb had landed in the camp, wrecked the place and killed some RAF prisoners. It was suggested that if any of us had been on that raid in particular, we were advised not to mention it, as feelings were running high. It was understood by the inmates during the raid, that the bomb had been jettisoned well before the aircraft reached the target, so hitting the camp which was well clear of the city.

The replacement camp for Frankfurt was repositioned at Wetzlar where it was intended to erect new huts, but in the meantime, the accommodation provided was a series of tents. This was no problem to us, as the weather was warm and we did not expect to stay there for very long.

When we were all showered and changed, fit once again to be amongst human beings, we were allowed into the tented camp where we were allocated eight to a tent. This was to be ours until we moved out again for our journey to a regular prison camp. Up to this time we had not received our promised meal, although we knew that some people had been called to the mess tent already, so it was with something like anxiety we waited for our turn, hoping there would be enough left.

An hour passed before the rest of us were called out for tea parade. We hadn't been aware that the mess tent was not big enough to take us all at once and an explanation earlier would have allayed our fears that we had been forgotten. One friend was so weak that he found the waiting too long and collapsed while on parade. We were satisfied that this was caused by hunger as he recovered very quickly when given something to eat.

It would be difficult to describe the feeling I experienced as I entered the mess tent. Tables were laid out for a feast, so impressive after our weeks of starvation. I can't recall being so excited at the prospect since I was a young child attending a Christmas party, when everything was magic, I had almost given up hope of ever eating anything substantial again.

A description of the meal may give cause to wonder at the effect it had on us, as it consisted of barley soup, potatoes, spam, bread, butter, jam and two cups of American coffee. To be in that situation, is the only way of fully understanding our reaction.

Finally, the meal over, we returned to our tents, lay back on our beds and smoked cigarette after cigarette until our throats were sore. No longer did we have to worry where the next cigarette was to come from, they had been placed in our kit-bags during kitting out.

Just before lights out, an announcement was made to the effect that one party of Americans and one party of British prisoners were to leave next morning for their respective Stalags. The names of those concerned had been posted on the notice board.

No examination results were ever scanned so avidly as were those lists. There was quite a rush, as everyone wanted to see and it was with great difficulty that I pushed forward, to discover that Nat and I were listed among those to go.

CHAPTER 13

Morning came and the start of yet another journey. I had been a prisoner just over three weeks and already seen the inside of four places of imprisonment. How many more journeys and camps was I likely to see? I hoped that the forthcoming move to a Stalag would be the last one, except for the eventual return home, however long it might be. As there was no likelihood of the war ending in the next week or so, I considered it inevitable that I was to experience prison camp life, if only for a short while. I was however much better off than people who had been captured in the early years, they had to put up with news of defeats and setbacks. Our thoughts were tempered by the knowledge that at least our forces were in Europe again and advancing.

A slight boost to our morale was the thought that our families might soon learn that we had survived. This of course depended on the Germans who may or may not have posted the cards we had written the previous day.

On arrival at the station, we looked for, but could not see any coaches for our transportation, The reason was simple, there were none, we were to travel in horse boxes. If I remember correctly, the official capacity was six horses or forty persons. Prisoners are apparently different to persons as forty five of us were crowded in. Perhaps the scarcity of our luggage was taken into account as this left more room for bodies.

Once we had become settled as comfortably as was possible, we were issued with fifty cigarettes each and a Red Cross parcel between two. We were told that this would have to last us for three days. When we discovered we were to spend so long under these conditions it caused quite a stir, although we realised it would be futile to complain.

I am certainly not anxious to travel in such a manner again as it was by no means comfortable. After running for twenty miles or so, the engine would shunt us into a siding, where we stayed for anything from one to twelve hours to wait for another engine to pick us up. When one did arrive, it left us in little doubt, as the action of hitching up was usually so violent that we were often thrown off our feet. Our opinion of the engine driver, his friends and the German Railways was better left unsaid.

Generally our progress was quite slow, except for one occasion when we were hitched onto a heavy Panzer Unit on its way to the Italian front, then it moved fast enough.

During the three days we were on the train, we saw five or six ambulance trains bringing the wounded back from the Front, for hospital treatment. We were told that they had been fighting on the Russian front, but wherever they had been, there were some very horrible sights. The majority of the injured we saw were in a similar age group to ourselves, late teens or early twenties, although some looked very young.

Strangely enough, even though the wounded Germans realised what we were, there seemed to be no animosity between us, instead there seemed to be a fellow feeling that we were both in trouble. It was obvious that they had no cigarettes, so whenever possible, we managed to pass some over to them. On one occasion, we were stopped opposite a hospital train, whose occupants seemed particularly poorly placed. We were waiting for quite a long period right alongside them, so it was decided to make a collection of cigarettes for their benefit which was taken across to the hospital train by one of the guards. I feel certain that if we had been allowed to mingle with them, we would have made some very good friends.

That three day train journey seemed to last for ever as the countryside was virtually featureless, consisting mainly of endless plains and forests. There must have been some towns on our route even though we didn't see them, perhaps we were diverted around the built up areas.

As far as we could tell, we had been heading in an Easterly direction for many miles. We had started from Wetzlar, which we knew to be roughly in Central Germany, so we realised we must be either heading into Poland, or very close to it. We were being taken a very long way from our own invading forces which did little to raise our spirits.

Just short of the Polish border, we stopped at a small place called Bankau in Upper Silesia near the town of Kreuzberg. We didn't appreciate this at the time, all we knew, we had arrived somewhere out in the wilds. The scenery was flat and uninteresting, not that it would concern us very much as we knew we would be seeing little of it. If only we had realised then how wrong we were.

CHAPTER 14

Our approach to the camp was made from a road which ran alongside it and the first impression of the place which was to be my home for an unspecified period did not exactly inspire me. I don't know what I expected a prison camp to look like, barbed wire certainly, with guard posts dotted around perhaps and people living in barrack type blocks. This appeared to be nothing like it, true the barbed wire was present, but the camp itself seemed to consist of huts not much bigger than dog kennels. There was no movement from inside, which made me think we were opening up a new camp. This could present difficulties as there would be no one experienced in camp life to guide us. Not a pleasant thought.

Passing through a very large gateway, we were ushered into a small compound situated between the outside wire fence and an inner one. We were counted and recounted to ensure that none had escaped, then we went through another equally imposing gate into the camp proper.

This was not the end of the official reception, as then we had to go through the full camp joining procedure. We were no longer in transit, we were to become permanent residents. First our kit had to be laid out on a table so that it could be thoroughly searched, then the ordeal of having photographs and fingerprints recorded had to be endured. From there we reported to a clerk who documented our personal particulars such as weight, height, description, in fact anything which could be used to identify the prisoner concerned.

Finally each new prisoner was given a metal tag to be worn around the neck, which was imprinted with a personal prison camp number. I was intrigued to notice that the number was printed twice, once on the top half and again on the lower half, but this time upside down. Across the middle of the plate was a line of perforations. I wished I hadn't asked for an explanation as it was slightly sinister. In the event of the prisoner dying or being killed, one half was to be buried with the body and the other half returned to the next of kin.

While we were being subjected to the joining procedure, the camp suddenly burst into life, prisoners came pouring out of the small huts, then assembled for roll call in a clearing in the centre of the camp. I assumed that everyone had turned out although there were not very many present. My allocated number should have given me a clue as that was number 311 which meant there were approximately three hundred inmates prior to our arrival. Another pointer was the newness of the buildings, they had not been erected very long.

Just as soon as the roll call was over, nearly everyone crowded up to the trip wire which separated us, scanning the people in our party searching for friends or crew members. It was while we were standing staring vacantly at the crowd in front of us, that I heard Nat's name being called. At first I could not see who it was, but finally located the person. I was astounded to see Ron our Flight Engineer who was bawling his head off to Nat, then when he saw me, he started waving violently. I would find it difficult to describe the relief that Nat and I felt on discovering that at least one other crew member was still alive.

When all necessary checks had been completed, the trip wire was removed and we were permitted to enter the main camp, fully fledged Prisoners of War. It was natural that we should make straight for Ron, who met us wreathed in smiles and full of questions. I am afraid that we were unable to give him very many answers as we ourselves knew so little, in any case, we had a great number of questions to ask him.

First things first, we had to find the hut allocated to us, so that we could dump our kit, then talk. Ron who knew the layout, helped us with our bags while directing us towards our new abode.

Once having settled in and introduced ourselves to the others sharing our hut, we went along to visit Ron. It was a reunion marred by the thought of the fate suffered by the rest of the crew. I had been told by the Germans that the Rear Gunner and Bomb Aimer were dead, which left doubts regarding the Skipper and the Mid-Upper Gunner. I think we all agreed that giving due consideration to the state and condition of the aircraft when we baled out, we were almost certain to have been the only survivors. This fact was proved conclusively later.

Apart from meeting Ron again, I was very surprised to meet people who had been on the squadron with us, as it was assumed they had been killed. Another surprise was meeting people I had known earlier during training. Thinking about it, I don't know why I should have been, as we were all in the same business and I can think of no reason why I should be the only one to finish up in a prison camp.

The first day was naturally rather strange. We had to learn the routine to be followed, and the rules concerning Do's and Dont's, also we had to familiarise ourselves with the layout of the place. This was fairly straightforward as basically it consisted of a perimeter wire fence surrounding an area approximately two hundred yards square. Inside this, ten feet from it, another similar fence had been built, both were roughly fifteen feet high with tops pointing inwards.

To enable guards to maintain a watch over us, towers were placed at intervals around the wire. One was placed at each corner and six more along the sides. These were equipped with searchlights so arranged that any part of the camp could be illuminated if necessary. Later on machine guns were fitted. To prevent prisoners from approaching the wire, a trip fence made of white painted laths was erected within fifty feet of the wire and anyone crossing this was liable to be shot.

The huts were arranged in lines so that they all faced onto broad avenues. Each of these avenues was controlled by one of the guard towers where a sentry was on duty at all times. In the middle of the compound was a large open space, suitable as an exercise area, which also contained our fresh water supply in the form of a village type pump. At the Western end of the clear space, a large hut had been built for use as a cook-house.

The daily routine was fairly straightforward as at eight in the morning we collected hot water from a field kitchen sufficient to make a cup of coffee, then at nine o'clock a parade for roll call. Between midday to half past one another issue of hot water, plus soup and boiled potatoes. At five in the afternoon we were subjected to a second roll call followed by an issue of such rations as were available, for example, jam, sugar, syrup and sometimes cheese. Whatever else may have been issued, there was always a bread issue of some sort. Just before lights out we were given more hot water for a final cup of coffee.

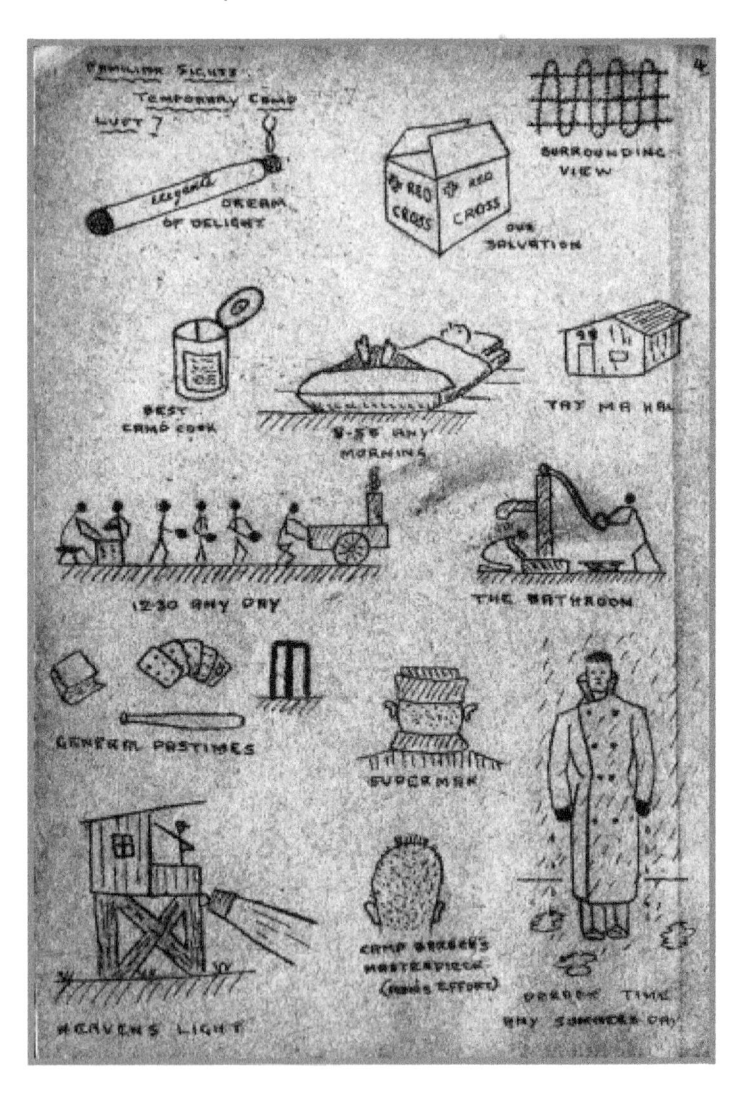

Lights out was signalled by the Camp Leader whose duty it was to walk round blowing a whistle, which also meant we were to remain in our huts until six o'clock next morning. The only time this rule could be broken legally was a requirement to visit the latrine. Following the final whistle, the camp would then be patrolled all night by guards with dogs.

A thing that gave me food for thought was the size of the camp and the number it was designed to hold. As mentioned earlier there were three hundred prisoners previous to our arrival and we numbered forty five. Altogether we only managed to occupy a quarter of the camp so the Germans were anticipating the capture of a lot more aircrew.

The camp itself was on sandy soil, built in an area which had been part of a pine forest, The huts which I have described briefly were made up with sections of matchboarding bolted together, with roofing felt covering the roof. They were designed to hold six people each and measured twenty feet by ten feet round the base, seven feet high at the ridge. Two windows twelve inches by nine were our only means of illumination during the day. By night we made our own, using fat melted in a tin, with a piece of shoe lace as a wick.

The windows were made so that they could be slid open, but in very hot weather these gave insufficient ventilation. We overcame this problem by jamming a tin under one corner of the roof to lift it a few inches, as this did help the air circulate.

The furnishings consisted of six wooden stools, a table, a witch's broom and a basin made out of compressed paper which they readily replaced when the bottom fell out. The beds were mattresses of coarse sacking material stuffed with wood shavings. As these shavings were brittle, the mattress which started at a reasonable thickness, soon became little more than a skinny pad full of dust and gave practically no cushioning effect from the floor.

HUT COOLING SYSTEM
MODERN VERSION

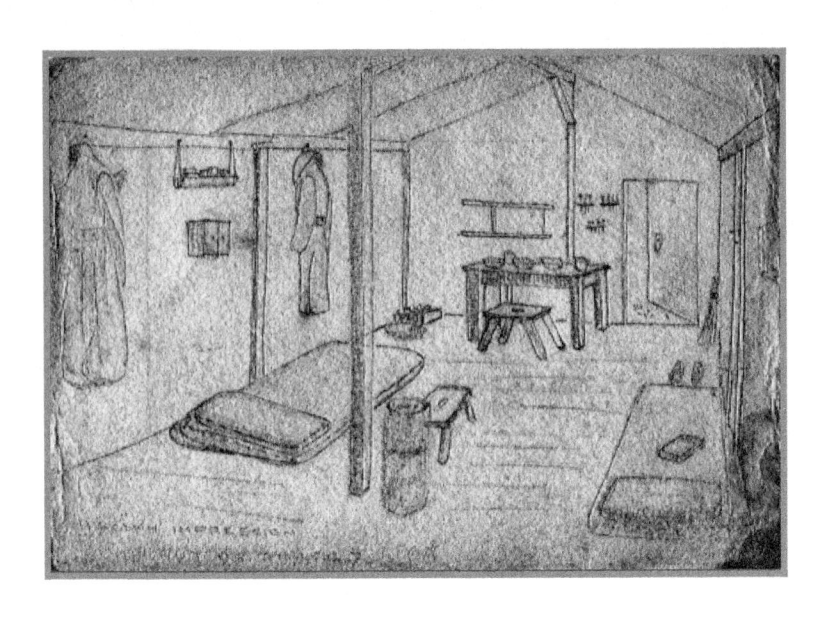

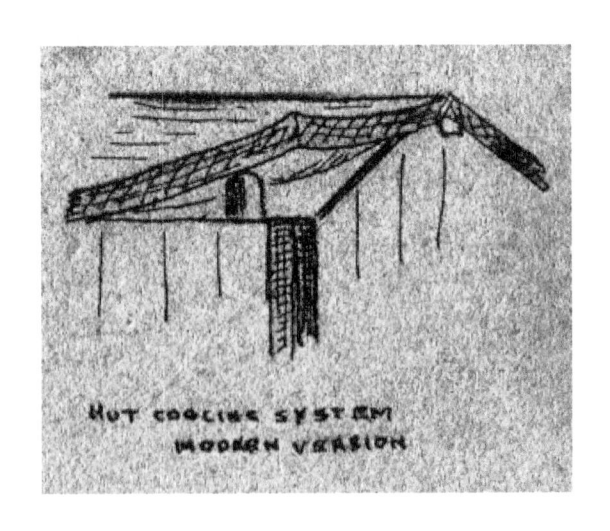

MORNING TOILET SET UP

As a personal issue, each prisoner was given a knife, fork, spoon and soup bowl. The knife was the most useful implement as it could be used for several purposes. Apart from its intended purpose, it was used to cut up old food tins for the material used in cooking utensil manufacture. The cutting of tin very soon produced a jagged edge to the knife, which could then be used as a wood saw. Quite by accident it was discovered that some knives were magnetised, which meant we had crude compass needles available to us. Needless to say that these were not used as tools, but carefully segregated in case the they were required.

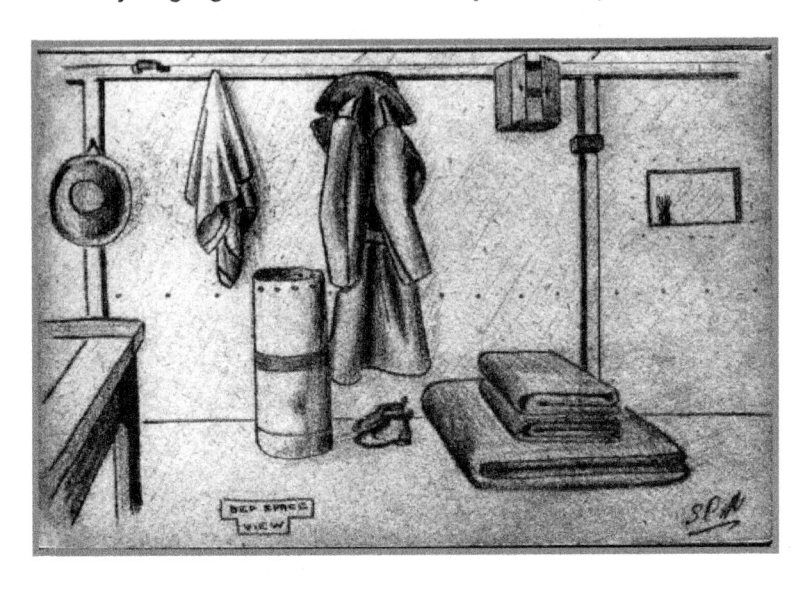

We found this quite amusing considering the trouble the Germans had gone to trying to locate secret compasses, hidden about our clothing. The people not quite so amused perhaps, were those whose trouser buttons had been ripped off by the searchers, when it was discovered that some of these were in fact disguised compass needles.

Another small benefit unwittingly supplied were the nails which fixed the hardboard lining of the hut to the framework. These could be prised out for use in our various activities, and providing care was taken, the gradual dismantling of the hut was not noticed.

About fifty yards from our particular hut was one of the latrines, whose basic design was the same as our living huts. They were erected over a deep pit and the floor cut away to leave a big hole in the middle. On the two long edges of the hole, horizontal poles were fixed to be used as seats, and each pole could accommodate up to six people side by side. To make life a little more comfortable, underneath the pole which was two feet off the floor, boards were fixed, which enabled the user to press his heels against them and so retain his balance. Between the poles was a wooden partition, not there for modesty but to give the person a means of support while attempting to sit down on the pole.

An unfortunate entered this latrine one dark night, unaware that a fellow prisoner intent on carpentry had removed the section of the partition he tried to lean on. He had to be rescued from the bottom of the pit.

Due to the proximity of the latrine to our hut, we became an assembly point for one type of 'nuisance' activity. As mentioned earlier, under normal circumstances, we were not allowed to walk about outside after the ten o'clock whistle except to go to the latrine. This was excuse enough. As soon as things were quiet someone would call for a latrine party and ten to twelve people would assemble in a line outside our hut. At a given word, we would run around the corner still in line, arms outstretched, playing aeroplanes. As soon as the nearest searchlight picked us up, there would be a shout of 'Corkscrew', away we would go, zigzagging all over the place, while the Searchlight operator went stupid attempting to keep us all in his beam.

As soon as we were in the latrine, we would suddenly go silent and sit patiently waiting for about ten minutes. By this time the guard in the tower would get jumpy and start calling up the dog handlers, using his searchlight to do so. As the handlers got to within twenty feet of the latrine, we would burst into song and march out in a long line back to our huts. The first few occasions we did it, the guards were startled and the dogs went mad, as they were not quite sure what we were up to. This activity certainly kept them on their toes and was just the start of a whole series of 'nuisance' activities.

The pump which supplied our water, was the only source we had and any required for the cookhouse was transported in large water jugs. It was unreasonable to expect our volunteer cooks to collect the water themselves, so parties were organised on a daily basis to carry out this duty.

Before the camp had been completely opened, the pump was contained in the closed off section which meant that the people collecting water had to be escorted by an armed guard. To get to the pump, it was necessary to pass through a trip barrier which separated the occupied and unoccupied sections of the camp, and to do so without authority was a sentence of death.

On one occasion when I was involved as a water carrier, our guard was the German Warrant Officer an extremely hard looking man. Once assembled, we moved off towards the trip barrier, and as we got close to it, the duty sentry moved it to let us pass through. I thought that the Warrant officer was going off his head, he halted our party, then stormed up to the sentry screaming abuse at him. We wondered what had happened, until a Dutch friend explained to us that no one was to remove the trip wire until expressly ordered to do so by the escorting guard. If the sentry was daring enough to act without orders again, he would be immediately posted to the Russian front.

Later when the camp expanded, we were able to use the pump quite freely, not only for drinking water but as a means of taking a bath. The procedure for bathing required two people, the one needing the bath and an assistant. The assistant's job was to pump the water, so as soon as the person to bath was undressed, he would start pumping like mad. The bather then held his hands tightly over the pump outlet, so building up a large force of water. When the pressure was sufficient, the bather would let go and dive under the pump outlet, to be soaked by the deluge. After applying soap to the body, the whole pumping process had to be repeated to rinse off. As I remember, it was not as good as a bath - which was not available to us - but more effective and quicker than a shower and as we were not equipped with showers either, it was the best we had.

THE BATHROOM

Eventually all internal barriers were removed and the camp was opened up completely, a real benefit for us but it also gave rise to some depressing thoughts as it meant more aircrew were being captured. There were so many arriving, that a strange defeatist attitude started to develop and one which was difficult to avoid. It was believed by some, that if their squadron friends or colleagues had not been taken prisoner, then they must have been killed. This was based on the thought that everyone was shot down at some time or other and no one avoided it. True the casualty rate was high, but not as high as it seemed to us locked away in our distant camp.

The main benefit gained by the removal of internal barriers was the ability to be able to walk about more freely and play football or cricket in the open compound. This helped a great deal as boredom was something which had to be avoided. As far as we were concerned, we were perhaps facing years of captivity, possibly life sentences, so it was essential to get organised in a way which would make our existence more tolerable.

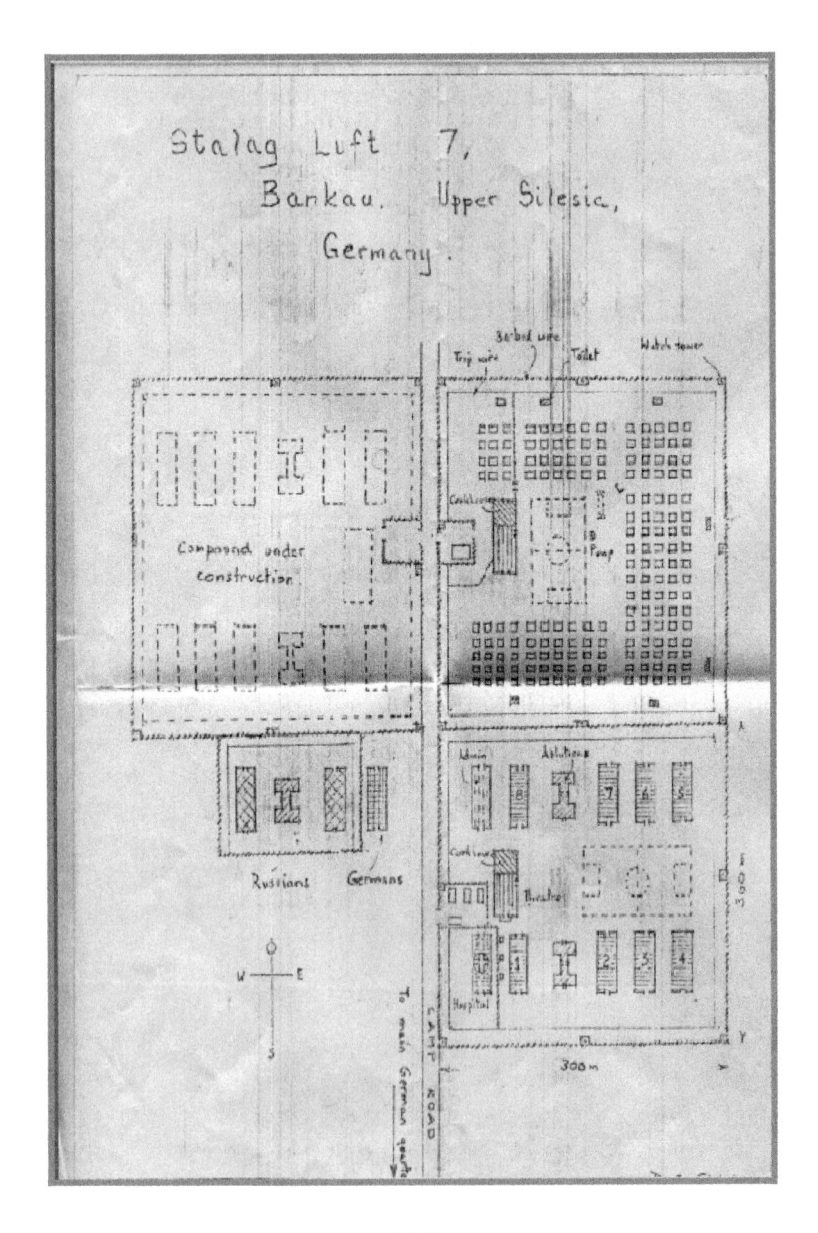

CHAPTER 15

There were many things we had to learn if we were to make a success and survive in a sane manner. Skills had to be developed in things not considered by some before, for example, mending and washing clothes, cooking, catering, making shelves, cupboards, baking tins, in fact anything necessary which was not supplied by the authorities.

In one sense, I suppose we were developing some form of civilisation for ourselves, as we had been removed from our normal ordered life, where a great many things had been done for us. It was fairly soon recognised amongst the small groups which formed, as to who were the best administrators, who to go to if a baking tin was required and who was the person good at woodwork. A few people concerned themselves with none of this, but simply lay on their beds brooding for hours, they weren't even trying to survive. An important thing missing from our lives, was any form of entertainment which could be enjoyed by the majority. Sports like football and cricket were for the few and walking around the perimeter wire soon became boring. Without conscious effort an entertainments group did start, but in a small way. A few of us gathered between the huts one day to listen to anyone who was prepared to sing a song, recite a poem or perhaps tell jokes. It was nothing spectacular, simply an attempt to entertain one another with the talent available. It was pleasant just sitting in a circle and by listening, be removed from our private thoughts awhile. This small start was a nucleus for more sophisticated entertainments groups which formed eventually when we were supplied with musical instruments and facilities for concerts. In the early days, anyone however unqualified he may have been as a performer was received with appreciation. Later, the standard attained was quite high, as there were professional and semi-professional people in the camp.

If entertainment was important to us, so was the skill of cooking, if only to introduce variety into our daily menus. We were all extremely grateful for the food and cigarettes supplied to us by the Red Cross, but not all the food was ready to eat. As an example, we received dehydrated eggs, rolled oats, tinned bacon and several other things of similar nature, hardly palatable in their uncooked state. Not only did we learn to cook under difficult conditions, there was the added interest of attempting new recipes, or trying to improve on existing ones.

Apart from the Red Cross issues, we did receive food from the Germans, but these were so meagre we could not have survived had we received nothing else. Most of the rations supplied by the Germans were already cooked and issued to us on a daily basis, in the form of a stew or soup. One of the dishes most frequently served up was a sort of boiled pea mash which never looked particularly appetising, especially to a new arrival.

One evening after rations had been issued, I noticed six bowls of peas piled up in a hut doorway. Thinking that the inmates were in some trouble, I asked if they were sick as they had left their food untouched, I was informed that the pea mash contained maggots and were unfit to eat. I asked if I could take the bowls away so that the group in my hut could pick them over. They were pleased to see the last of them, so I returned to the hut in triumph, bearing the bowls of maggoty peas. My colleagues could not believe their luck and in a short space of time, peas and maggots had been consumed. It took our benefactors another two issues before they realised that peas with maggots were a standard pack.

Our own cooking efforts presented two major problems, one was what to cook the food in, and the second, how to make a suitable fire. The first was solved by salvaging tins from Red Cross parcels and using the tin plate as a basic material from which utensils were made. A great deal of effort went into making a cooking utensil, as not only did it have to be water and oil tight, it also had to look presentable to satisfy the critics. In addition, it was a matter of pride to produce a better looking article than anyone else and there was a certain amount of friendly rivalry which developed.

Before making something like a baking dish, it was necessary to select three food tins of equal size, preferably without dents in them. By using a tin opener and a jagged table knife, the tins were cut up to produce useable pieces of tin plate. As each piece measured approximately nine inches by four, the three had to be joined together to make a piece large enough from which the utensil could be made. This was achieved in the following way: Taking the middle plate first, the two long edges were folded over about a quarter of an inch, but not completely flattened. The same treatment was given to one edge of each of the outside pieces, then the three pieces would be hooked together by engaging the turned up edges and then hammered flat to make a seam. To ensure a good joint the work was placed on a flat surface and the seam beaded or ridged by using a simply made tool. This only consisted of a piece of wood with a groove cut in the bottom, which when placed over the seam and tapped with a stone, formed a very good seal. On this large plate, the required design was marked out and the sides folded up. As no soldering or riveting was available, the plate could not be cut to form a corner, instead the surplus material was folded around rather like tucking in the blankets on a bed.

OVEN (HOT 9% MODEL)

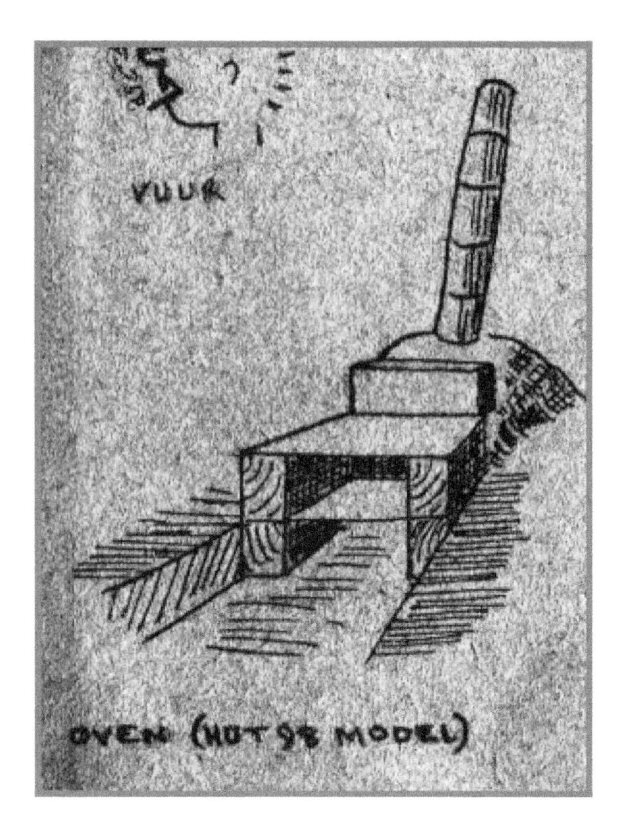

The construction of a suitable cooking fire presented as big a problem as that of the cooking utensils. My first attempt was a hole dug in the ground, an oven made of tin plate placed over the top, a chimney of tins to help create a draught and then earth packed over the top of the oven. This worked fairly well until it rained, then cooking had to be abandoned as water running down the hole put the fire out. One bright bunch decided to overcome the problem of the rain by lifting the floor of their hut and lighting a fire on the ground beneath. They were stopped in time just before the hut caught alight.

The appearance of a 'Blower' made all the other cooking devices obsolete. This was a small portable forced draught cooking fire designed by a prisoner of unknown origin. It consisted of a baseboard about five inches by fourteen at one end of which was a circular fire pot and at the other an air compressing fan. The two were connected by an air duct. Materials used in construction were those which we could either find, or already had in our possession, and, some very useful machines were produced. In the 'Blower' that I built, the fire pot was made of tin lined with clay and the grate a piece of tin with holes punched in it. The compressor was another large tin which contained a rotary fan driven by a geared crank wheel. The construction of the fan was fairly critical as the blades which were fixed to a longitudinal axle had to be curved and also just fit into the tin. Air inlets, supplied the air for compression. The air ducting was made of cardboard from a Red Cross box and had to be tapered to help compress the air.

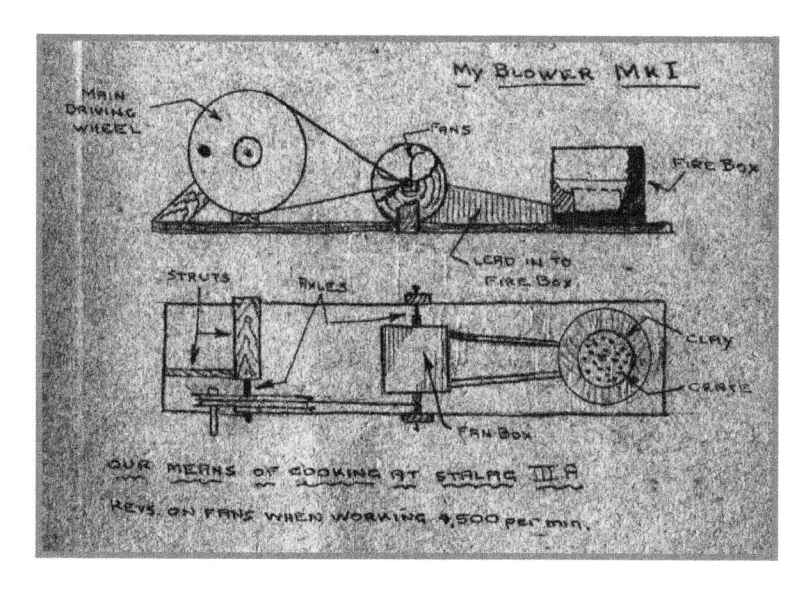

The standard operating test was to place a piece of paper on the grate and blow it into the air using the fan. A major drawback to an efficient blower was the flimsiness of the fire box as the heat generated was so fierce, that a replacement had to be made every few days. One day a German guard brought in a masterpiece of a 'Blower' which had been manufactured by a local firm and was really good to look at. It must have cost the new owner many cigarettes in bribes and I admit we were rather envious as we gathered around in admiration.

We asked for a demonstration, to see how a properly made piece of equipment should work. What a disaster it proved, as no matter how fast the owner turned the handle, the piece of test paper in the grate didn't even stir and as far as I know, the machine never did work properly and was abandoned.

Discussing menus, methods of cooking and means of entertainment was only a secondary objective in our lives. We had a duty to perform and that was to escape, at least those were the original aims. This situation changed when orders in code received on secret radios, instructed us to remain where we were in camp. Owing to the intensity of the fighting in Europe, escape would now be extremely dangerous. In case we had any doubts regarding the authenticity of such messages, it was only necessary to read notices posted by the Germans themselves. It was stated quite clearly, that any prisoner caught in a war zone would be shot on sight or on being recaptured. They carefully avoided stating where the war zones were situated.

This meant that we would have to concentrate in our duty to hinder the guards and in a small way the German War Effort. We didn't mind upsetting them in the least, but for their part, failure to do their duty had dire consequences. It seemed that a standard form of punishment for them was a spell of imprisonment, then duty on the Russian front.

The first major eruption that I can remember, started with the feeling that something serious had occurred and were quite concerned when summoned to report on parade immediately. The German authorities were there along with our own camp officials, and nobody seemed to be smiling.

Calling for silence, the Camp Leader announced that a serious situation had arisen as a revolver had been stolen from a guard and it was to be handed over immediately, otherwise the retaliation would be severe. It was emphasised that providing it was returned at once, no further action would be taken.

As was expected, despite repeated appeals, no one made a move to step forward. A big discussion then developed between the British and German officials while we waited rather anxiously, as the situation was so serious.

At last a decision was made which required our co-operation. The Germans had given permission for our Leader to attempt to solve the problem in his own way, if that failed, then they would take over. The plan settled on was fairly simple, as the Camp Leader and his assistant were to sit at a table, while we filed past one by one, to be asked where the gun was hidden. Sometime after he had found out he would then inform the Germans who would be standing out of ear shot.

We all lined up as directed and commenced to file past the table positioned in the middle of the compound. There were many anxious faces and just as many anxious discussions as to what would happen to us should the gun not be recovered, as we were certain it would not be.

I am not sure how many had passed the table before the Leader shouted with great exultation that he knew where it was. The Germans hurried over, demanding to know the answer and were rather stunned to discover that it was resting in the bottom of the latrine pit. The problem now became one of recovery. The Germans first insisted that the culprit be sent down, but it was pointed out that they would then know who was responsible and punish him. This would not do, as the discovery was made as an act of faith. The Camp Leader then suggested that as we all knew who the guard was who had been careless enough to lose the revolver, he should be the one to go down.

This seemed like a good idea and it was a very sad looking guard who was brought out to suffer what he knew was going to be a most unpleasant fate. There was no lacking in volunteers who offered to help with the recovery, but only a few were chosen to lower him.

It appears that none of them were very strong, as although he was lowered very quickly, they had to make several attempts to get him out. He was then escorted tethered by ropes, to the pump, where he was washed off by his prisoner escort. It was rumoured later that the Camp Leader himself had engineered the whole thing.

An incident which developed quite by accident, concerned a record playing session in one of the huts. By a means unknown, one of our friends obtained a wind-up gramophone and two of the latest swing records. These must have been supplied by the Red Cross as such records were forbidden in Germany. As our friend wished to share his good fortune, he invited several of us to visit his hut during the evening. At the appointed time we arrived and somehow all managed to squeeze in. Once the music started, it was magic and transformed a normal evening into a very memorable one, perhaps because the entertainment was completely unexpected. I am sure that most of us had put such thoughts of music out of our minds. Although the music was good, the greatest effect was the reminder of normality which we were lacking, cut off as we were from the outside world.

We stayed so long listening to the records which were being played repeatedly, it was almost curfew time before we returned to our own huts, very pleased that we had been able to share in such an evening.

Next morning we were surprised to see the 'Ferrets' enter the camp armed with pick axes, crowbars and shovels. Their job was to seek out tunnels or any other illegal proceedings in order to destroy them. We wondered who had given cause for this visit, especially when they converged on our meeting place of the night before. Once there, they proceeded to take the hut apart, pulling up floorboards and probing underneath but finding nothing. They were acting in the belief that a group of people gathered as we had been, meant a conspiracy of some sort.

Later that day all those who had been present at the previous evening's meeting received instructions to report to the same hut at eight o'clock that night, I was quite mystified and enquired of the others as to why we had been summoned, but they were equally puzzled. To make matters even more mystifying, we were told to bring English Red Cross boxes, not American ones, only English would do. In addition to this, we were to wear great coats, despite the fact it was a hot summer's day. It was going to be one of those situations where it was better not to be too inquisitive.

When we reported properly equipped, it was explained to us that although the 'Ferrets' had found nothing, we were going to give the impression that there really was something for them to worry about. We were told to wait in the hut for a few minutes, hold the box under our coats to create a bulge then walk down to the latrine. Almost immediately we were to return, swinging the empty box which was then to be folded flat and to make sure that it was easily seen. This was to be carried out several times until told to stop. It was not surprising that we received some very curious looks from the other prisoners while we did so, although none asked what we were doing.

The Germans were now faced with a problem, as we had been so blatant in our activities. We were either brazenly digging a tunnel, or covering up for someone else's scheme.

They must have decided it was the former case, as early next morning, the 'Ferrets' came in with their digging equipment and proceeded to dig up a quarter of the camp. As they found nothing at all, they may have realised that it was a hoax, however, they took no further action as far as I know.

Not so very long after this event, another one occurred which surprised nearly everybody. On leaving our huts one morning, we noticed that there were fresh traces of sand spread along the paths between the huts. A quick check proved that it was spread everywhere. The subject was being discussed by everyone, as we all wondered who could be so foolish as to advertise the fact that an excavation of some sort, had been, or was taking place. Soil disposal from such projects should be more discreet and gradual.

This did cause some smart reaction from the Germans, as this time they probed the whole of the camp. It took a considerable time and caused a great deal of inconvenience all round. To say they discovered nothing would not be true as under the very last hut, our school hut, they found the answer. A practical joker had simply dug up loads of sandy soil from beneath the floor and spread it carefully all along the pathways.

Following this discovery, the Germans did respond, in fact they lost their cool completely and issued orders that no holes of any sort were to be dug by anyone and any already dug were to be filled in. The punishment of course affected us all as it meant that no goal posts or cricket stumps could be left in the ground, all pits dug for cooking had to be filled in, in fact no holes at all.

We waited a while to see what developed, wondering how we were going to manage under such a sweeping order. Before any posts could be removed, the order was cancelled, not because the Germans had relented, but because it was an infringement of the Geneva Convention. This prevented any collective punishment being meted out for one person's misdemeanour. I don't doubt that it was a hard won victory for our Camp Leader and his staff, but we appreciated it.

The only other incident of this nature that I saw, was concerned with a large hole dug quite near to our latrine. I had been walking around the camp for some exercise and noticed several prisoners standing in a group looking down at something. It was obviously amusing as they came away laughing. I edged my way through the small knot of people to find out what it was that caused the amusement. All I could see was a deep hole which was either dug for a new latrine or a rubbish pit and I didn't think that particularly funny. I was about to move away, when a German guard pointed to something and commented on the English sense of humour. On top of the pit was a notice which said; 'Tunnel - Private - Keep out', and below this was an arrow pointing downwards. At the bottom of the pit was an opening about eighteen inches square let into the sidewall.

The Germans stopped laughing when they discovered it was not a joke and was in fact a tunnel halfway to the wire and passing between two guard posts. I am not sure that it was a genuine bid for freedom, I prefer to think that it was a demonstration to the Germans, what could be achieved by people who were determined enough.

The mention of freedom recalls a very strange experience I had one night when I thought my spirit was freeing itself from my body. It crossed my mind that perhaps I was dying which I found difficult to accept as I didn't feel ill, but then I didn't know what to expect and maybe this was it. The strange feeling occurred just after I had settled down for the night and as it was in the temporary camp, I was sleeping on the floor. As usual, I closed my eyes and tried to visualise my family at home, wondering what they were doing. I don't think I was asleep, in fact I am almost certain I wasn't. Try as I might, I had great difficulty in visualising my wife, except as a very small figure in the distance. I then tried hard to bring the image closer to see if it was her, but all I succeeded in doing, was getting an inverted image which was so close it was frightening. Because it was so disturbing, I attempted to put all thoughts out of my mind and settle down to sleep. This fact alone was enough to convince me later that I was wide awake at the time, unless I was dreaming within a dream.

Quite suddenly I had a sensation of floating, and looking down I could see my body still on the mattress. It was so novel, as I seemed to be floating about five or six feet up. I knew I had to get back to my body immediately, as if I got too far away I would never return and my body would be classed as dead. By great mental effort, I willed my return and all too slowly, this was achieved.

I lay in bed wondering if I was still alive and if so was I seriously ill? I discarded the thought of waking the others until I could prove to myself that I needed treatment. Getting out of bed, I went to the door just to get outside and breath fresh air. I didn't want to wander away in case I needed help but simply rested in the doorway. After a short while, I concluded that I wasn't about to collapse, so returned to my bed in the hope I wouldn't be troubled any more. Fortunately I went to sleep and by morning felt quite normal physically, although mentally I was very troubled. I spoke to several people about this, but there was nobody who could give me a satisfactory explanation as to what had happened.

Several years later I was quite startled to read an account written by a Tibetan monk who claimed to have had such experiences quite frequently.

I think it was true to say, that apart from a few aches and pains, the only other thing I suffered from was a mild form of dysentery as did the majority at one time or another. I possibly suffered from this complaint on two occasions but general stomach upsets were fairly frequent. At first, we reported to the medical hut whenever we suffered, but subsequent to a visit I made, it was discovered how to treat ourselves.

The first real bout that gave me concern, attacked me almost without warning. Severe pains in the stomach caused me to curl up on my mattress and I felt dreadful. A visit to the latrine did no good at all, so I crawled back to my bed in misery. After a while I knew I had to get help of some sort and a visit to the medical orderlies was necessary. I am not sure how I managed the fifty yards to the medical hut, as I was being violently sick and could barely see or walk.

At last I reached the door and staggered in, certain that I would be rushed off to hospital because of the dreadful malady I was suffering from. The medical orderly in attendance took one look at me and said; 'Take this powder, it is recommended by the German Medical Officer, I was taken aback, as I expected more concern to be shown. The powder which looked like soot, was piled up on a dessert spoon and had to be swallowed dry. It nearly choked me but I managed it. I was then instructed to return to my hut, lie down and eat nothing for twenty four hours. That was not at all difficult to comply with the way I felt and neither did I mind drinking coffee without milk.

As I lay back on my bed, I was absolutely convinced that the medics were off their heads, giving me such rubbish. Strangely enough, from then on, I began to feel better and by next morning, I felt as fit as ever. Colleagues of mine concluded that the powder was carbon based, so it was decided that in future we would treat any such upsets ourselves. Our remedy was quite simple, we placed a piece of black bread in the fire, burnt it to a cinder, powdered it up, then used it in the manner prescribed. From that time, we never suffered for very long, as at the first onset, we would give ourselves the treatment.

We were discovering that there were a number of things which were taken for granted in normal living. We had basic items supplied but the small things which made life more tolerable were missing, so it was a case of either make them or do without. I think a lot of us realised that even given tools and equipment, we didn't appreciate how some of the simple things were made, but with our limited resources and a lot of thought we improvised.

When I first arrived in camp, shaving brushes had not been issued, so I decided to make one for myself. After a little searching, I found a piece of wood suitable for a handle and some coarse string for bristles. By the time I had tied several short lengths of string to the handle, I had quite a respectable looking brush. A good soaking in water made the bristles very soft and the final product was as good to use as any I could have bought. As a matter of fact, I continued to use it, even after I was issued with one from the Red Cross.

There were a number of things we could make, but an item such as a box of matches was beyond our capabilities. As they were considered to be an undesirable item for a prisoner, we had no chance of receiving an issue from the Germans. This lack of matches was quite a drawback for the smoker, as the only way a light for a cigarette could be obtained was from another prisoner. When things were normal it was no problem, as there was always someone nearby who would be smoking, but during an air raid alert, the situation was different. Orders were given that, under no circumstances were prisoners to leave their huts, but remain inside until the 'All clear' had been sounded. The punishment for an infringement was to be shot on sight. It seemed that to be shot was the principal punishment for a great many misdemeanours.

The combination of the two factors, no matches and the threat of being shot, gave rise to a very risky but exhilarating game and that was, to get a light for a cigarette during an air raid warning. At the first alarm, everyone would make for their respective huts to sit and wait for the raid to pass. There always seemed to be a strange atmosphere of silence and an air of expectancy. I think that every time, we hoped that this one would be the final raid and one which was going to free us, but it never came. More often than not we heard nothing at all and it was during such times that people got bored, although none so bored as the smoker without a light.

The would be smoker going to the door of his hut would shout;
'Has anyone got a light?' back may come the answer, "Hut ninety four'.
'Too far, is there anyone else?' this time hut ninety six might volunteer.
'Okay hut ninety six, open your door wide, I am coming over.'

Making sure that no guards were in sight, the person concerned would launch himself like a rocket, out of his own hut, into the other, stopping abruptly before he wrecked the place in his charge. After regaining his breath and receiving the light he came for, he would prepare for departure, but not too soon in case the guards were waiting.

Eventually back he would go to his own hut, perhaps faster than before, as the thought of a well-aimed bullet acted as a spur. Perhaps it was all done as an act of bravado although at that time, we didn't bother to analyse our actions.

On odd occasions, we would hear a rifle or a machine gun being fired during a raid, although only one prisoner was ever killed and that was a slightly different story with more sinister implications.

Despite attempts to keep ourselves occupied as much as possible, frustration and boredom remained as our enemy. Anything slightly unusual, normally gained the attention of most prisoners, as it presented something new to think about or look at.

For some reason, it was with only mild curiosity that I noticed new wooden buildings being erected next door to our camp. I took no real interest until it was disclosed to us that the new construction was for our benefit. It was to be a permanent prison camp, unlike the camp we were in which was obviously very temporary.

The news was received with mixed feelings as we were pleased to have new and improved facilities, but depressed to think of any form of permanency, as all we wanted to do was leave altogether. We had arrived in July, full of hope that our release was only weeks away and now another door was being closed behind us. It seemed that we were being placed even further out of reach of freedom. Continually we had been looking for signs of weakening in the German 'War Effort'.

Little things gave us hope, for example, if more prisoners had to share a loaf, this maybe meant they were running short of food. If Red Cross parcels were late it was taken as a pointer to the decaying state of their railways. Anything which gave us hope was seized upon as a sign of their eventual surrender. To hear the news that we were to be moved to the new camp, indicated to us that they were still confident and it was a sad blow to our morale.

Finally we had to console ourselves by the thought that if we were to stay, we needed the extra shelter that the new places would provide. Our present huts were quite small, without adequate insulation and no means of heating. Neither roofs nor doors fitted properly and the wooden floors we slept on were getting rather cold.

As the first days of October arrived, so came the first hints of what winter could be like here on the border of Poland. We now became a little more anxious to move and wondered why we had not done so as it seemed as though the new camp was finished.

It was revealed that Russian prisoners had been building the new camp and like ourselves, had decided to play our game of causing problems. During the construction stages, several spades had disappeared. The Germans didn't like the implications as they realised that the Russians had buried them for our future use.

We were grateful for their attempts to help us, but I am afraid the plan misfired as it was pointed out that until all spades were recovered, the camp would not be occupied. There was little we could do about the situation except hope that the Russians would return the hidden spades as it was now getting much colder in our small shelters.

Finally the message was passed that the camp was now clear and ready for occupation. All we had to do was wait until we were given the order to move. At last the day arrived when we were told to pack our things and assemble for the transfer. It was then the thirteenth of October, which meant that I had been in the temporary camp exactly three months to the day. I wondered how long the next stay would be, not too long I hoped, I also hoped as I had done once before, that the next move we would make would be home. I could see no other reason for moving again.

Packing took very little time as our belongings were few, even so there were cooking tins, blowers and blankets to be taken. I was just about ready to go when a prisoner, quite unknown to me, gave me an odd looking piece of wire and instructed me to take it through the search. When I enquired what it was for, I was told to mind my own business and simply deliver it to the owner when we had settled in. I later discovered that it was part of a radio being smuggled through in small pieces. With nothing left to do, I followed the others to the assembly point preparatory to starting our journey to the new camp.

CHAPTER 16

The short well guarded journey was over and we had arrived at our new accommodation. This was quite different to the old place and more as I imagined a proper prison camp should be. Once inside the compound, I with several others, were directed to a barrack block, where we were divided into smaller groups and allocated rooms.

VIEW FROM MY BUNK
NEW BARRACK BLOCK

The barracks, which were constructed of double skinned matchboarding, were built on stilts about three feet off the ground. This made it easy for guards to go underneath to listen into private conversations, or check for tunnels. It also meant that the passage of air kept the buildings quite cold and with winter approaching, we could have well done without it. Each hut was about thirty five feet wide and eighty feet long. The interior was divided by a central corridor which gave access to four rooms either side. Each room was designed to house sixteen men, but for some unknown reason, our particular room was only equipped with fourteen bunks. To make things more confusing there were fifteen men in the room, so one had to sleep on the floor.

This peculiarity caused problems during the late night room check. There were two lines of four barrack huts facing each other on either side of a large exercise compound. In the middle of each row was a wash house and toilet with the added facility of showers. A vast improvement on what we had been used to, even if there was no hot water. The design of the wash house left something to be desired, it was more suited to the tropics, as there were large gaps between roof and walls for ventilation purposes.

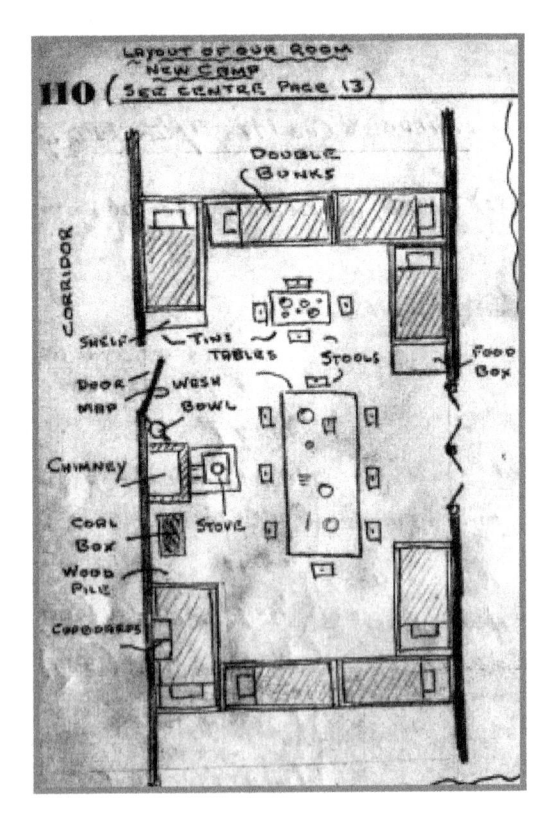

The cook-house, another large wooden building, was across the end of the two lines of huts, so forming a 'U' shape. Two more large buildings completed the major part of the camp, one was used as a sick bay and the other a concert or entertainments hall. A final but significant addition was a very small wooden hut, designed to be used for solitary confinement.

There were other buildings just outside the compound which did not concern us greatly, as they were German living and administrative quarters. The camp layout was straightforward and basic, quite in keeping with the interiors of the barrack huts and the furnishings within. Each room contained eight double bunks, except ours which had seven, two wooden tables, stools, a small iron stove and a single light bulb which was very dull indeed. The room itself was approximately twenty feet by fourteen which gave adequate space for the occupants.

The beds themselves were worthy of note because of their simplicity. At first they appeared to be double bunks but they were in fact one bed stood on top of another. Each bed was simply a wooden frame supported by four legs and into the frame were fitted five boards on which to lie. The boards were six inches wide and fitted across the frame. This meant that there was an awful lot of space left between the boards. Not only were they insufficient in number, they were also loose in the frame.

When we first saw them, we knew there had been a mistake as nobody could sleep like that, so a request was made for the full quota of boards. Back came the answer that prisoners in other camps found the number sufficient and so would we. It transpired that this was a form of mass punishment in retaliation for an occurrence in another camp. Apparently escape teams needed boards to shore up tunnels, so prisoners were asked to donate bed boards for this purpose.

When the scheme was discovered, the Germans decided to reduce the number of boards to an absolute minimum and five was the number arrived at. Faced with the knowledge that we would get no more bed boards, we had to decide on a suitable arrangement to ensure a reasonable weight distribution. The main points requiring support, were, head, shoulders, buttocks, backs of knees and feet. This still left a lot of unsupported weight, but it could just about be done with five. It must have taken quite a bit of research to arrive at that number.

Having positioned the boards as required, it was then necessary to arrange the mattress on top without disturbing them. The mattress incidentally was still the same as used in the temporary camp, a sack full of wood shavings. Getting in to bed was quite a problem at first and it took time to acquire the knack. It was important to locate one of the boards before getting in, then by kneeling or leaning on it, the weight of the body had to be distributed carefully, trying not to disturb boards or mattress. For those on the top bunks, it was particularly difficult at first, but as with many things, we soon learned how to do it without too much of a personal risk.

On more than one occasion though there would be a shout in the night followed by loud thuds and curses as somebody's bed boards took off in opposite directions. We didn't need to be told that a restless sleeper, folded up in his mattress, had been deposited on the one below.

One night I fell through mine so hard, that when I landed on the lower occupant, we went through his bed as well. What a shambles, not only had we unshipped our bed boards, nearly all the joints in the framework had come apart and we virtually finished up with a bundle of wood. We switched on the light and attempted to sort out our beds and bedding as it was impossible to do so in the dark. This attracted a very irate guard who wanted to know just what we thought we were doing and insisted that the light be switched out. We were equally irate and also insisted that we had to have light. If he wasn't prepared to let us have the main light on, then he could stand there with his torch while we rebuilt the bed. Very reluctantly he complied with our demands and stood there shining the torch wherever we needed it. He was very pleased to leave when it was completed, as I don't doubt that had he been seen by his superiors, he would have been in trouble. Thankfully the bed stayed intact until the morning, when we had to rise and get ready for the morning Roll Call parade.

The parade itself was simply to keep a check on numbers present and was part of the routine to which we had become accustomed in the old camp. In the new place, there were minor differences mainly due to the layout. For ease of counting, prisoners paraded in groups or divisions outside their own barrack block which meant that there were roughly one hundred and twenty prisoners to each division.

The Camp Commandant and his Warrant officer, both members of the Luftwaffe, stood in the middle of the compound with our Camp Leader and Man of Confidence. The guards then walked round, counted us, reported the numbers present and when everything was satisfactory, we were dismissed to carry out whatever activity we were involved in.

It sounds straightforward and simple, but it was not quite so and I believe that the guards dreaded our daily parades, but more of that later. There was a final check last thing at night, when guards came to the rooms to count us.

Another change in routine occurred when the Germans realised that during very bad weather, we could all stay in our barrack blocks to be counted. This was more for their benefit than ours, as standing in the middle of the parade area, they were much more exposed, than we were in our groups. They also discovered that if we thought they were suffering discomfort, we would prolong the parade in some way, by being awkward.

Everyone was becoming quite adept at this, because as mentioned before, it was our duty to do so and daily parades were a very good way of keeping several guards occupied for longer than they wished. It was our custom to parade in three ranks, whereas the German drill formation was in ranks of five. Unfortunately we were very dull and never understood anything they tried to teach us. Many times have I seen guards near to despair attempting to get us into a sensible order for counting.

They would be fretting and fuming, giving orders in German, which we refused to comprehend, while the German Warrant Officer waited impatiently, wondering why the fool of a guard couldn't carry out a simple task. At no time did he attempt to take over even when a shambles developed. He possibly realised that things would only get worse if he did.

On one occasion a guard attempting to get a line of prisoners covered off with the line in front, gave the order for the line to move. He forgot to tell the first man to stand fast. As a result of his action, they moved out completely into the next division. The guard watched amazed, unable to give the order to stop as he was becoming so hopping mad. Going over to the other division, he shouted that everyone was to get back, which they did, although the other division came as well. If we hadn't sorted ourselves out, I doubt if he alone could have done so. At last peace was regained and the count continued as though nothing had happened.

Another method of spoiling the count was by standing to attention when ordered, then lean sideways against the next man, which gave the impression of a group of Siamese twins on parade. Even more peculiar effects were produced when prisoners stood with legs wide apart so that the left foot rested against the next man's right foot and the right foot against the other neighbour's left foot. In this manner, pairs of feet lined up and so did bodies, although they didn't match. It was surprising just how difficult it was to analyse what was being done, as it looked so unnatural. Invariably under these circumstances, the count would be incorrect and require a repetition.

The disruption was not only confined to the day time parade but occasionally happened during the late night count as well. Our small contribution was made easy due to there being only fifteen in our room instead of the normal sixteen. Add to this the language difficulties and we had ready made confusion, particularly as the Germans could not readily accept irregularities.

When the guard was due to arrive for the late night count, we would perhaps import a body from the next room, thus giving a total of sixteen which would satisfy the guard. We would then explain that we should only have fifteen and the sixteenth man was a visitor. This always caused turmoil. Another means of doing so, was by exporting two of our people to another room. We would apologise for the discrepancy and promptly go in search of the missing persons, with the guard following us in an attempt to restore some sort of order. We were often able to make our room count last up to ten minutes or more. Before doing this, it was important to judge the nature of the guard to see how far he could be pushed, then not go too far, they were only human after all and could have got very nasty with us.

Apart from Roll Call parades, there were very few demands made on us by the authorities. There were other parades but these were quite willingly attended, for example when Red Cross parcels were being issued. Nobody would miss those unless of course sickness prevented it. The parcels were normally issued once a week and could be either English or American. Each type had its merits although

American parcels were in great demand for the cigarettes, as they always seemed to be fresh. For a reason we could never understand, the English cigarettes were in paper packets and more often than not felt damp, so would not smoke very well.

The variety of food though, seemed much better and enabled us to create some reasonably interesting dishes. The German rations which were issued daily, were not received with the same enthusiasm as attended the Red Cross issue, although it was still food, despite the doubts cast on some things we received. We had improved our living conditions with the move from the old camp but the rations were still the same.

Two items I remember quite well as will a number of other prisoners, The first I knew as Romanian dehydrated vegetables, which were so vile that I doubt if much of it was ever eaten. We did try to use it in various ways although the smell and appearance put most of us off. Maybe they were appreciated in Romania but if this was the case, why send them to us? It was not in a prisoner's nature to intentionally waste anything although there were exceptions and this was one.

A close runner-up to the vegetables was the German issue cheese, which I believed to be a means of exercising mental cruelty. It came in the form of individual cheeses which were about two inches in diameter, one inch thick. The outside casing looked like yellow crepe rubber and contained a mixture of goats' milk cheese and caraway seeds, Anyone who was warped enough to accept them was banned from the room. We insisted that they were stored in a place where we couldn't smell them, which was no easy task.

Following one such issue, one of our room-mates, Ron our Engineer, decided that he had a strong stomach, and a diet of cheese would be good for the health. Despite our protests, he downed three or four, claiming they were excellent. We could tell from his actions that he was not enjoying it but he insisted they were very tasty. Eventually we went to bed, that is all except Ron who disappeared outside for a while, then came back and crawled into bed. He did not stay long before he was up and away again. This was continued through the night which rather disturbed our sleep and in the morning when he awoke, he was the shadow of his former self and swore never to eat the cheese again.

Despite Ron's experience, a very knowledgeable person decided that the right way to eat them was to cook them. We tried hard to dissuade him, then when it was apparent his mind was made up, asked him to go somewhere else, all to no avail. We watched fascinated as he heated the cheese in one of his cooking trays, wondering just how he was going to deal with it. Quite suddenly the crepe rubber melted and spread all over the pan, while the odour, already bad, increased in intensity. All at once, he realised that even he couldn't face it and attempted to remove it from his dish. He hadn't reckoned on the tenacity of that cheese, it stuck hard and as far as I know, he had to ditch the lot as cheese and dish would not part company.

Meat was a much more acceptable food than either of those previously mentioned although the quality was never as consistent. I don't know if it was general practice, but on the rare occasions when meat was on the menu, a runner from the cookhouse would appear in our room to brief us. He would first ask if anyone had stomach trouble as we were to be given meat for lunch, which had been condemned. As no one ever admitted to being ill, he would then define the state of condemnation. The first grade was meat condemned by the British Medical Officer, the second grade was meat condemned by the British Medical Officer and our own voluntary cookhouse staff. The final grade was condemnation by the British Medical Officer, our own staff and the German Medical Officer. Despite this, I don't recall anyone ever refusing to eat it, we knew it was well cooked.

Bread, an essential commodity issued daily, was always shared out in our room with a strict ritual, closely observed by all inmates. Normally it was a two kilo loaf, thick in the middle and tapered at each end, which had to be divided into equal portions, otherwise bitter arguments would ensue. To make matters more difficult, the number of people sharing a loaf would vary according to the allocation decided by the Germans. At times it would be six to a loaf, sometimes maybe eight. One person would cut the loaf into sections or slices, a committee would decide that all amounts were equal, then two, would decide who was to receive which portion of bread. The careful division of all rations we received was an essential activity, as none of us wanted more than the next man and made very sure that we didn't get any less either. In addition to this, it prevented fights developing amongst disgruntled people.

The person cutting the loaf certainly had the most difficult task and because of this, was normally entrusted to those few who were more adept at using cutting tools, as precision was of prime importance. As a guide he would use a piece of wood marked off as a measuring stick, Its length was equivalent to that of a standard loaf and was divided up on one side into six divisions and on the other side into eight. This worked well providing the shares were of this nature, should any changes be made a new stick would have to be produced which required lengthy discussions. When cutting, compensation had to be made for irregularities in the loaf and where necessary pieces would have to be trimmed off or added to make the portions equal. Once the cutter was satisfied, the portions would be placed on the table for inspection by the committee, who then handed responsibility to the two who were to do the allocation.

To make the selection of portions, the method used was similar to that employed by children in their games. One person would point to a pile of bread and ask who was to receive it. The person doing the nominating had his back to the table so as not to favour anyone. We considered this to be the fairest way as no one could be biased in favour of another. This activity may be considered excessive unless it is borne in mind that to deprive a prisoner of a portion of his rations, was the equivalent to unjustly relieving a person of his earnings.

The rations may not have changed since our move from the old camp although the method of cooking had. There was no longer a need to build fires outside, neither were blowers required any more, as most of the things we cooked were done on the stove in the room. This was a small cast iron affair which stood on a block of concrete against the wall which separated our room from the corridor. The chimney was brick built and protruded into the corridor where a small flap gave access to the flue. The art of cooking on this particular stove, was also an exercise in tact and diplomacy, due to the small top which gave little room for more than two baking dishes. As there were fifteen of us, it meant that we had to come to an agreement very quickly as to how the cooking was to be done. Quite often it meant that dishes had to be rotated during the cooking, to give all a fair share of the hot spots.

It was decided that if we divided up into three or four groups this would facilitate the cooking, providing that all in one group could agree on the menu for the day. This naturally developed into the requirement for a caterer and a cook. The system worked very well, but still the stove top was very crowded.

OVEN BUILT BEHIND STOVE
(NEILLS BULMER & Co.)

One day, someone who had been giving a lot of thought to the subject, came up with the idea that we move the stove away from the wall, so as to use some of the space behind. At first we were reluctant to do so as if anything was broken, we would be without means of heating or cooking. Finally when it was agreed, the task proved much easier than expected and we were able to pull the whole thing forward by about nine inches. By means of one or two bricks, some clay and sheets of tin plate, a double oven was fitted to the space at the back. This was a vast improvement on the old arrangement, as not only had the cooking capacity increased, new recipes could be tried. There was no longer a necessity to fry everything, as food could be baked in the oven at the same time.

On one occasion, when the stove was completely full, one of our colleagues needing more space decided that provided the food was properly covered, it was possible to get it heated by placing it in the flue. As mentioned, access to the flue was done by opening a flap in the chimney in the corridor. This flap was sometimes used for this purpose and sometimes for flue cleaning, but one prisoner discovered another use for it. After we had occupied the barracks for a few weeks, the stoves which had been alight continuously, accumulated soot in the chimneys. It was due to the fuel blocks we were given, as they produced more smoke than heat. Sweeping them was not a job for the guards to do, so a local civilian sweep was called in. As each block was being swept, the inmates were ordered to stay out of the building, so there was little else to do but stand and watch him at work.

It may or may not be a German custom, but this sweep thought it a good idea to stand on the roof and push his brush down the chimney from the top, so causing a lot of soot to finish up inside the building. Maybe he thought it funny, although the joke was not shared by all, as one prisoner got very angry about it. When no guards were looking, he slipped into the building and located the chimney being swept. As the brush reached the bottom, the prisoner opened the flap of the flue and grabbed the brush. The sweep started pulling like mad, afraid he was about to lose it. During one long pull, the prisoner inside suddenly let go, which completely caught the sweep off balance, so causing him to tumble down the roof. Fortunately for him, it wasn't very high, so as he fell off, it did little more than hurt his pride.

This action certainly stopped him from sweeping the soot downwards, as after he had been pacified by the guards, he decided to continue, although this time sweeping from the inside. An enquiry was made regarding this episode but the culprit was never discovered, as happened so often in these circumstances.

The stoves may have burned brighter after the sweep had been, but space was still limited and although we were able to do most of our own cooking, we still drew hot water from the cook-house. Owing to the location of our block, we had the shortest distance to go for water, so our water collectors were normally very early in the queue. Our system was to detail a person daily to carry the water, as one person doing the job permanently was not ideal, because it often meant standing in the rain or cold.

When it was announced that water was being issued, people carrying jugs, would erupt from each room all anxious to be first, and it was always quite a scramble. One day, right on the time hot water should have been issued, the Air Raid sirens sounded and those waiting to collect water had to stay where they were. The rule still applied, that nobody was allowed outside during the period of an Air Raid alarm. No one was prepared to return to their room and wait, as to do so would mean losing a place in the queue. Looking across to the other blocks, I could see groups of people standing just inside the door, ready to run at the sound of the "All Clear".

After a reasonable period, I was thankful to hear the siren sounding, as it meant we could resume normal activities. I thought it was not so loud as usual, until I realised it must be the one in the local village. Almost immediately there followed a rifle shot, which puzzled us, until the truth was discovered. A Canadian who lived in the block opposite us, was absolutely determined to be first and burst out of his hut at a run, sure that it really was 'All clear'. He didn't get far, as he was blasted by a guard using dumdum bullets, a big hole blown in his back. Despite the danger, two of his colleagues rushed from the block and dragged him back inside, but it was too late, his injury was too severe.

When we heard the news, we prayed he would live but unfortunately he eventually succumbed to his injury. This was a very black day for the camp as we all knew that the shooting had not been an enforcement of an order, just plain murder.

The parade that evening was the most sombre I had ever attended and to make matters worse, there seemed to be one person missing. This brought remarks from the prisoners that perhaps the murdered man had been overlooked. It soon became obvious that the guards were becoming as jittery as we were and they certainly felt ill at ease with our sullen lack of co-operation. At last the dreadful day ended and with it, the final chapter in one man's life.

CHAPTER 17

Life carried on in different ways for different people, some simply brooded on what had happened, which served little purpose. We could not change the violent environment in which we lived, but we could with the help of others, do something to make life more pleasant. Very soon the majority of us were once again concentrating on our various interests, anxious to subdue disturbing thoughts. We still had to live and face the future.

In addition to food which we had been receiving from the Red Cross, other articles started to appear in greater quantities, for example, shaving brushes, razors and toothbrushes, items which we really appreciated. In addition, there were such things as musical instruments, greasepaints and material to help create a theatre. As our shows became more sophisticated so even more equipment appeared and I understand that even the Germans supplied us with some things. This would not be too surprising, as they had very little in the way of entertainment themselves and depended on us quite a lot.

Gradually, the small entertainments group which had started in the temporary camp, blossomed into a dramatics group, an orchestra, a piano accordion band and a harmonica band. I became interested in the dramatics group and although the parts I took were small, I did my best to play the roles given me. Perhaps my enthusiasm was greater than my acting ability, which might have been said about others as well. It didn't seem to matter, we were all doing our best. In addition to the dramatics group, I also joined the harmonica band as a performer, but regarding the orchestra, my role was helping out with a little of the backstage work.

Rehearsing and acting in the stage shows, gave us a great deal of enjoyment and we played to packed houses, who judging by the applause, enjoyed it as much as we did, Not only did our people have a good time, the Germans also crowded in, not as guards, but as audience. On one occasion we had to put on a special concert, as the Commandant who wanted to see it, was unable to attend the regular showing.

At the end of each performance, it was customary to follow tradition and sing the National Anthem which was sung with much greater feeling than that normally displayed at home. I suppose it was to be expected that eventually it would be banned and it was when it finally happened, it acted as just one more reminder that we were in fact prisoners with few rights. At the end of the concert which immediately followed the ban, we wondered what would happen, would the show simply stop without any final ceremony and were we supposed to just walk out. Coming onto the stage, the compère announced that as we were aware, our National Anthem had been banned, so from then on we would sing 'Land of Hope and Glory' in its place. The gloomy mood lifted and it was sung with such fervour and pride that we nearly raised the roof. The Germans may have realised the meaning of the words although no attempt was made to stop us, I am sure that if they had done so, life for them would have become much more difficult.

The various concerts were much appreciated and was often a subject for discussion. During one such conversation, the subject of musical talent was raised, when Bob Burns one of our room mates declared that he was a musician and his main instrument was a clarinet. When it was suggested that perhaps he should join the newly formed orchestra, he declined as he considered that they were still not organised and in any case they had no clarinets.

One day, to our surprise, a member of the orchestra walked in with a clarinet, presented it to Bob and asked him to prove that he was as good as he claimed. Bob then explained that he wouldn't play it without a new reed. This objection was soon overcome when reeds were produced. Fitting one to the mouthpiece, he attempted to play. Even to our untrained ears it didn't sound very good, which proved to our satisfaction that he had been exaggerating.

He seemed quite hurt by our attitude and often explained that he really could play. He told us that the reeds were much too hard for him but should any decent reeds turn up, he would show us. An easy thing to say of course as none of us would know a good reed from a poor one and we were of the opinion that he was over-estimating his own ability.

We soon lost interest in the subject and had almost forgotten it until one day he came in and announced that some new reeds had arrived. Apparently, these were just about the standard he required. It was with idle curiosity that we watched him fit one of the new reeds to the clarinet and start to play. We listened, astounded at his skill as it was beautiful to hear. I for one wished that I had never questioned his ability.

Now that he was satisfied with the instrument, he joined the orchestra and in a very short time took over as leader. He had to make good, as the competition from the other forms of entertainment was increasing rapidly and reaching a high standard. He justified his claims by organising the orchestra and producing some excellent music. Some of the credit for the standard of the music must go to the arranger, as without his skill, the music which may be technically correct, would sound uninteresting. We were very fortunate in having at least one good arranger in our midst. Although musical instruments were available, sheet music was not, at least, the type we required. Anyone who could remember a new tune would be cornered by him, then made to repeat the melody over and over again, until it was written down. From this would be produced sheet music for the various instruments, which was no mean task.

Once the orchestra was established the need for a motif became apparent and the leader's initials BB were settled on as a monogram. It was pointless having a motif if it could not be displayed to advantage and the obvious place to have it was on the front of the music stands. In their original state they were not very attractive, so it was decided that a touch of colour would not come amiss.

I offered to do what I could to decorate the stands and was immediately accepted for the job. To help me in my task, I was given a roll of paper and poster paints. Using various Disney figures copied from the newspaper, I drew them holding various musical instruments and to make things more attractive, used different coloured backgrounds. I am pleased to say that when all the stands were decorated, it made quite a difference to the general appearance of the orchestra.

At the end of each performance, the posters were removed from the stands and rolled up for future use. They could not be left where they were, as the stands were also used by the Piano Accordion band and they had their own ideas.

I know little about the organisation of this band as I was not involved in any way, but it was a major contribution to our entertainment. Like the orchestra, considerable effort must have been made to produce a band at the standard achieved. The style of music was quite different to that of the orchestra although both were very much appreciated and to sit in on a concert was to forget the outside world for a while.

Although the Harmonica band was not the size or complexity of either the Orchestra or the Piano Accordion band, it matched them both in enthusiasm. When I first joined, it seemed to be a bit disorganised which I suppose is typical of many new organisations. In the beginning the selection of tunes we were to play was a problem, owing to the varying levels of skill of the performers. As we had no music of any sort to work to, tunes we wished to play had to be learned by heart. Discussions then took place regarding musical arrangements followed by constant practice to make sure it all fitted together. I am sure that we all enjoyed our practice sessions despite the hard work, and the applause received during concerts, repaid us with interest.

In addition to stage shows that were produced as a way of entertainment for the masses, there were also intellectual activities in the form of lectures or courses given by experts. Anyone was welcome to attend, as they were not only of educational value to the student, they also helped to keep the experts in practice. Several subjects were covered, such as advanced mathematics, law, geology, or perhaps architecture. In some cases, where the subjects were mainly theoretical and did not require tools to practice with, prisoners were able to prepare for examinations, in the hope that they would be able to qualify after the war.

A small group of people whose interest was quite different to that of the majority, claimed that they were being neglected. This group consisted of several artists who thought that the entertainments organisations were benefiting from Red Cross supplies, whereas the items they needed, pens, pencils, inks, paint and paper were not available. Because of this shortage, they were not able to practice their skills, so made application to be supplied with them.

Soon after the request was made, some materials arrived and the artists promised to put on a show of their talents. They must have worked very hard indeed as shortly afterwards it was announced that an Art Exhibition was to take place. I think it was true to say that even those people not particularly interested in art attended the showing and came away amazed at the skill shown. I am not sure what I expected to see, certainly not the quality of pictures which were on display. There were cartoons, portraits, advertisements, landscapes in fact all forms of art. It was obvious that some, if not all of the artists were professional in civilian life. I can still vaguely recall one drawing of a girl's face which was so good, that from a few feet away, it could be mistaken for a photograph in black and white.

I don't know if the Germans had ever considered the other skills which could be developed, as now the prisoners had the means of practicing the art of forging official documents, I suspect that this may have been the original reason for the request for materials. I don't think that this concerned the majority of us though, as I doubt if much thought was given to anything but the Art show and its effect. The display certainly had its effect on me as it must have done to others, no longer were these people simply prisoners, they were artists. It was of course accepted that there were many different types amongst us, but a person who could not display his particular skill, was just another prisoner. A trapeze artist could only talk about his work. A range riding cowboy, no matter how good he was on a horse, made little impression, as neither were able to demonstrate their ability. I suppose that the proverb 'Actions speak louder than words' could well apply in this case.

Not all scenes were depicted on paper, nor were they presented on stage as some took place in the billets, in other words, there were domestic scenes. It was to be expected, from a group of people who were under a certain amount of stress and our particular room was no exception. We could quite often avoid the guards we didn't want to meet and even shut them out of our minds, whereas we who shared a room, were constantly in contact with each other. Any irritating habits or behaviour became magnified until in some instances, quite serious fights developed. One such situation arose in our room one morning.

I forget the precise details, except that one of our colleagues had done something to annoy us and when confronted with it, maintained that it was nothing to do with us. He was quite right I suppose and the matter should have rested there. Unfortunately the problem was resurrected, and became more than another room mate could bear. Suddenly leaping on the offender, he grabbed him by the throat and started to strangle him. Under normal living conditions we may have reacted much quicker, but as it was, we looked on with mild interest at this display of fearful temper. It was not until the person being strangled, fell to the floor in a semi-conscious state, that we realised the seriousness of the situation and its implications. We were in fact witnessing an attempted murder.

This had to stop, so grabbing the attacker, we pulled him away and went to the aid of the other one who was now fighting for breath. Fortunately this action cooled the temper of the attacker, but despite this, he still resented the other strongly. The problem was resolved when the two were sent to live in different barrack blocks and had no need to meet each other again.

Not all domestic scenes were so violent I am pleased to say, otherwise life would have been intolerable. There were however minor incidents of a nature experienced in many households and the following is a typical example. As may be imagined, cooking for several people in the manner previously described was not at all easy. Because of this, we had to organise our meals so as to prevent clashes with each others' interests.

When a meal had been cooked, it was removed from the stove and normally eaten right away. One gentleman, a Scotsman, did not seem to consider food to be very important and was often late for his meals. It was not solely lack of interest, as his activities as pianist for the theatrical group often kept him busy. One day as usual, we had finished our meal and were settling down to our various interests. There was one exception, Sandy, who was particularly late and had not yet turned up for his meal. The cook for his small group was a bit put out, as his efforts were not fully appreciated, but reluctantly left the bowl of stew on the fire to keep it warm. If it was ruined, it was not the cook's fault.

Still a little put out, he decided to wait no longer and go off for a wash. On his return, he was even more put out as he told us that someone had stolen his bar of soap. He hung his towel above the stove, checked the stew which was still being warmed then returned to his bunk. He sat there a while brooding on the lack of interest shown by some and the dishonesty of others.

At the time, I was engaged in producing the posters for the music stands and had spread my paper and paints on the table. I did leave a small space for Sandy, should he eventually return for lunch. At last he turned up to be greeted by the disgruntled cook, wondering where he had been as the meal was ruined. Neither appreciated the others point of view, Sandy not realising the cook's difficulties and the cook not understanding that Sandy had been busy. There was a stony silence as Sandy sat down opposite me to eat his lunch. I tried to ignore the atmosphere and continued to daub paint on the poster, using my spare shaving brush which was excellent for the purpose. Peace at last.

I worked away quietly, idly noting that Sandy had picked up his cup of coffee, which by now must be cold. I wondered why he was staring at it in such a strange manner until in an ominous voice, he wanted to know why it had turned jet black. In a flash it dawned on me that I had washed my paint brush out in his coffee cup by mistake. I thought he would strike me.

At last we managed to calm him down and accept my apologies. Not an easy task considering that the cook was muttering to the effect that it wouldn't have happened if he had turned up to meals on time. Again things became quiet as we all resumed our interests until it was realised that something else was amiss. It was Sandy again, who fishing around in his stew with a spoon, had recovered one bar of toilet soap, which had dropped from the towel above the stove. Sandy was speechless, especially when the cook claimed it was his soap and took it away from him. The place was hardly fit to live in for quite a while after that.

It was not that Sandy was a trouble maker, far from it, but he did come close to being involved with the guards, It developed in quite a simple way and was partly due to his role as pianist. It so happened that the piano he was using, was a grand piano which had in fact seen better days. Every time it was moved it needed retuning, also the pedal mechanism kept falling off. There was no connection between the two facts and is only mentioned to describe the state of the piano. Sandy was more concerned with the pedals than the tuning, as the latter could be easily remedied. If the pedals were damaged they would have been difficult to replace. To make certain they were kept safe, he stored them beneath his bunk amongst our empty tins and timber which were materials for our various projects.

Just prior to the storage of the pedals, it had been announced that prisoners were only allowed to have small quantities of wood and no more than five tins of any shape or size. The reason for this was fairly obvious to us as timber could be used to shore up tunnels and tins joined together would make good ventilation trunking. These were essential items to us as we needed tins to make or replace our cooking utensils and wood to construct cupboards and shelves. In common with other prisoners, we seldom threw away usable materials.

As a result, we began to make a fair collection of items, especially if we included the piano mechanism. We certainly had more than five tins each which we intended to hang on to and we also meant to keep any wood that had been so carefully hoarded.

We had doubts as to what to do when we heard that there was to be a search for unauthorised collections of wood. If we had tried to conceal it somewhere, we would most certainly have lost it, as it would have been discovered either by Germans or other prisoners. A decision was made, we would display the permitted amount of timber then hide the rest behind numerous tins and hope that we could get away with it.

The day of the search arrived and we waited anxiously as the guard entered the room and started his hunt. We showed our co-operation with the guard by pointing to the small amount of wood on display under the bunks. He was quite happy and ignored the number of tins. When it came to the tin search the following week, we repeated the exercise, although this time, we dragged the wood out and built a barrier in front of the surplus tins. This worked quite well, as we had judged the situation correctly, the guards only searched for the items they were specifically briefed for on any particular day and ignored anything else.

As I remember, the items to be searched for were always announced beforehand which made it easier for us. We did however come unstuck, or at least very nearly. The search was on for timber and Sandy had just started keeping the piano pedals under his bunk. The guard went round the room peering under bunks, quite satisfied with what he saw, until he arrived at Sandy's bunk. Cautiously he stretched out his hand and pulled forth the piano pedal mechanism. It seemed that he was not too sure what it was, except that the framework was made of wood. This made Sandy guilty of holding more than his quota. A very serious matter and something he should investigate further. It was a little difficult, as he did not speak English very well, although the message was getting across that he was not satisfied.

He studied the contraption which was in the shape of a wooden harp, with two brass pedals positioned at the base. These controlled two brass rods, which passed up through the harp to where the piano should be. He still looked puzzled, so jokingly Sandy described it as a secret weapon. The guard wasn't at all sure of his ground now, so to cover his confusion, he pressed one of the pedals.

Sandy reached out and implored him not to press them both together otherwise there would be an explosion. The guard looked quite alarmed, put the thing down and hurried from the room, saying something about an officer. We would have found this more amusing if the guard had simply laughed about it instead of being so serious over the matter.

We thought little of it until a few minutes later the guard returned with a very severe looking German officer. In excellent English, he demanded to know from Sandy what he had been telling the guard, so out came the pedals and the story of the bomb was repeated. The officer looked at Sandy as though demented, then turning to his guard ordered him from the room.

We wondered what this implied, was Sandy to be arrested? Once he was alone with us, the officer asked Sandy, who he thought he was making a fool of, with the piece from the grand piano. It was explained that we didn't think the guard would take the matter seriously as it was so obviously a joke, unfortunately it had misfired. The officer was now satisfied and accepted our apologies.

When he was about to leave, he thought to ask how Sandy had the pedals in his possession. He explained that as he was the pianist it was his duty to look after the piano. The officer then became very interested and wanted to know more about Sandy as he himself was also a musician. I don't know how long the officer stayed, but the two of them talked non-stop about music, discussing their likes and dislikes. It was apparent that they had a great deal in common and when they finally parted, were on very good terms.

The inspections for wood and tins became fairly routine and after a while gave little cause for concern except for the invasion of our privacy, but who could expect privacy in a prison camp? Apart from such minor inspections, our rooms where we lived, were a kind of sanctuary where the authorities seldom ventured.

Then came the disturbing news, the Gestapo were coming to report on the camp as a whole. Prior to this visit, we were to be inspected in our rooms by our own German officials. The German Colonel asked us to cause no trouble during the visit as things would become unpleasant for everyone, Germans included and by his manner, it was realised it was not so much a threat as a plea for a temporary truce.

On the day of the preliminary visit, we made sure that our room was tidy and no incriminating evidence present. Just to be on the safe side, we rolled up the map which doubled as a door blind. Theoretically there was nothing wrong, as it was only a copy of a similar map in the German news paper.

When the inspection party arrived, they seemed satisfied that all was in order, except for minor items which had to be rectified. The stove being away from the wall, did concern them a little, until we explained its purpose. As the Colonel was about to leave the room, he happened to notice the roll of paper stuck to the door, above the window pane. He naturally enquired its purpose although he was quite sure that it was only a window blind. When he was told it was a map, he was quite visibly shaken and insisted that it was unrolled for his inspection.

He was even more surprised to see that it covered a very large area of Europe. Obviously he wanted to know how we had obtained it and its purpose. He seemed satisfied with the explanation. It had been copied from a map printed in the official party newspaper the Volkischer Beabachter and was used to trace the progress of the war. He then wanted to know where we got our information from and knew we were lying when we said it was from the same newspaper. I am sure that he was aware that our information originated from BBC news broadcasts received on secret radios. Obviously we were more likely to accept our own news than the propaganda issued to the German public. We were told to remove the map and hide it during the official visit and restore it again when they had gone.

The moment the Gestapo arrived in the compound, the word passed round like magic and it seemed to me that there was an uneasy calm about the place. Their reputation was enough to prevent anyone stepping out of line during their visit. My brief brush with them when first captured was enough and whereas I had been threatened with one of their prisons, others had actually experienced them. We realised that the guards themselves were very wary of the organisation and had no desire to attract their attention in any way.

We had been warned that the Gestapo were likely to visit each individual room and it became apparent that they were doing so. The inspection party, which consisted of the visitors and our own German staff could be seen moving from building to building. It was obvious from the time they were taking that it was more than just a formal glance. At last we heard them enter our hut and begin to visit the rooms. It was bad enough hearing them approaching, but when they entered, their very presence seemed chilling.

I know this was the effect they had on me and it would seem that I was not alone as even the guards were subdued. We were very thankful that we had hidden the map before their visit and even more thankful when they finally left altogether. They must have been reasonably satisfied with our side of the organisation, as we heard nothing further.

The departure of the Gestapo must have come as a mixed blessing to the authorities, as having got rid of one threat, they were faced with our disruptive tactics again. Not all disruptions were pre-meditated, some just started naturally and grew from there. One such situation originated with the discovery that there were junior ranks in our midst. I am not sure if this happened before or after the Gestapo visit, but whatever the case, I am sure they would have not been too pleased had they known of the situation that developed. In itself it was not too serious, but it did demonstrate a defiance of the German authority.

Having made the discovery of the junior ranks, the Germans wanted them sorted out and identified. It seems that the names and ranks were known, but they wanted the bodies that matched. We were rather concerned, as it would most probably mean them being separated from us and perhaps sent to another camp. Our theories proved wrong, as all that the Germans wanted, was a working party. In accordance with the Geneva Convention, they were entitled to use these airmen on work which did not contribute to the war effort.

Eventually the order was given that the airmen were to assemble next morning properly dressed and ready for work. We wondered how they would be employed, where they would be taken and especially how they would be treated. I hoped that they would get better treatment than some of the slave labour gangs I had seen.

When the dozen or so working party assembled next day, they were far outnumbered by spectators who, like myself, wanted to see what these airmen looked like. I studied the first one a Leading Aircraftman, who seemed familiar but I had been under the impression that he was a warrant officer. Another airman, I had believed to be a Flight Sergeant. As a matter of fact I knew them all and had always been under the impression that they were either Senior NCO's or Warrant officers. I was a bit bothered about this until I noticed that some of them were having difficulty with their uniforms which didn't seem to fit properly. I suddenly realised that the whole thing was a put up job and that they were who I thought they were. The masquerade was arranged by the 'Nuisance Organisation' who were set on making more trouble.

Eventually after a roll call in which they answered to unfamiliar names, the party were surrounded by armed guards and prepared to march off. We all wished them well and hoped it wouldn't be too long before we saw them again. The inner gates opened and they passed into the Vorlager (the space between the inner and outer main gates) where they halted while the gates were closed behind them. We waited for the outer gates to be opened, but no move was made to do so. What an anticlimax as that is where they were to be employed, in the vorlager. We now realised that if they were going to be put to work where we could see them, it should be worth watching.

I have witnessed many farces staged by professional actors, but none have matched the performance that was put on by the working party. There was a big difference between the two types of performers, actors played in farces to amuse an audience, while the prisoners did so to confuse an enemy.

The job proved to be quite simple. It was only necessary to erect a few small sectional huts of the type we had lived in while at the temporary camp. To start with, the walls had to be bolted together, the roof dropped on, then the floor sections fitted in. Work started, watched closely by the guards, who were not there to give technical guidance, only for security reasons. They either didn't know or care how the huts should be assembled as long as they weren't affected. That was a false hope, as in no time at all they were involved in arguments and requests for instructions. Two people carrying a section of wall easily carried by one, put it down on its end and tried to make it stand up. They gave up after a while and went to fetch a second piece, which meant that they had two pieces to deal with, thus a much more difficult task. They tried to get the guard to help them, but he stood back as he was only there to watch.

Eventually a roof section was added to the collection and after a great deal of struggling, they managed to form an arch. No bolts were put in, they were simply propped up, then quite satisfied with their efforts the two workers went for more pieces. Inevitably, while they were gone the assembly collapsed and on their return they stared in disbelief at their ruined efforts.

Approaching the guard, they accused him of sabotaging their work, which he of course denied. To make matters more confusing, the conversations were carried out in a little English, some German and a lot of sign language. Turning to the spectators crowding the wire, they appealed for witnesses and a big argument developed among the prisoners as to who was responsible.

Some blamed the guard, while others blamed the prisoners which developed into a shouting match. The guard who found the situation a bit too much for him to handle, decided it might be better to wander off and guard a different pair of workers.

Another guard approached a worker who was sitting on a tree stump smoking and demanded he return to work. The prisoner objected strongly and informed the guard that he was governed by British Trade Union rules, which demanded a five minute break for every ten minutes worked. No amount of argument would persuade him to work, so that guard also decided it was better to look elsewhere for a more co-operative worker.

While all this was going on, with guards trying to explain that walls should not be assembled inside out and a hut only four feet long wasn't right, the lads inside the camp, were as busy as the working party outside. When no one was looking in their direction, workers would toss a section of hut over the wire, to a waiting group. It was immediately hidden from view by a press of prisoners and rapidly carted off somewhere to be taken apart for other purposes. I saw so many pieces come over the wire that I would say that for every two huts assembled outside, one finished up inside.

It took two days for the authorities to realise that the working party was not genuine and demanded that things were put right. No mention was made of the huts that were lost, but either they didn't know or didn't care very much. I am sure they knew as we did that we had received instructions not to escape, so perhaps no harm would arise from possession of the stolen wood.

Although many prisoners would think twice of escaping into what was becoming a very hostile Europe, the thought that we were ordered not to do so was depressing. It meant that our only chance of freedom was not likely to occur until either we were recaptured or the war was ended. It was rather difficult not to dwell on freedom at times and when it did occur I found it best to be alone.

This of course was not entirely possible, but at least I was able to get away from my room mates for a little while. The walk was rather limited, I agree, although going round the perimeter a few times was reasonable exercise. On one such walk, when I was feeling a little bit down, I wandered slowly along the trip fence and gazed out into the fields beyond, where a few peasant women were working. It was all very quiet as apart from these field workers, few people were ever seen in the area. Maybe the locals were discouraged from getting near us. The fields themselves were quite large and the view rather uninteresting as it was so flat and open.

As I walked, I contemplated on the fact that there was only a few yards between me and freedom, but those few yards were extremely dangerous ones. Just to step over the trip fence meant death - only one step was enough. The thought had an evil fascination, rather like standing on a cliff top, Wondering what it would be like to fall. My walk was not helping me to dispel my gloomy feeling so I carried on a while as I was in no mood to return to the room.

SURROUNDING VIEW

When I got to the tree, I stopped. I had often seen this tree before and had given it little thought, which was surprising as it was the only one in camp. It was hardly a tree, more of a sapling, but at the time it was in leaf. I thought that if I could rest beneath it, I would be able to imagine I was out in the country and escape from my surroundings. It was quiet when I sat down and everything seemed peaceful especially when I leaned back and looked up through the leaves. No barbed wire or anything else was in sight only the vast expanse of sky and hemmed in though I may have been on the ground, there were no barriers above me. Thoughts like these had to be put aside, as dwelling on captivity could be very distressing and did affect some prisoners very seriously. After a short period of rest I felt a little more settled and returned to my room.

CHAPTER 18

Life carried on in camp, with the hope that we would all be freed very soon, as with the speed of the approach of both East and West fronts, it was obviously not going to be long. Several forecasts were made by the experts, but none were right and we had to continue waiting.

From time to time, we could see flashes of light on the Eastern horizon, which made us hope that it was Russian artillery approaching. We would watch them for quite long periods, trying to convince ourselves that this time it was not simply another thunderstorm, but the real thing. We were fooled every time, although it was only because we wanted to believe it. The self deception gave us something to hope for.

If any of us thought very seriously of how we were going to achieve our eventual return home, I don't know as I can't recall ever having discussed it with anyone, I am sure that many of us hoped or thought that the Germans would quite suddenly stop fighting, the gates would be opened and we would be free. The idea of actually being involved in a battle was something best not to be considered.

Hope is a wonderful thing to have and our greatest hope was based on the fact that everything would turn out alright in the end. If we had known what was to come, we would have spent some sleepless nights.

There were various ways of keeping ourselves occupied while waiting for the freedom we all so longed for, such as the sports and theatre entertainments already mentioned. In addition to this, other small private organisations were set up. Some people opened a small Swap shop, where it was possible to exchange unwanted Red Cross items for others of a similar nature. The swapping was done at a price of course and that price was usually paid in cigarettes. One person opened a 'Crown and Anchor' school, which was a quick method of gambling cigarettes away.

Ron our Engineer had his own good idea, which not only gave him another interest, but it also brought him a small income. This came about when he was discussing the question of haircuts with another prisoner, who then asked him if by any chance, he could cut hair. Ron agreed that he could and would do so, providing some scissors could be found. When these were eventually supplied, a chair was set up in the compound and a queue formed, all waiting for Ron the barber. The fee for a haircut was to be paid in cigarettes - a valuable commodity.

At last the haircutting session started and I watched with interest as he displayed his talent. He had never mentioned anything about this skill before, but nevertheless, he was doing quite well. He had completed his fifth hair cut when I saw him talking to the next potential customer. Without warning the queue disappeared as if by magic and Ron was left standing by the chair, scissors in hand, completely alone. Eventually he picked up the chair and walked back towards our billet, looking more than a trifle crestfallen.

Once back in the room, I asked him what had made his customers disappear. He explained that as the sixth man prepared to sit down, he asked Ron how long he had been cutting hair,
'About twenty five minutes I would think'.
The customer was quite puzzled.
'No, I didn't quite mean that, I only wanted to know how much experience you have had?'
'I've told you', said Ron, 'about twenty five minutes'.
'Is that all?" said the customer rising rapidly, 'then I think I have changed my mind' and as soon as he could, he retreated hastily with the other customers following him.

Strangely enough, Ron set up shop again a few weeks later and this time was quite successful. I for one was very pleased, as not only did it benefit him, it helped me as well from the extra cigarettes he gave me from time to time.

Another activity which several people took part in, developed from a simple and harmless concoction known as a 'Klimbash'. Klim was the trade name of dried milk supplied to us in American Red Cross parcels and formed the basis of a tasty drink. Having mixed Klim and sufficient water to form a paste, raisins would be added then left to soak for a while. The resulting drink was much appreciated, despite the extravagant use of the milk powder. The more knowledgeable amongst us soon realised that soaking the raisins for longer periods, resulted in fermenting juice which could intoxicate if drunk in any quantity.

I suppose it was only natural that quite a lot of this would be produced in time, which proved to be the case. If the Germans had not known previously what was going on, they were soon made aware that all was not well when a prisoner or prisoners were seen walking about in an intoxicated state.

I saw one in a very happy condition, who was escorted out of sight quite quickly and taken back to his billet. Shortly after this, we were notified that all raisin based drinks were banned and any stocks held were to be destroyed. This seemed to be a bit unreasonable until we learned that prisoners in other camps had discovered a means of distilling an extremely dangerous potion. This was so disastrous it had caused blindness, insanity and even death. To make sure we obeyed their order, we were informed that a thorough search was to be made and anyone discovered with the illegal drink would be punished. It was unlikely that anyone who had produced the drink in quantity would waste it by throwing it away, so it was a case of find it if you can, which made us wonder who would win.

The appointed day arrived and we were confined to our rooms, while guards were positioned to ensure that nothing could be hidden in a building once it had been searched. One by one, the buildings were all carefully examined and as ours was the last but one, we were held in for quite a time. The last hut to be searched was the hospital, but as most of the inmates were in bed, it didn't concern them too much and they soon left. Finally the guards and search party were removed as nothing had been found and honour was satisfied on both sides.

Despite this result, the Germans were still of the opinion that there had been a stock of liquor just prior to their search and they wondered how it had been disposed of.

Some months later, an Austrian corporal approached a friend I was with and pleaded with us to tell him if there had in fact been a secret liquor stall. At the time of the search, the Germans were convinced that they would find some. I knew nothing at all and admitted the fact, although my friend who had been working in the hospital during the search, decided to reveal all. By this stage of the war, it didn't matter very much if they did find out, so it was no betrayal of a confidence. He asked the Austrian if he remembered standing in the hospital corridor and saying; 'We know it is somewhere, but we just can't find it'. The Austrian replied that he remembered it well. 'Did you notice the extraordinary number of fire extinguishers in the corridor?" asked my friend, 'those contained gallons of drink and anyone using one on a fire, would have had the shock of his life.'

I have no idea what happened to the drink when the search was completed, I can only assume it was returned to its owners and as far as I was concerned, that was the end of it. I must admit that as the temperature was dropping, we could have all benefited from something like it to keep us warm. Our rooms were quite chilly as the stove was unable to combat the cold draughts which blew through the cracks in the wooden walls. To make matters worse, we were not getting enough food. Quite often I would wake up in the morning, aching all over where I had been so cold lying in bed. Moving about was the only way to keep warm.

Perhaps it was due to the cold that another problem arose which was more of a personal crisis affecting those in our room. Someone came in with the news that lice had been found in a few of the billets. We assumed that some people were not so anxious to be clean now that it was getting very cold and were reluctant to visit the wash-rooms.

This was quite disturbing news, but fortunately none in our room had been affected up to that time and it was our intention to stay that way. The answer to this was quite simple, we would all have to shower. Although the solution was easy the decision to act upon it was a very brave one and only reached after fairly lengthy discussions.

It may seem strange that we even hesitated to use the showers but there were several things to be taken into consideration. We were in a fairly low state of health due to lack of food, also there was a foot of snow on the ground outside. If that was not enough the temperature was below zero. As for the showers themselves, they were situated in the draughty unheated toilet blocks and were only plumbed for cold water. Our room as mentioned before was inadequately heated which meant we would get little comfort on returning from the shower.

The next step was to examine the showers, to help us decide on the procedure to adopt, as we realised that the longer we took over the operation, the greater the loss of body heat. It became apparent that we would not be able to undress and dress in the shower room as apart from the draughts blowing through the place, there was nowhere dry enough to leave our clothes. We decided that the best way was to undress in our room, which in itself was a bit of an ordeal, then put on a greatcoat to walk to the shower, a distance of about forty yards. Fortunately a channel had been dug in the snow which helped a bit and also we were loaned some flying boots.

This was quite a bonus as trying to walk through snow in ordinary boots without socks was a very unpleasant thought. As I remember, we decided to go in pairs, more for moral support than any other reason, as one on his own might well lose his nerve at the last moment.

When it was my turn to go, I did as planned, undressed in the room, donned the greatcoat and flying boots, then with my companion, stepped outside into the snow. Dressed as I was it seemed colder outside than I had expected, but it had to be faced. On reaching the shower, I turned the cold water tap on full, removed my coat and boots then stepped under as quickly as possible. This required some care, as to slip on the duckboards which were covered in ice, would have been too cruel to endure.

At the instant the water hit me, I realised I had been foolish to even entertain such an idea. I might have given up even at that stage, had I not been encouraged to put up with it by my partner. As soon as I was wet all over, I left the shower long enough to apply soap to my body. This perhaps was the worst stage, as not only was I cold and wet, the wind howling through the building greatly increased the discomfort. Having once covered myself with soap, I had to wash it off, not a very pleasant thought, as the first dousing had been shock enough. Gritting my teeth I stepped into the freezing downpour once again and very hurriedly rid myself of the lather. It was little consolation to me that my companion was suffering to the same extent, it didn't make me any warmer. It was a great relief when I was able to turn the water off and reach for the towel.

Getting dry was quite difficult and took a long time. This had to be done fairly thoroughly as neither of us fancied putting a greatcoat on while we were still damp.

The trip back to the billet was conducted with greater speed and enthusiasm than our outward journey, as even our cold room was better than being outside. We were extremely thankful when we stepped through our door as we knew our ordeal was over. I don't think I had ever been so cold before as I was at that time, in fact it took me about four hours to get back to anything like normal.

Finally the memory of the discomfort we had suffered began to fade, until once again we thought it necessary to repeat the exercise. Not for us the trip to the delousing centre to suffer the indignity of antiseptic baths and have our clothes steam cleaned. Those who were treated in this way were quite distinguishable by their crumpled shrunken clothing as they looked more like scarecrows than anything else. I may have been fortunate, as later on although surrounded by prisoners with lice, none ever affected me. Perhaps even lice can be choosy, who knows?

We had assumed rightly or wrongly that the lack of cleanliness was responsible for this situation. If it was so, then perhaps a contributing factor could have been the unserviceable toilet block. Fortunately it was not ours that had suffered the failure but the one on the other side of the compound. It did affect us in a way though, as everyone had to use the same facility. On a cold bleak winter's day it was no fun standing waiting for a place to become vacant and I am sure that some prisoners never bothered at all.

I often wondered why the other toilet block was not in use, as it appeared to be alright. All we had been told was that the building was not to be used. To make sure that the order was not contravened, the entrance was securely boarded up. It may have been the plumbing which had failed, although ours remained in working order, despite the low temperature. Another thing which puzzled me was the apparent lack of interest shown by the Germans regarding a repair to the fault. I quite expected to see a working party of some sort make a start on rectification, but nothing happened.

Eventually it was revealed that the block was closed because the roof was unsafe, although how it was unsafe and why was not made known to us. We still had to tolerate our overcrowded facility as there was little we could do about it, except moan. Finally it became just another small annoyance, which could be added to a long list of others, which we had learned to accept.

As was common in our camp life, while we were feeling a bit disgruntled over one upset, something else would happen to divert our attention from what had seemed so very important at the time. The next event to gain our attention was centred on a group of Canadians who lived in the block opposite us. They had applied for tools, such as spades, pick axes and buckets to dig an ice rink. I understand that this was refused initially, until they pointed out that the rest of us were allowed goal posts for our games of football, whereas they were being denied the facilities to partake in their national sport. When eventually the tools were supplied they set to work and for some time were busy digging out a large level square.

Those of us not involved watched and wondered how they were going to achieve such a thing. It seemed that they just kept digging and digging without any great advances being apparent. Quite often they could be seen hacking away at the ground which due to the cold, must have been like rock. Even late in the afternoon as dusk was falling, teams would still be at work while we were gathered in our rooms where it was a few degrees warmer. They apparently knew what they were doing, as despite critical comments from onlookers, they continued, oblivious to anything else. It seemed strange that they never asked for help in the project, as several people would have been only too willing to give a hand in something constructive.

They even seemed to withdraw into their own small group and discourage any interference. Some British prisoners interested in skating did actually offer to help as they wanted to take advantage of the facility when it was completed. They were rather annoyed when told to build their own if they wanted to skate. This seemed a bit unfriendly, as the rink was apparently going to be quite a big one.

Eventually the hole was big enough and deep enough to satisfy them, but it still needed to be filled with ice. There must have been some very sympathetic Germans in our camp, as one day, long fire hoses were produced and plugged into a high pressure water supply. The rink builders then held the hoses pointing into the air so that the water fell in a spray onto the prepared area. As the ground was so cold, the spray froze on impact and gradually the ice built up until it was thick enough to stand the weight of several skaters. We still considered that the Canadians were crazy to put up with the hours of digging the hard ground, then standing outside in the freezing cold with hoses, just to go skating, it just didn't make sense.

Whatever we thought made little difference as it was a very satisfied group of Canadians who stepped onto the completed rink to start skating for the first time. I assume that their skates came from the same source as our other supplies, through the Red Cross. It was not always possible to tell, as sometimes items were procured by bribing guards or even blackmailing them.

Despite our thoughts regarding the project, it provided quite a lot of entertainment to people, not only those skating but spectators as well. Another plus factor was the closer approach to a civilised way of living. One day while watching the activities, I happened to remark to a companion that the people constructing the rink seemed to have dug out a remarkable amount of earth for such a shallow pit. In answer to my comment, I received a swift kick in the ankle. I was puzzled, but kept my peace as obviously something strange was going on. The feeling was strengthened when I noticed some fresh soil in heaps on the edge of the rink and yet the construction had been completed for some time. My companion was none the wiser than I as to the reason, but at least he was older and had more sense than to ask questions.

The skating continued to keep people amused and it gradually took its accepted place in our day to day living. Due to the existing weather conditions, it was perhaps the only outdoor activity which could be practised easily, as the others were no longer suitable. It was still possible to go walking which was one way of getting necessary exercise and a means of keeping warm.

The ice rink and its construction soon lost its power to remain a topic of conversation until the time of the raid. Without warning, the peace was disturbed by a great commotion occurring in and around the Canadian living quarters. As I remember, the guards had surrounded the place and were also inside it, while the occupants were turned out into the compound.

There was a great deal of speculation as to what was causing so much activity. A big fight perhaps or maybe a fire, although somehow that didn't seem to be the answer. At last the story came back to us that a secret room had been discovered. Although I never saw the room I was told that it had been excavated by the Canadians and was beneath one of their barrack rooms. It had been so well constructed that it was considered to be undetectable by even a careful observer, which led to the belief that an informer was at work. One prisoner already under suspicion of collaborating seemed to be a likely person and from then on, was avoided more than ever. He incidentally was not the only suspected collaborator in camp. If the account I heard was accurate, then the whole project had been very cleverly managed and executed.

I mentioned earlier that the stove in our room had been moved to create space for an oven, the prisoners in this case, had done a lot more to theirs. By a careful piece of engineering, they had made it so that in one billet, the slab of concrete on which the stove rested, could be lifted up and swung to one side. Beneath this was a ladder which led down into a large underground room. It was illuminated by tapping the mains and the whole thing shored up by baulks of timber. This explained the dangerous roof in the toilet block as the supports had been stolen for the purpose.

The reluctance of the Canadians to permit outsiders to help with their ice rink was also explained. This was their real reason for obtaining excavating tools, also they needed somewhere to dump the soil which they had extracted.

The purpose of the room must have puzzled the Germans as it did not lead anywhere and was not occupied by anybody even though it was designed to do so. The explanation given for the existence of the room, concerned an incident which happened a few weeks earlier. The Germans had interviewed several prisoners of Jewish origin and asked them if they were of the faith. Those who admitted to the fact, were marked down for segregation. It was then learned that once this was achieved, they would be moved to an unknown destination, which sounded very ominous indeed.

The Canadians thought they would thwart the scheme by excavating the room and making it large enough to hide the Jewish prisoners when necessary. Just prior to their intended removal from camp, they were to be whisked away out of sight and placed in the underground room, in the hope that they would remain safe and undiscovered. It turned out that the Jewish prisoners were never segregated or moved, either because of the publicity, or because other events of a more serious nature developed.

The Ferrets must have really delighted in finding such a place as they had spent many months in fruitless searches probing for non-existent tunnels and looking for illegal activities. Now they knew such things existed and it wasn't all a myth. Of course it must have been less of a pleasure to them when they reflected on the fact that the digging had been going on for weeks apparently undetected. I had discovered that fresh soil was being dumped on the ice rink boundary, they supposedly constantly alert for such possibilities, had not even seen it. The Ferrets and the guards must take some blame for the oversight, but what of the higher authorities who had quite willingly supplied prisoners with digging tools. Perhaps they were avoiding trouble by giving in to prisoners' demands for various facilities, although a little supervision would have avoided such problems for them.

Just about the time that the skating rink was under construction, we were on parade as usual, when it was noticed that the Ferrets were passing along behind the assembled ranks. It was quite possible that they were looking for the roof timbers which had been removed from the toilet block. Whatever they were doing, they were extremely unwelcome, particularly as our rooms had been left unattended while we were on parade. If they had not already realised how unpopular they were, it wasn't going to be long before they discovered the fact.

Their normal escort was a Corporal who it was reported, belonged to the Gestapo, but whatever the truth, he was not trusted, It had been snowing recently and the snow was lying several inches deep, so making their progress difficult. As they plodded by, a prisoner threw a snowball which hit the Corporal on the back of the head. In a rage, he turned with crowbar upraised, ready to strike the supposed offender. Instantly the rest of the division moved away, leaving the prisoner and threatening Corporal in isolation. The German Warrant Officer, alerted by the shouts of the prisoners, screamed at the Corporal to stop and from a distance of about forty yards threatened the Corporal with all dire things. During the harangue, the ferreting party didn't move a muscle.

Finally the Warrant officer was satisfied and with a curt order, they started to move on. It was quite obvious, even from a distance, just how angry and resentful they felt, particularly as their own Warrant Officer had sided with us. In a sullen mood the group continued to their place of duty, quite unprepared for the avalanche of two hundred plus snowballs aimed at them by the rest of the division. It was not worth their lives to complain in public again, even though some of those snowballs had been packed very hard indeed and must have really hurt.

It was a surprise to me that no action was taken against the prisoners, for what was really a physical attack on the guards, but may have been looked on as a purely high spirited action. It was that without a doubt and I am sure that those who did the snowballing gained a lot of personal satisfaction by being able to retaliate in some small way. The fact remains however that it could also have been considered a punishable offence.

There were other Germans who were distrusted or disliked by the prisoners and it would have been a great pleasure to have meted out similar treatment to them as well. One such person appeared in camp towards the end of the year. A very smart well spoken German Officer, whose command of English was very good indeed. Reputedly, he had been an

Intelligence officer at Sagan when the twenty two RAF Officers had escaped. There was no way we could verify the fact which would have made little difference even had we been able to. He had a very sorry tale to tell and many times repeated it to us. He knew all about the officers making their escape bid, and also admitted that they had been shot on recapture. It had all been a mistake, apparently due to some action of his, although what that really was, we were never told.

Because of this tragedy, he had been banished in disgrace and as further punishment, posted to our camp for a spell of duty. There were very few among us who trusted him and the majority were very careful what was said when engaged in conversation by him. This seemed to happen all too frequently, as he was always around chatting freely to everyone and being extremely friendly. Not only could we not trust him an inch, we wondered what sinister reason was behind his posting to our camp. He certainly didn't act like a man disgraced or in sorrow for the lives that had been lost, in fact he was almost jovial when he wasn't being apologetic. His manner was quite different to any other German officers I had been in contact with. They were either severe, arrogant, or distant, which was to be expected of them when dealing with prisoners. This officer's attitude was of an easy-going nature, one who regarded discipline and that sort of thing as a bit of a bore.

Quite often I saw him wandering in and out of the ranks talking to prisoners while we assembled for roll call, He would ask after our welfare or make a comment about the necessity to parade in the cold, anything it seemed, to make personal contact with us. He was one of the boys. The questions didn't appear to be particularly pointed, more of a general nature, so it was difficult to guess what he was doing.

He didn't stay with us very long thankfully, but disappeared as he had arrived, almost unobtrusively. If he had been as genuine as he tried to appear, he would have mentioned to someone that he was leaving, but there was no word. We wondered if he had discovered what he had come to learn or had he departed finding nothing amiss? Looking back, I wonder now, if the purpose of his visit was a propaganda campaign to persuade us that the shooting of the officers at Sagan had been quite unintended. How many more camps had he visited, or how many Sagan Intelligence Officers were making the rounds?

I think that this particular officer's danger point was his smooth approach and treating us as equals.

Another German, a guard, could never be accused of this approach. He also spoke very good English and had been a butcher in London for ten years. He seemed rough and tough, hardly the type to gain the confidence of a prisoner, although he was still able to listen in to and understand prisoners' conversations. He, in common with other English speaking guards could sometimes be seen, resting outside a barrack block, apparently taking things easy. It was quite obviously an eavesdropping exercise, so as soon as it was noticed, a prisoner would approach and engage the guard in noisy conversation.

I hadn't seen our London butcher for a few days and mentioned it to a fellow prisoner who gave me the reason for it. One Sunday, when all was quiet, he was seen staggering across the camp compound in an extremely intoxicated state. On his head in place of his uniform cap, he was wearing a silver Communion Chalice. To make his indignity greater, it was one loaned to the camp by the local church and he had removed it from our church hut.

We never saw him again which was not surprising as he was most likely put in the cells, then sent to the Russian Front. This seemed to be a standard punishment for offenders. He was the guard I had in mind when I drew 'Superman' on the page of 'Familiar Sights' in the original diary.

CHAPTER 19

To be sent to the Russian Front under any circumstances was bad enough, to be there in the winter must have been a real test of endurance. As winter was now upon us, the armies facing each other to the East of us were experiencing great hardships. Already we had received a foretaste of winter, cold rain, snow, bleak winds, grey skies and icy nights, but worse was to come.

I doubt if there were many, if any in our camp, who had experienced a mid-European winter, but we all knew that they were often far worse than those in Britain. Under normal circumstances, the Canadians would be less affected by the climate, while most Australians and New Zealanders had little experience of snow and ice. They would be badly hit. Obviously we were not facing the rigours that the troops in the field were experiencing, even so, standing on parade in the open was not the most pleasant thing to do. To make matters worse, we were without gloves, so it was natural for us to put our hands in our pockets. This seemed to offend the Germans in some way, but we would argue with the guards that our hands were suffering. After much complaining, it was accepted that we would be permitted to parade with our hands in our pockets, providing we removed one when called to attention, I believe this order had been recommended by our friendly ex Sagan officer, so perhaps he had done us a little good.

The permission to parade in such a manner was posted on the board for all to see and was one of several slightly unusual orders. Another order informed us that we were not to smoke after being called to attention, while another informed us that we were not to mutilate our uniforms as they were Air Ministry property. I am not sure if they meant the German or British Air Ministry.

This last order was published to combat the manner in which some people were doctoring and decorating their uniforms. I cannot understand why the Germans concerned themselves so much with our appearance unless they felt that anyone looking like a clown, would not respond to discipline. Without some form of order, things could soon get out of hand.

I did see several people who had modified their clothing prior to the order and some looked quite weird. A service greatcoat with a zigzag hem would not have been approved by either of the Air Ministries, neither would a field service cap turned into a fancy looking coronet.

I only hope that those who altered their uniforms, did not suffer later on, as we were to need all the warm clothing and protection we could get. The reference to the published orders is a reminder of one which appeared earlier when the weather was much warmer. This informed us that we were to keep our clothes clean and in order and unless items were being washed, we were to appear in full uniform. This regulation caused considerable amusement as it laid itself open to a lot of misinterpretation and misinterpreted it was.

One unrehearsed comedy developed on a particularly warm day, when most of us were on parade. A late comer, who obviously had arranged it so, appeared wearing a greatcoat and shoes, As if nothing was amiss, he ambled past the assembled British and German authorities, preparatory to taking his place on parade. The Colonel at first stared in disbelief, then on recovering his composure, told our Camp Leader to call him over for an explanation. The prisoner acted as though he was very surprised that they should pick on him and with an enquiring manner, approached the officials. When ordered to remove his greatcoat, he did so, to reveal the fact that he was naked except for two pieces of material tied as a loincloth. The visual shock was too much for the Colonel who demanded to know the explanation. It must have been difficult to hear over the waves of laughter coming from those of us who could see what had happened. He had obeyed the rules implicitly, and to ensure that everything was clean he had washed the lot.

A few more people tried similar things later, but as with all stunts, frequent repetition becomes pointless. Even if some prisoners had decided to continue this form of ridicule of the rules, the advancing cold weather would have acted as a deterrent. I could not imagine anyone willingly standing on parade without his trousers, when a snow laden East wind was blowing.

The same East wind was affecting our daily lives, as no longer did we spend very much time out in the open, but concentrated more on indoor activities. To contemplate the view when snow was lashing down and the wind was howling across the compound, made us appreciate the shelter we had. At least we were inside and dry, even if not very warm. Anyone wishing to venture outside for long would have been crazy.

We began to accept the fact that Christmas was coming and that we were going to spend it in the prison camp. In the summer and autumn, we had looked forward to our early release, with this weather our hopes were rather dashed. We felt that there would be little action on the Eastern Front until Spring and that was where we had been looking to for our salvation.

If we were staying, then we had to make plans for a small celebration with our room mates. First it was agreed that we would make a Christmas cake, then we thought about a pudding. Our first set back was a lack of flour, which was where our ability to improvise came to the fore, we thought that if we allowed bread to get dry, it could be reduced to a powder, then with water added, we could make a sort of paste. This was to be the basis of both the cake and the pudding. To this end, we each saved a portion of bread from our daily ration and placed it in a container ready for the big day. Milk was no problem as we had the powdered variety, while fruit and sugar were also obtainable from our Red Cross supplies. Of course these commodities had to be saved very gradually.

It was extremely difficult to save food while feeling hungry, but we were determined we would do our best at Christmas. Not only was it necessary to save for our pudding and cake, we also had to consider what we were going to have for the various meals that day. Once decided on a menu, we then had to ensure that we could meet it. The general items on our Christmas menu were quite standard products although it would be difficult to say the same for our specialities the pudding and the cake.

I have no hesitation in saying that they were both very unique and will not be found in any cookery book yet published. It is quite unlikely that our recipes will be copied by anyone else. What is more, should they try, it is most unlikely that either would be recognised as what they were intended to be. The recipe for the pudding was as follows:-

> PUDDING
>
> 600 GRAMMES GERMAN BLACK BREAD (CRUMBED)
> (APPROX 1½ lb)
>
> 6 OZS AMERICAN RATION BISCUITS (CRUSHED)
>
> ¾ lb PRUNES ¼ lb MUSCAT RAISINS.
>
> ¼ lb MARGARINE
>
> 3 OZS SUGAR.
>
> STEAMED FOR 5 HOURS. BEFORE SERVING BAKE IN OVEN, USING MARGARINE TO PREVENT BURNING. (THIS WAS RATHER TOO HEAVY FOR ONE MEAL)
> MILK POWDER, BUTTER, SUGAR, COCOA, MIXED UP AS SAUCE

Sauce for above, mix up milk powder, butter, sugar and cocoa. The recipe for the cake was even more exotic:-

> CAKE
>
> 600 GRAMMES BLACK BREAD (CRUMBED)
>
> 8 OZS ENGLISH TINNED BISCUITS (CRUSHED).
>
> ¾ lb MUSCAT RAISINS ¼ lb PRUNES
>
> ½ lb MARGARINE 2 TINS EGG POWDER (12 YOLKS)
>
> 6 OZS SUGAR
>
> 1 OZS COCOA + POWDERED MILK
>
> KERNELS FROM 1 lb OF PRUNE STONES.
>
> PLACED IN WELL GREASED PAN, THEN COOKED IN SLOW OVEN 4 HOURS. REMOVED FROM TIN, COOLED OVERNIGHT.
> ICED WITH MIXTURE OF POWDER + CONDENSED MILKS BUTTER + SUGAR. (EXCELLENT CAKE, VERY RICH + FULL OF FRUIT)

Place in well greased pan, then cook in slow oven for four hours. Remove from tin to cool overnight. Ice with mixture of powdered and condensed milks, butter and sugar. I think that if an attempt were made to eat such things now, they would be found to be indigestible, inedible and unrecognisable. Despite all of these facts, we were very proud of our efforts.

I can remember very little about our Christmas festivities if they could be considered as such, except that we attempted to make it a very special day. Somehow, despite our surroundings, it did seem that we had captured the spirit to a certain degree, it was no ordinary day. Possibly, we made it special by laying the table in an orderly manner and all sitting down to eat together. In other words, we were trying to act as we would have done, had we been at home.

At the time of the event, I recorded our Christmas Day menu, which on reading, sounds as if we had some very good meals. We did our best I admit, but what the menu doesn't show are the quantities of the various items, they were just a little sparse. Just for completeness sake, I will list the menu for Christmas Day 1944, in our room at Luft 7, Bankau Upper Silesia.

CHRISTMAS 1944

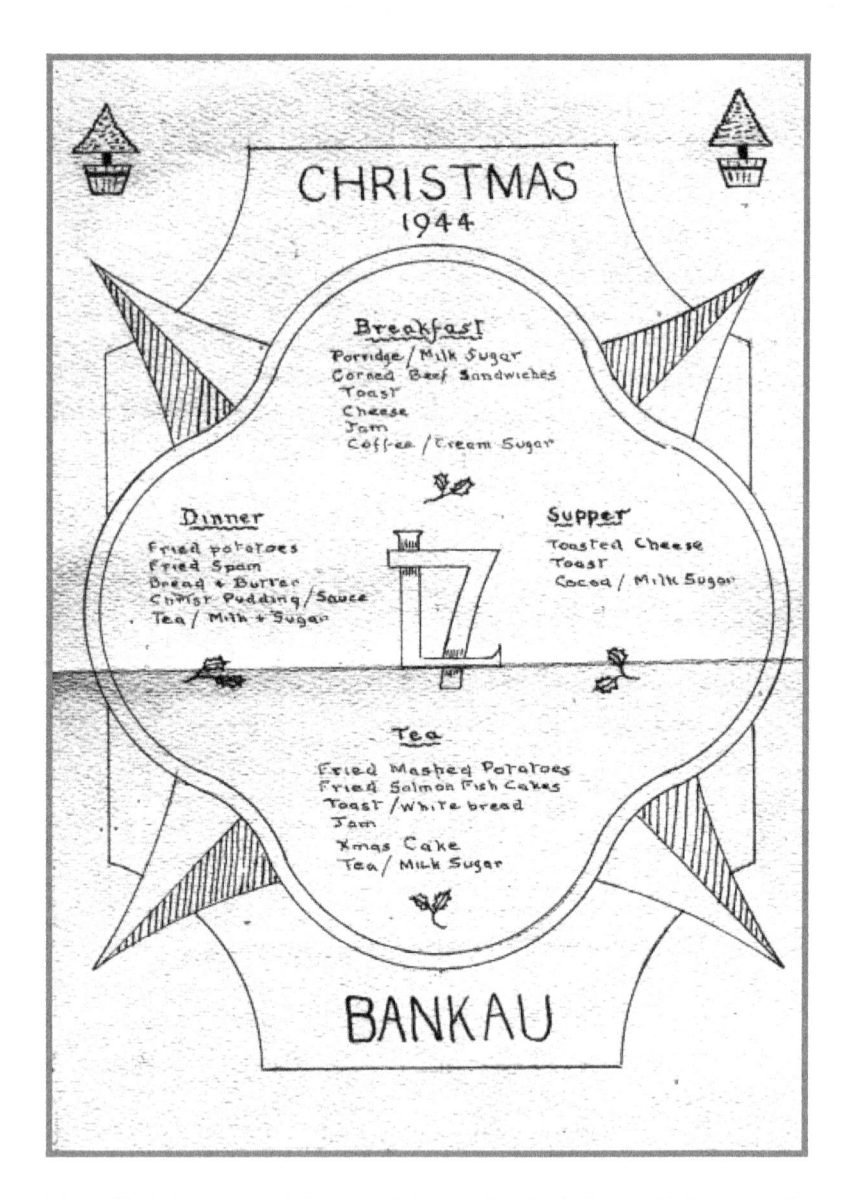

Breakfast
Porridge / Milk Sugar
Corned Beef Sandwiches
Toast
Cheese
Jam
Coffee / Cream Sugar

Dinner
Fried potatoes
Fried Spam
Bread + Butter
Christ Pudding / Sauce
Tea / Milk + Sugar

Supper
Toasted Cheese
Toast
Cocoa / Milk Sugar

Tea
Fried Mashed Potatoes
Fried Salmon Fish Cakes
Toast / White bread
Jam
Xmas Cake
Tea / Milk Sugar

BANKAU

The Christmas pudding which we had at the midday meal, proved a little too much for us, so we postponed eating the rest until the next day. I don't think it was the quantity, so much as the quality and the way it was cooked which beat us. The method of preparation and cooking is worthy of note.

On Christmas Eve, all the main ingredients were humped together, stirred around a bit, then placed in a tin. This in turn was then put into another tin full of water and boiled for the prescribed period. On Christmas Day, it was my intention to boil it a little more before serving. I think I must have rather overestimated our ability to maintain our strict cooking roster as I discovered that I had nowhere on the stove to put it. Not to be cheated of our speciality, I placed a cover over the pudding, went out into the corridor and put it in the chimney for an hour or so. I would hasten to add that this was not the best treatment for a Christmas pudding of any sort. I doubt though that our pudding would have been any better however it was cooked.

The Christmas cake was a much better product than the pudding and was more like a fruity stodge. The icing was a little unorthodox in that it was a pale yellow, not too surprising considering what it contained. The prune stone kernels were used as decoration and just as inedible as any plaster Father Christmas or Robin, these being the more usual form of decoration.

This day had been the first Christmas in captivity for most prisoners in our camp and we all fervently hoped that it would be the last one as well. I don't think that I let it depress me too much, in fact I was rather too busy during that period to have a great deal of time for brooding.

I was fortunate that I was involved in the entertainments, as it really gave me another interest, particularly as we were putting on a pantomime. A lot of time was spent in the theatre either rehearsing or general preparations for the show. It didn't really matter too much what the concert consisted of as long as everyone enjoyed the performance. As I remember, it was more of a series of sketches, with the accent on topical humour. Jokes which were told and sketches acted out, may well have left many audiences at home sitting in stony silence, ours were there to enjoy themselves.

In one small scene for instance I was supposed to be Jack of Jack and the Beanstalk. I had to complain that I had climbed to the top of the wretched beanstalk, but couldn't get down for flak. I thought this line so corny, I held my nose. For some reason, this brought the house down. I don't think that the script writer appreciated my action at first although he agreed to retain it when he saw the response.

I think that the performance on New Years Eve must have been the biggest and best as the place was crowded with prisoners as well as on and off duty guards or anyone else who could squeeze in. I was really enjoying the show both on and off the stage, as when I was not actually performing, I did as the others did and left the stage to sit in the audience. It was a while before I realised I was sitting next to a guard, I noticed that he was enjoying the show as much as anyone, even if he was a little puzzled at our hilarity. He looked to be a son of the soil, more used to farming than soldiering and he was several years my senior.

It was approaching midnight and the end of the Old Year, the time for linking of hands with the singing of Auld Lang Syne. It was a very awkward situation, how would he react if I offered him my hand? I felt that if I failed to do so, it would have made a difficult situation more embarrassing. Inevitably the time arrived and as the traditional song started. I turned to him and offered my hand, After a moment's hesitation, he took it as though it was the most natural thing for enemies to join in an expression of friendship. I am certain there was no animosity between us at that instant despite the differences in our military and political alliances.

Whatever else we may have felt privately, we all looked forward to the New Year, in the hope that everything would turn out well and in our favour. This would be difficult of course as the Germans' idea of a favourable development was entirely different to ours.

When all the celebrations and concerts were over, we settled down again into our usual routine. Once more we concerned ourselves with our domestic problems, regarding food and menus, or how to keep warm. The situation on both the Western and Eastern Fronts were still of great interest of course, particularly as we were between the two. We scanned the paper when available, listened to secret radio messages and tried to assess the accuracy of rumours which abounded in plenty. Not all rumours were optimistic ones and for every optimist there was a pessimist. I am afraid the pessimists had a chance to press their views, as it did rather seem as though things had gone quiet.

We had of course anticipated that there would be little movement during the winter months, so we should have been prepared for some reduced activity. The fighting had not stopped, far from it, but to those of us who were sitting waiting, it seemed to be a very slow process.

Quite dramatically the situation changed and we discovered that the Russians were very close to us. We had the feeling that something big and exciting was about to happen, maybe because the guards seemed edgy. Perhaps we were on the verge of being released, although how it would actually come about was not very clear.

Something did happen, but certainly not what we were expecting. On the seventeenth of January, 1945, we were told that we were going to be evacuated within the hour as the Russians had broken through; the time was eleven o'clock in the morning. I remember the date well as it was my twenty second birthday and I wondered if I might see my twenty third.

The news was quite a shock to us as it meant our hopes of release were dashed. We were thinking that freedom, or the chance of it, had been only days, or perhaps even hours away, now this. For weeks we had been waiting and hoping for the Russians to come, never imagining that we would be included in a German retreat. I think that many of us believed that we would be either recaptured, or simply abandoned by the Germans. We wondered what this move would mean to us and what was going to happen, as the whole idea seemed incredible.

The fact that we were to leave at such short notice was not too difficult, as we had so little to pack, but what appalled most of us, was the thought of leaving in such very bad weather. It was bitterly cold, it had been snowing heavily and the winds were very strong. Our state of health, lack of rations and inadequate clothing meant that we were quite unprepared to venture out in these conditions on a journey of unknown length or destination.

To make matters even more hazardous, we were to be travelling in an area which either was, or could become a battle zone. I know that we had often looked at the outside world with longing, but we had never anticipated going out of the gates in this manner.

As if matters were not difficult enough, the Germans had informed the Camp Leader, that for every man falling out of the column, five would be shot. Although I may have known this fact at the time, I can't recall having heard it, although it is written into the official report of our march. This news must have added greatly to the worries already facing our Leader and would have certainly increased our troubles if the threat had actually materialised.

As it may be imagined, we were in a state of turmoil, with prisoners wandering about asking questions that had no answers, while others brooded about the unknown that was to be faced. This kind of thought was common among most of us, and I doubt if any prediction made then, subsequently proved to be accurate.

We could not settle to routine as it was pointless if we were to be moved out at any instant. If we packed our few personal possessions, what were we to do? Just sit and wait? We were in such a state of indecision that we were not even sure if we would have time to prepare a meal before we went.

After many rumours and counter-rumours, we were officially informed that our departure was delayed, although we were not given a reason. I wondered as did others, if perhaps the attack had not been maintained, but this seemed unlikely, so perhaps our retreat was cut off.

It was rather worrying not knowing what was happening to the outside world and it was undesirable to find out the hard way. We had waited so long for the Russians to come, but now they were supposedly on our doorstep, we were not feeling quite so confident. There seemed to be no signs of a battle raging nearby, neither had we seen any movement of troops. They must have been in the vicinity somewhere, so was it all going to erupt suddenly? We felt rather defenceless.

The delay was certainly a welcome one to those who were sick, as it did enable our Medical Officer to have some of them removed to German civilian hospitals. Although a few were prepared to go to hospital rather than face a forced march, only those considered to be genuinely sick, or unfit to travel were accepted. Borderline cases were asked if they would like to join the march. One patient had made up his mind that whatever his state, he was going to march with us.

He had been under treatment for weeks suffering from something which was causing him to be jaundiced. His treatment had consisted of starvation, feeding well, no smoking, in fact anything that could be thought of. He was looking very frail and it seemed that none of the treatment had been successful. The doctor tried to dissuade him as he considered that his patient was simply not strong enough to survive the coming ordeal, as ordeal we knew it might well be. The patient had other ideas as he decided that if he was going to die, then he would rather be with us than possibly isolated in what was about to become the front line.

Despite the fact that we had been told officially and despite the fact that people were being sent off to hospital, it still seemed impossible that we were actually leaving. It was difficult to accept at first because we had so hoped for release, but common sense prevailed and we knew that we had to leave. Once we had accepted the fact, we began to consider practicalities, at least that was the procedure adopted by myself and my small group of friends. We knew we were going out on the road for an unspecified period and to an unknown destination, we had to prepare for it.

We had to think carefully of what we should take with us, as our future needs were purely guesswork. Food and clothing were important and so perhaps were blankets. Some things would have to be discarded as being nice to have but of no particular value. Weight and bulk were also a consideration as we were obviously going to carry our own, there would be no transport.

The two most important items, food and clothing were our greatest worry, with food taking priority over the clothing. We were in a far worse state for food than we need have been, owing to an order that had been issued a few weeks prior to this proposed move. The Germans had insisted that all Red Cross tins were opened at time of issue, which meant that we had to eat perishables right away.

Because of this ruling, we were caught out with no reserves of food to take on the march. We had several opened tins, such as rice, butter, cheese and jam, which normally would have lasted us for three or four days until the next issue, but now we had a real problem. Our departure was delayed, not postponed, which meant we could go at any time day or night and any opened tins of food not eaten, would have to be left behind. We could of course eat up everything we had, then be delayed for a few days, which would have left us in a very sorry state as the German rations were insufficient.

Judging by the general atmosphere which was developing, it was obvious that our departure was imminent, so we came to the decision to finish up all the remaining food. It was an extremely difficult thing to do, as for months we had been carefully rationing our supplies. We had not dared to eat more than we had allotted ourselves for a particular meal and here we were about to break all the rules. In one sense it was almost like someone suggesting that we change our religion.

I think we realised that if we did eat, at least we would be starting on the march with a full stomach, even so, there was a feeling of guilt as we started on our first tin of food. Once started, it was difficult to stop and the only reason we did so, was because the food ran out.

We didn't actually start on the food until the afternoon as for quite a while after hearing the news, we were full of indecisions, but then the eating started. I remembered that I had a tin of creamed rice in my small store and suggested that someone share it with me, maybe because I was rather reluctant to start it on my own. We had not eaten very much before my partner in crime suggested adding a tin of jam to give it more flavour. This was sheer luxury and by the time we had finished that lot off, my conscience was not worrying me nearly so much.

Very soon, a tin of something else was consumed, followed by other items, until we had almost finished everything. By normal standards, we had not really eaten a great deal, but to us it seemed extreme. Despite this, when a friend walked in with some tins of food that he was unable to eat, we gratefully accepted it.

There is one thing which stands out in my mind, a very minor event, but I doubt if I will ever forget it. When evening came, someone produced a tin of condensed milk, sugar and cocoa so that we could have a drink before going to bed. It was anticipated that any not used would be thrown away, so we were invited to take whatever we wanted. I don't know what the others did, but I piled my cup with each of the ingredients, to such an extent that I was almost ashamed of my greed. It had become liquid chocolate and even before I tasted it, I could imagine what it was going to be like when I drank it. I had just picked up the cup and was standing near the table when the lights went out, leaving us in total darkness. Puzzled, we stood and waited to see what was going to happen, as nothing seemed to be amiss.

We were not left in doubt long as we discovered that the Russians had mounted an air attack which seemed to be directed at the local railway. I felt foolish just standing there, cup poised in the air, as I knew that I really should be lying on the floor with the others. Carefully I reached out to place my cup on the table, trying very hard not to spill any. Just as I was almost there, I happened to look out of the window in time to see a house blown apart by a direct hit from a bomb, I let the cup go and dived for the floor, only to be joined by my beautiful mixture of cocoa, I had missed the table by a foot. Frustration and disappointment knew no bounds. I could have wept as I had used it all up in this marvellous concoction, so there was nothing left. I vowed that should I ever get back to England, I would one day, make myself another cup of cocoa like it. Funny thing, I can't stand sweet drinks now.

Perhaps the only thing normal that day was the time for lights out, which meant of course retiring to bed. As I lay there, I was wondering if we would be called out during the night, but we slept undisturbed. Undisturbed that is by outside activities, although many thoughts were passing through my mind as to what may happen in the immediate future. Morning came without further incident and I started the day with an unsettled feeling.

It was dismal, the organisation had failed, things were being broken up and discarded, in fact the camp looked a most depressing place. I regarded the room we had been living in for the past months and it seemed strange to think that in a day or maybe two, we would no longer be there. What was to happen to it, would it be burnt down, smashed up in the fighting, or occupied by Russian troops? What of our possessions that we had collected or made, such things as cooking tins, shelves, or our storage cupboards. They had meant so much to us because they had been made out of sheer necessity, using improvised tools and materials,

These things would mean little to strangers and would most likely be destroyed without much thought for the effort put into producing them. Although the room was our prison, it had also been our home, where we could get a little privacy and rest, a place we could retreat to. What of the future, no prospect of rest, privacy, or any form of normality at all.

Late in the afternoon, I was idly wandering around, when I thought I heard a piano playing softly and it seemed to be coming from the theatre building. To me it was uncanny as I thought that the place had been smashed up to deny the Russians a safe building. Approaching, I entered quietly and looked around at the place where we had spent so many enjoyable hours. The scene was one of devastation, windows smashed, the stage wrecked, things torn and damaged were thrown about, in fact a most depressing sight. There at the piano amid the gloom, was a prisoner I had not seen before, playing the piano in a very pensive mood. He acknowledged my arrival but continued to play. The tune as I recall, was the Warsaw Concerto, a rather dramatic piece of music under normal circumstances, in this situation it was very moving indeed, I stood entranced as I listened, not wishing to break the spell and as though it was all part of the performance, I heard the sound of heavy artillery in the distance. When the music was finished, we parted without a word, too full of our own thoughts, to say anything to each other.

We were probably the last two people to visit that theatre, as the news came that evening informing us we were to be on the road at five o'clock next morning, thus started what has been up to now, the worst experience of my life.

CHAPTER 20

Morning came and we were ready to move. I had packed my kitbag with the few things I intended to take, although I am afraid the articles were few and the two and a half day's rations we had been issued with, looked quite inadequate. I had a sense of foreboding while waiting and it was in a sense, a relief to receive the order to fall in outside. We were about to find out what was going to happen to us, the guessing was over.

Conditions were far from ideal, it was very dark, bitterly cold, snow on the ground and a gale was blowing. I was thankful for my long American greatcoat which was buttoned to the neck, as without it I wouldn't have lasted long. My field service cap with its flaps pulled down, protected my head, only leaving my face exposed. My legs were freezing as my trousers had seen better days and I only hoped that my boots which were soled with pieces of timber, would be capable of prolonged use, I had my doubts.

Apart from my greatcoat and cap, the only other really serviceable piece of clothing I had was my big white fisherman's jersey. I was very pleased it had never been taken from me as it was now worth its weight in gold as a barrier against the intense cold.

Once our barrack block was empty, we moved out through the gates only to be halted on the road outside. We had been the first division to move out, which meant that we would have to wait for the others to assemble. We waited and waited but nothing much seemed to be happening, which made me think that something had gone wrong. We were standing so long that the cold was starting to penetrate my clothes. I prayed we would move soon, but we didn't, we continued to wait. At one stage, with my back to the wind, I was being blown across the road and try as I might, I couldn't keep my footing on the glass ice. I managed to stay upright for a while until with gathering speed, I was thrown into a ditch full of snow. This just added to my misery and made me feel even more dejected.

Almost unnoticed, others had joined us on the road, yet still we waited. I assumed that the guards were searching the camp before we were allowed to leave, just to make sure that no one was hiding. They had threatened that when the billets were supposedly empty, they would open fire with machine guns. They intended to spray the huts with bullets and anyone hiding would almost certainly be killed. I didn't hear any firing, but even if they had done as threatened, the wind would have reduced the chances of the noise reaching us.

At last we were all assembled, prisoners and guards, ready to move westwards in a great straggling column of more than fifteen hundred souls. At the rear was our Medical Officer and three orderlies, whose task was to try to help those who fell by the wayside. The only medical equipment available was that which they carried on their backs. Had I known this at the time, I would have felt even more concerned than I was. At last the order to march was given and off we went, heading into the unknown.

A lot of the details of the march, have now been long forgotten, but some things do stand out in my mind and will always be remembered. The sequence and some small points of the events I will attempt to describe, may be a little inaccurate, although the essential facts regarding the situations did occur. As I remember, it was still bitterly cold and dark as we moved off. It was not snowing, which was a blessing although we were walking on hard packed snow and ice, which was not particularly easy. I was not so troubled by the biting wind now that I was moving, as at times I was not only sheltered by trees and hedges but also by the marchers in the column around me.

Armed guards were placed at close intervals along either side of the column, while others were at the head and tail of each division or group of marchers, I don't know where all the guards came from as I felt sure there were many more than I remembered in camp. A number of the faces were quite unknown to me. I suppose it was only reasonable that they would need extra guards for such a large mobile group.

I had imagined that as the Russians were so close to us we would have seen sights of frantic activity, troops moving into defensive positions and civilians fleeing their homes. Instead of this, everything seemed quiet, and when we arrived in what I believe to be the town of Kreuzberg [(now Kluczbork)], the few people we saw appeared to be carrying on as normal. It is possible of course that we were the last group to be evacuated and all intending to go had gone. Later on in the march, I found quite a number of people who were either oblivious to the Russian advance, or appreciated what was happening but decided to stay and take a chance.

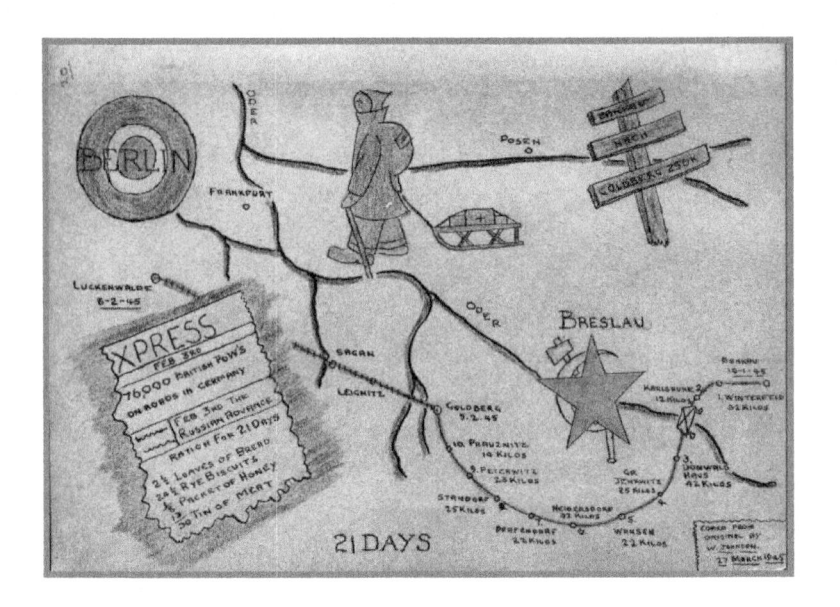

We marched for hours that day, not knowing where we were going, how long we would be on the move, or what was to be our final destination. I believe it was true to say that the Germans guarding us were no wiser than ourselves. All we really knew, was the fact that we were in retreat. It became pretty obvious later, that no set plan was involved, as the Russian movements were naturally unpredictable and we kept changing direction to avoid encirclement. At some time during the day, I teamed up with Tom who had been working in the sick bay. This meant I had someone to talk to, which I welcomed as it kept me from dwelling on our sorry state. Alongside us was a red headed New Zealander who had been walking with Tom for some time. I noticed that he was pulling a sled and wished that I had made one for myself. Fortunately, he suggested that I might like to put my kit on board, provided I took my turn at pulling.

This was a great help, as although my kit bag contained little more than two thin blankets and my POW diary, it had begun to get cumbersome after a few miles. The sled was not quite so easy to pull as I had imagined, even so, with three lots of kit, it was considerably easier than carrying one kit bag. In one sense, it seemed easier to maintain a better balance when walking on slippery ground, than it was to do so with a kit bag on the shoulder. The sled was quite a sturdy one and appeared to have been made from bed boards. It was not exactly a professional job, but it served us very well for the time we required it.

There were some prisoners who would have welcomed a sled, even more than I did, as they had really loaded themselves with anything they could lay hands on. In a very few miles, many had realised their mistake and relieved themselves of their burdens. Prisoners had overlooked the fact that they were suffering from malnutrition. In addition to this, the limited exercise available in camp meant that we were not physically prepared for a forced march. Our progress was littered with discarded articles of clothing, personal items and even musical instruments which people had been reluctant to leave behind. I saw many people carrying some very expensive piano accordions, but even these were eventually cast aside into the snow. Somehow it seemed almost indecent to see such things simply dropped by the roadside.

It is easy to be wise after the event and criticise someone's actions, but if the march had only lasted two or three days, many musical instruments would have been saved. If this had been the case, those who had carried them would have been praised for their efforts. I did see one person who kept his accordion for quite a long time and even discarded essentials to reduce his load, then even he had to finally discard his valued possession. As far as I know, he was left with nothing. I only hope he survived. I thought him rather foolish to act in such a manner, but now looking back, I wonder what I would have done in similar circumstances. We all needed something to cling on to, something which was familiar and belonging to part of one's life. To be forced to throw away something which has meant so much, is a form of surrender and an admission of defeat.

My talisman was my diary and nothing would have made me part with that, so I was fortunate that it was something easily portable. Every time I repacked my kit bag before starting on another march, I made sure that the diary was safe and protected from the damp. It didn't matter about my blankets, or any other items, they could get wet and often did but my diary stayed safe. Its loss would not have created any great security leak, or been of particular interest to anyone else, although its importance to me was the irreplaceable record of an important part of my life.

That first day of our march was not a pleasant one. We had not known what to expect but we were learning fast. On reflection, although the weather was bitterly cold, it was not nearly so severe as that which was ahead of us. There was no snow that day, just the searing wind, which proved to us how inadequate our clothing was. We had been halted at intervals, which gave us a chance to rest and at the same time eat from the rations we had been given. There was no lying or sitting down, we just had to stand until ordered to move again. In no time at all, our legs were aching and our bodies tired due to the unaccustomed activity. The short breaks were welcome as far as our muscles were concerned although our bodies didn't like the chill wind, so each halt was received with mixed feelings.

We seemed to go on and on without any sign that we were to stop anywhere, it all seemed so open and devoid of suitable resting places. There was no indication of what was intended and as far as we knew, we might just keep walking all night as well as all day. Finally, at twenty past four in the afternoon, we stopped at the small village of Winterfeld [(now Zawiść)], a very apt name for the existing conditions. It was obvious that we were going to remain for a lengthy period, which might give us a chance to have a proper rest. It was disclosed that we had covered a distance of eighteen miles and that we had been on our feet for eleven hours. Not very much for fit and trained infantry perhaps, to us it was gruelling.

What a great relief to discover that we were to be billeted in small barns. I for one didn't care what it was, as long as I could get out of the wind and sit or lie down somewhere. Once inside the barn to which I was allocated, I was crouching down arranging my blankets on the floor, when I realised that the backs of my legs felt sore and stiff. On investigation, I discovered that due to the intensely cold wind they were raw and bleeding, so that blood had run down into my socks and boots. Seeing my sorry state, an older prisoner took pity on me and gave me a spare pair of long underpants he had been carrying. I had always scorned such things in the past, but having had a taste of the effects of exposure, I accepted them gratefully and what a world of difference they made.

Our resting place was not the most comfortable, although we were all very pleased to be inside. I was still cold even when wrapped in my two blankets which were very prickly and not exactly thick. I was of the opinion that the previous owner had been a horse who obviously had discarded them, which is how I got them. It was cold, but not so cold that I couldn't get off to sleep, as I was so tired from the day's marching. It was necessary to get as much rest as possible as it was felt that our journey was to last a great deal longer than suggested by the two and a half day's ration issue.

We were retreating on foot, whereas the Russians were most likely being transported. Our only hope of escaping them was if they stopped a while to consolidate their positions. When at a reasonable distance ahead of them, we would need transport if we were to finally avoid being overrun. I believed that at the time, they were too close to us for comfort, so it was an uncanny feeling to lie down to sleep knowing that the Russians were approaching and that we could even be caught during the night. I hoped that should this be the case, they did not mistake us for resting German troops.

We were not permitted to rest for long as in the early hours of the morning, guards came in shouting for us to get outside. It required a great deal of willpower to get my legs moving again, but eventually at four o'clock in the morning we were assembled outside in the bitter cold. As we moved off, I wondered how long this journey would last and how we would fare. I was already feeling weary, although not as weary as some who were several years older than myself. Weary or not, when it was my turn to pull the sled, the reins were handed to me and I had to get on with it.

I believe that it was on this day, we came to an area where there was no snow on the road. It was my misfortune that I had charge of the sled. Trying to pull it along a dry road was extremely hard work and I wished that I could leave the road. After a while, I discovered that other people with sleds had been given permission to move over to the snow, so without further hesitation I joined them.

Eventually when we reached the end of the dry patch, we were back on the road with the rest of the column. As we arrived in the village of Karlsruhe [Karlsruhe im Oberschlessein (now Pokój)], the order to halt was given. This was most unusual, as normally when we were given a few minutes rest, it was out on the open road. To my surprise, it seemed that we were to be billeted in an abandoned brick factory. As it was only ten in the morning, something strange was happening, and why the halt after only thirteen miles? We had been of the opinion that our original departure from camp was a panic decision and here we were in the middle of nowhere doing nothing.

It was obvious that we would not stay long as there were no amenities for us, which was not surprising as the village was only a small one. Despite our doubts about stopping for long, we had to take our opportunities to rest when we could as we had no idea when the next chance might be.

Our fears were not without foundation as after a rather uneasy day, we were told that we would be moving out that evening. We didn't know exactly when it would happen, but we hoped that whenever it did, it would only be a short distance and one which would give us better accommodation. Shortly after being issued with a cup of coffee, we were ordered to move. Prisoners were protesting to each other that they were in an unfit state to continue which no one doubted although there was little we could do.

The Camp Leader and Medical officer took their protestation further as they approached the German officials stating that the men were inadequately fed and rested. Despite this, they were told it was an order which had to be obeyed.

Although I wasn't aware of the details at the time, we were in fact being supplied with two field kitchens and a form of transportation for the sick. The field kitchens were each capable of cooking for two hundred men, so the feeding of more than fifteen hundred would present problems. The transport for the sick was quite remarkable as it was an open horse-drawn farm cart, only capable of carrying six men. It was certainly an improvement on our previous situation but still grossly inadequate.

Before we had been on the road for very long, we were told that we would be crossing the river Oder that night, a severe blow to our hopes of spending it under shelter. None of us had any idea how far the river was from our present position and none of the guards could or would tell us. It was becoming quite apparent that we were on a forced march in every sense of the word and a feeling of urgency was beginning to affect prisoners and guards alike. We were further told that the bridge was mined, and ready to be blown up in order to hinder the Russian advance.

It was essential to our well being that we crossed the bridge before a given deadline. I cannot remember the exact time it was meant to be demolished, but I believe it was to be five o'clock in the morning. This was no help to us as we had no idea how far we had to travel to it, which tended to increase our anxieties. The fact that we were approaching the bridge so close to the deadline, indicated that we were the last people in that particular sector, not a very pleasant thought. I imagined that their own troops would have been withdrawn earlier to set up a new defensive line.

Once having done that, others would have to take their chances. True, our guards were Germans, but I don't doubt that the authorities would have sacrificed them and us if we didn't make it in time. Not to do so, could have resulted in greater losses on their part. By this time, we realised that if we were caught in the open, things would go very badly for us, as in the dark, the Russians could be forgiven for assuming we were Germans in retreat.

To me, our journey seemed endless and pointless, just a continual movement to nowhere. It was not snowing at the time although everything was covered in snow. The area seemed bleak and open, with no visible features to relieve the monotony of the scenery. I recall walking along a road which was covered in hard packed snow and ice, nothing in sight in any direction except flat whiteness. The air was cold, hard, and still, a sort of stillness which gave me an unearthly eerie feeling. In a sense it was like moving across a very large ice bowl, covered with a lid of black sky. The air was so cold, it was difficult to breathe and no matter how I covered my mouth, it hurt my lungs as I dragged the air into them.

I knew that the others were suffering in the same manner, which was perhaps a help to me as if they could carry on, so could I. The temperature at that time was minus thirteen degrees centigrade, by far the lowest I had experienced up to that time. It was a creeping cold which seemed to get into my clothes and stay there. This was not too surprising, considering the fact we had been exposed to these conditions for several hours. Add to this, our inadequate clothing and lack of food, then it became a wonder that so many people were still on their feet. We had started at eight o'clock in the evening and by two o'clock in the morning, we were all at our lowest point, or so it seemed.

On the first occasion we were told to halt for a rest, we asked permission to keep moving because of the intense cold. The guards were of the same opinion as they readily agreed and at no time did we stop moving, until we reached our destination. True, our progress was painfully slow, more of a stagger than a walk as was proved when it was discovered our average speed was only two miles an hour. We were afraid that if we stopped, we would never move again, but just freeze where we stood.

It seemed that even this was too fast for some people, as I was suddenly aroused from my torpor by a prisoner shouting in a very excited manner. It seemed that he had worked his way up to the front of the column from the rear. He called on us to stop as we were going so fast that the column was stretching back for a very long way. According to his story, people were dropping in their tracks by the score, so it was essential that we halted. It was a very disturbing thought indeed although equally disturbing to think that he expected us to stand still while stragglers caught us up. I thought at the time of his apparent reserve of energy.

Here we were, barely capable of moving, people in the rear were dropping with exhaustion, yet he had been able to overhaul those of us at the front. I thought that he was being an alarmist and hopefully overstating the truth. It must have been the opinion of others, as although we may have slowed down a little, I can't recall stopping to wait for them. We didn't know it at the time, but we were to keep continually on the move for something like thirteen hours, over a distance of twenty five miles. Our travels earlier that day, were now a long way in the past and had only happened in a dream. The early part of the day was totally disconnected with the nightmare we were experiencing during this second stage of the day. I am sure I can speak for the majority when I say that not only were our bodies becoming numb, so were our minds. We were plodding on relentlessly with little thought other than how we were going to make the next step.

It was with regret that we would see a person collapse in front of us, not for his sake, for our own. It meant we would have to make a detour around the body as treading over it took too much energy. Some people made a supreme effort to struggle to their feet and rejoin the marchers, although not all did so of their own free will and had to be persuaded forcibly to do so. On one occasion I saw the Medical Officer literally kicking a prisoner who was lying on the ground crying, as he wanted to be left alone to sleep. It was as well he finally came to his senses, otherwise he would have died where he had fallen.

For those really beyond helping themselves, there was a chance of a ride in the horse-drawn cart which was following, providing of course it wasn't full. According to reports, I heard that to make room for extreme cases, others were put back on the road providing they could move. For those left in the cart, not much could be done, except give them a rest in the hope that they would recover naturally. If not it was hoped that they would survive until they could perhaps be removed to hospital. I still don't understand how the Medical Officer and his orderlies were able to, not only stand up to the rigours of the march, but physically help others to do so. They must have had a hidden strength not available to the rest.

I began to get the feeling as we progressed through the night that nobody but ourselves existed and we were alone in the world, so it was something of a jolt to discover a dead horse by the roadside. A sense of reality returned when we discovered more dead horses, presumably victims of the weather. A man by the roadside was also frozen to death, probably attempting to do what we were doing, fleeing from the Russians. He was unfortunate, as he was a civilian who had to fend for himself and his chances of finding shelter were minimal.

I gathered later that we had priority, possibly because we were a security risk and for no other reason, I wonder now if any of our people were left frozen to death in the same way, only to be discovered by the Russians. It is something we are unlikely to know as they are probably listed among those missing from the night's march. There were certainly some who never lived to see the river Oder.

Even for the survivors the river was nothing spectacular to see, except we had reached our goal. In one sense it was an anticlimax as the bridge was deserted. I had imagined that there would have been soldiers guarding it, ready to defend or challenge anyone approaching. This may have happened of course, although not apparent to us. As we prepared to cross, I saw a trench with three soldiers standing in it, seemingly in a defensive position. As it was still dark we could not make out if they were alive, but as they neither moved or took any interest in such a large body of men as ours, we assumed that they also had been frozen to death, of course they may have been the demolition party waiting to blow the bridge except that if it were the case, they were on the wrong side of the water.

As I walked on to the bridge, I had a distinctly uneasy feeling knowing that it was packed with explosives, and it was quite a relief when I reached the other side. I had no doubt in my mind, that if the order had been given to demolish the bridge while we were on it, then it would have been blown up along with prisoners and guards.

We were over the bridge, so now what would happen, we had reached our goal, what else was there to aim for? All we wanted to do was rest, as we had been on the road for eight and a half hours without a break. Common sense told us that we could not stay there as it was almost certain to become a battle area in the near future. There was no real alternative, we had to continue. Somehow, exhausted as I was, I forced my legs to keep moving so that I could stay with the others. We trudged on and on, not knowing when we might stop for a rest and I was starting to get desperate. As dawn broke, there was no sign of buildings or anywhere we could possibly stay, a most depressing sight.

Eventually, four and a half hours after leaving the bridge at Nikolas Ferry [Niklasfähre (now Mikolin)], we halted at a large farm. It was obvious we were meant to stay there, but I couldn't understand why we were out on the road waiting. One large barn just in front of me seemed to be an ideal place for housing most if not all of us, but it was locked up. Not only was the barn locked, I had the feeling that the whole place was locked up and deserted. I hoped that nothing had gone wrong so that we would have to start walking again, as I was aware I had reached my limit.

At last after some delay, a farmer appeared and unlocked the barn door, hopefully to let us in. Surprisingly, we were not given the order to move despite the agitation of some prisoners, no wonder, as the place was full of cattle. I had the feeling that they were reluctant to leave, although once started, they streamed out. It seemed to us waiting in the cold that the cows were going to take forever to vacate the barn, there seemed to be hundreds. At last it was declared clear for us to enter and very thankfully we moved towards the door.

Once inside, we looked around for a place to rest, not a difficult task as it was either a bundle of straw on the concrete floor, or a similar bundle of straw in a feeding trough. Our small group being among the first in, did have some choice in our resting place, which turned out to have mixed blessings. Gradually the place filled up with weary prisoners who, like ourselves, sank down thankfully on the first convenient bundle of straw they could find, many going to sleep immediately.

Those who walked in, were more fortunate than the casualties who had to be assisted along and in some cases, even carried in. At one stage I helped carry a Canadian friend of mine who had really suffered. He was waxen faced, had staring eyes and was as stiff as a board. I was almost certain that he was dead despite reports to the contrary, but as I never saw him again, I didn't know his fate. There is no doubt in my mind that whatever his condition, he would have been amongst those who were transferred to hospital.

I am afraid that there were many more casualties from that night's march, more than the few I saw carried into the barn. I heard later that there were twenty two prisoners missing. This rather surprised me as I would have expected more. The resting place our group had selected was against a wall and far better than those who had chosen to sleep in the feeding troughs. Latecomers were less fortunate as they had to bed down wherever they could, even in the main alleyways. In our general state it made little difference as one place was as good as another.

The mere fact that we had stopped walking and could rest, pleased us most, what is more, it was several degrees warmer inside than out. This of course was only to be expected, although where I was lying it was very warm indeed, a fact I mentioned to the group. I pondered on this awhile and started to investigate the straw around me to see how large the area of warmth was.

I wish I had never bothered as I discovered that it was not only warm, it was also very wet. It was too late to do anything about it then, as all the other suitable places were taken and in any case, we were too tired. We were so tired in fact, we didn't think our legs would support us long enough to move. We were proved wrong about that, they could and did, as was discovered later.

Once I had accepted the situation, I lay back on the straw and went off to sleep as though pole axed, to rest I hoped for several hours. It was not to be, as within two hours I was wide awake, disturbed by a lot of shouting and prisoners running about in all directions. It took a few seconds to identify the cause, a bull was on the rampage. It seemed that it was asleep when the farmer came in to turn the cows out and had been overlooked. On waking it had become frightened at seeing all the strange bodies around him, so started to charge. He may have been frightened of us but not nearly so frightened as we were of him. It was at this point, we proved our legs could and would hold us, as we were on our feet in an instant ready to run. I was in time to see the bull who was in the central alleyway, suddenly make a charge at the reclining figures in his path.

Everyone was alerted instantly, that is, all except for one who remained rolled up in his blankets asleep. The bull was about twenty feet from him, ready to charge this thing in his path. I watched fascinated not able to do anything to help, even though it was apparent that the fellow would be seriously injured if not actually killed. People shouted and screamed, but the bull intent on his victim, started to charge, head down, he went for the blankets and that is all he got, blankets. By the time he arrived at the point where the fellow had been, the said fellow was elsewhere, in fact he was half way up to the roof clinging to a supporting pillar.

The bull stopped, not knowing what to do next and as he was just about opposite us, we had similar feelings. We prepared ourselves to run or leap into the feeding troughs, in fact anywhere to put an obstacle between our bodies and his. It was fortunate for us that he decided to continue in the same straight line, until he finished up at the other end of the alleyway bellowing with rage. The farmer was quick to arrive on the scene, but not quite so fast in tackling the bull. Carrying a long pole with a hook on the end, the farmer crept very cautiously forward, then with a deft move, hooked the ring in the end of the bull's nose. Backing slowly, he eased his way down the alleyway to the door of the barn, watched anxiously by a very interested crowd of prisoners. At last, the bull and the farmer were outside, to the great relief of all concerned, as we were now able to continue our rest.

During this episode, explosions could be heard in the distance. They sounded rather muffled to us, so it was difficult to say whether it was the bridge being blown, or artillery fire. Strangely enough I think there were very few of us who cared one way or the other, as all we wanted to do was rest. As soon as we could, we returned to our slumbers, quite prepared to let the world outside carry on without our interference. I don't know how long I slept before I woke up, certainly long enough to have regained some of my strength.

Once awake, I was feeling so hungry I had to have something to eat, although whatever it was I had, it would most certainly have been very meagre, as the quantity of food we received was only one step from starvation. Several prisoners were awake by this time, discussing the situation and wondering what the next move would be. It seemed that during our sleeping hours, the world had passed us by. No Russian or German troops had come near us, at least if they had, we were not aware of it. There was little to do during our waking hours, except perhaps talk, no one felt like doing anything else.

A few people just sat and stared into space, apparently withdrawn into their private thoughts, stunned by all that had happened so far. I consider that I was very fortunate being involved in a small group. We could help each other, or give encouragement when necessary. The lone traveller had no one to help him or be concerned if he was suffering. Surprising perhaps, but it was possible to be alone, although surrounded by others.

We knew of course that we would soon be out on the road again, to endure once more the rigours of a march. What we didn't know though, was when we might leave, how far we would have to go, or what the weather was going to be like. It was appalling to think that we might be subjected to another march as severe as the last one, although there was no reason to suppose that it would be any better. I hoped that we would not be turned out that night, as somehow it seemed much worse when travelling by night. My hopes rose as finally darkness came and with it silence, as most people settled down to sleep, to wait either for the morning or fresh orders to move.

I am afraid that it turned out to be the latter as at some time between two o'clock and three o'clock in the morning, guards appeared, urging us to get ready to leave. According to a brief note in my diary, there was a considerable delay before we finally departed, in fact it was nearer to five o'clock. The official report blames part of the delay on the inability of some prisoners to locate their belongings in the dark. Because of this hold up, guards moved in and discharged their firearms as a form of encouragement to the prisoners to get moving. I can well understand their refusal to leave until the kit was found, as to attempt a march without maybe boots or a topcoat would be disastrous.

Even those of us with all our kit were not too anxious to step outside into what was a hostile world. Somehow, the barn had become a haven where there was no snow, no wind and no need to be on our feet all the time. As with all good things, the rest period in the barn had come to an end and I found myself outside with the others, ready to move. It was bitterly cold and snowing, not heavily, just enough to make us feel just that bit more uncomfortable.

At last the dreaded order to march was given and once again we were on our way to we knew not where. As it turned out, we did not travel far that day, only seventeen miles or so. In our tired state it seemed a lot further than that, and a lot longer than the six hours that it took us. Unfortunately the weather remained cold, which was a serious setback to some of those who had barely recovered from the previous march.

At one time I thought I might be calling for medical aid, as I could feel my face becoming numb and stiff. The first time it happened I didn't realise what it was and started to rub my face in an attempt to restore the circulation. When I discovered it was only an ice pack I was wearing, I felt greatly relieved as I had thought I was suffering from frostbite. The painful part of the de-icing process, was not so much the peeling of the ice from the face, as it was removing it from nostrils, eyebrows and eyelashes, It was a strange feeling to be walking along with eyes half closed against the wind, then discover that eyelashes were frozen and the eyes could not be opened properly. Once the face was de-iced, I felt much better, until it happened again.

I saw one man with a very thick beard, which had become so encrusted with ice it was solid. Another prisoner noticing this, grabbed him by the beard, then by waggling it about, made the man's head move as though he was a puppet. To the onlookers it was quite comical to see, and we needed some amusement.

There was nothing special about the day's march which stands out in my mind, just another day of almost mindless walking. Others may remember particular incidents, especially those who may have been taken ill, or collapsed with fatigue. The only really remarkable thing about the march, was its relatively short distance. Some time before midday, we were called to a halt in the village of Jenkwick [Gross Jenkwitz (now Jankowice Wielkie)]and detailed off to take shelter in various barns and buildings. I didn't like this very much, as I suspected that after a short rest, we would be moved again that night. It seemed to be a repetition of the sequence of events which led up to crossing the river Oder. If this was the case it would be disastrous. So many prisoners were suffering by now, we really needed a longer rest period.

The majority of the prisoners were housed in barns, but I was more fortunate. For a reason I can't remember, I found myself sharing a billet with some medical orderlies, as a result, I gave what help I could to those less fortunate. Shortly after we had settled in, a German officer was brought to us in a state of collapse. I recognised him as the officer who had discussed music in our room a few weeks earlier. We felt sorry for him, as there was little anyone could do, he was simply exhausted and needed warmth, rest and food. He was many years senior to ourselves and gave the impression that he was more used to the ordered gentle life, not this harsh existence. Most of us were in our early twenties and basically fit. Even we were finding the going very hard.

The rest did him good, although I believe it was more than rest which helped him recover. He was shown compassion by people who might well have refused to help him, but this was a man in trouble, not an enemy. Once he had returned to his duties, I lost trace of him as so often happened to many acquaintances during the march. Whether he recovered fully, or went to hospital, I have no idea.

Despite my fears that we might be called out during the night, we were in fact left undisturbed to sleep until morning. It may have been that the guards were as exhausted as we were, or perhaps even more so. We could plod along like mindless automatons, they had to remain alert in order to prevent escapes or the risk of being overpowered. I think there was little risk of us overpowering anyone, although I heard an unconfirmed report, relating just such an incident.

The small group of Russians who had been with us in Luft 7 had in fact left camp as we had under armed guards. In a very short time, the guards were overpowered and taken prisoner. I don't know how the story originated but it was a popular one to relate, and could have even been groundless, invented simply to keep our guards alert. True or not, it might have suited the Russians but it was not the thing for us to do. We were of the opinion that anyone trying to escape in ones or twos or even in groups were in great danger, as it was almost suicidal.

There were several hazards to face, the lack of food, advancing Russians, German patrols, German civilians, and worst of all the weather. This perhaps was our biggest enemy, as the blizzards which were raging, driven by bitter winds, showed mercy to no one. It is not true to say that it snowed continually throughout the march but the extreme cold persisted and anyone exposed to these conditions for long was unlikely to last.

The sight which met us next morning was most disconcerting, as a severe blizzard was in progress. We had no desire to venture out, but as no one was considering our feelings, we found ourselves assembled, once again ready to move. It seemed that whatever the weather might be, nothing was going to halt our progress. It was dark as we left, which made little difference. The snow caused us to keep our heads down, so that all we could see was the man in front. According to my diary, we travelled for seven and a half hours in these conditions, with the snow and wind battering at us all the time. As daylight came, the intensity of the blizzard became a visible reality. The snow, driven by a fierce wind, was being blown horizontally. This had a strange hypnotic effect and only added to our discomfort. It certainly made it difficult to walk in a straight line, particularly as we had the snow slamming into us as well.

It seemed to me that the countryside was so flat and exposed there was seldom any relief from the elements. At times, the mere sight of a tree in the distance gave me something to aim for, as it was an indication of progress, even if the destination was unknown. It was discovered that trees became very important. Not only could we note our progress by them, they also acted as a windbreak, even if it was only for the second or two it took to walk past. I can still vividly recall the time when walking as usual without too many thoughts in my head, I looked up to see a row of trees lining the road. They were single trees about twenty feet apart. It was like a gift from heaven, and as I approached, I could anticipate the relief I was going to get from the shelter of the tree trunks. Not for just two or three short seconds, but a whole series of them. What luxury it was to arrive and what reluctance to come to the end, to face once again the full force of the screaming wind.

At times it was easy to forget the purpose of the march and simply concentrate on achieving the next resting place. The armed men in the grey uniforms were like ourselves, simply walking because of an order to do so. This attitude was very quickly dispelled by an incident, which acted as a reminder that we were still very firmly under armed guard. Our small group was near the head of a section of marchers, being led by a guard who was a stranger to us. He was I believe, a warrant officer, possibly one we had picked up on the way. Whatever his rank, he was distinguished by the fact that instead of a rifle, he was carrying a sub-machine gun. I am not sure what happened, perhaps someone stumbled, or perhaps one prisoner spoke to another. The guard turned immediately, cocked his gun and threatened to open fire if there was any more disturbance. It was very uncomfortable being so close behind such a person as he didn't seem to be the type to make idle threats.

Fortunately for us, the column was in some disorder, so we were able to allow other prisoners to gradually overtake us, until we were some way back from the front ranks. One thing essential in our situation, was the will to survive, a very difficult thing to do without an objective in view. As mentioned several times, we had no idea where we were going, what we might become involved in, or even if we were marching to nowhere in particular, merely wandering.

Were we marching away from the Russians or towards them? Was there some haven for us to the West or just nothing? I did hear later that prisoners from some camps did just that, they were marched about aimlessly for weeks on end, until they were rescued by our forces.

It was not enough to simply aim for the next resting place, there had to be something more sustaining. The main aim of course, should have been to survive until eventual repatriation. Personally I found this too remote to contemplate and didn't dare look very far ahead. One day while plodding along, I was beginning to lose hope that we would ever arrive anywhere. We were doomed to wander forever in ice and snow. Once this train of thought started, I progressed to the possibility of failing to survive. Not a particularly pleasant thought perhaps, but neither did it frighten me. I considered the relief I would get from the cold wind, should I just drop and go off peacefully to sleep. Quite suddenly a phrase came to mind 'Death where is thy sting, grave where is thy victory?' and I was startled into awareness of the way my thoughts had been drifting.

This was what I needed, something to fight against other than the weather, and from that moment on, I really had something to sustain me. I was determined to challenge the threat which the phrase seemed to suggest. It often came to mind in bad moments and although I was never really sure of its true meaning, I knew that it was a reminder to me to keep going and not succumb.

There was more to the marching business than mere survival as creature comforts were also necessary. Trying to march with an aching stomach could become misery in itself, so it was essential to leave the column every so often to attend to the calls of nature. This was quite a serious business and one which was discussed with some interest as it affected us all. Whenever possible, it was desirable to wait until the day's march had been completed, so that a toilet or sheltered spot could be found, but it was not always the case. I must admit, it was a bit daunting to discover that the need was urgent and that the only place to go was the middle of a large field in a snowstorm. Discussions took place regarding the direction to face, how much clothing to remove and in particular, how to protect oneself from the snow. There was no question of modesty, that didn't come into it.

Normally the roads were deserted except for ourselves and even if people were around it didn't matter as they would take little notice. Some prisoners suffered severely, as desperately hungry, they started to eat snow. This upset their stomachs considerably, so they were frequently leaving the column to squat in a field. The discussions we had on the subject may seem amusing now but at the time they were of extreme importance as they were all part of our survival.

By four o'clock on this day, the twenty fourth of January, we reached Wansen [(now Wiązów)], which was to be our next resting place, and thankfully we moved into our billets, pleased that we had managed yet another day.

CHAPTER 21

Our arrival at Wansen meant that we had covered approximately ninety miles in five days. This was certainly more than I had anticipated when we first left our prison camp and it was quite apparent to all that we would have to continue for a while yet. At no time during our travels had we as prisoners, seen any other authority than our own guards. There appeared to be nowhere we could stop, even temporarily, where we could receive proper food, rest, or medical attention. We were in a wilderness only relieved by the occasional village and even then the places seemed to be deserted. In the summer months, it would have been a very lonely and desolate place, especially to those of us used to more densely populated areas, but covered in snow as it was, it looked far worse. I had the feeling at times that somehow we were lost, if not lost, then out of contact with the outside world.

Once again our accommodation was in keeping with our surroundings, we were billeted in a barn, which I suppose was the most sensible place that could be found. In general, barns were big enough to take large numbers of prisoners and fairly easily patrolled from the outside. Our particular barn was different to others we had stayed in, as here we had the company of several calves. They didn't appreciate our intrusion very much and kept telling us so. The one consolation we had, was the added warmth that we gained, but the calves didn't get too much out of our association unless it was the meeting with our New Zealand friend, the sled owner.

He had the advantage over us as with his farming background, he was able to speak their language or so it seemed. This became apparent when one calf overcoming his natural fear of us, decided to investigate these strange bodies sharing his straw. Our friend started to speak very quietly to the calf who stood stock still as though listening intently. Gradually other calves started edging up, until they stood in a semi-circle concentrating their gaze on him. He then started to address them all, talking in the same gentle voice. I can't recall what he said, except that it was soothing and may have even been hypnotic to them, whatever it was, they all listened patiently for quite some time. When he became tired and stopped, they drifted away as they had come, seemingly reluctant to leave him. He explained later that the animals enjoyed the sound of the human voice which may well be true in his case. Perhaps it was his accent that did it.

My experience of four legged beasts, has taught me that if I talk to them, they become more purposeful in their approach and begin to look menacing. I saw his control over animals once again, but that was later in the march. Despite the apparent friendliness of the calves, I am quite certain that if I was given the chance now to spend a winter's night in a cowshed, I would decline. This only goes to prove that values change with circumstances as we would have given almost anything then, to stay where we were for a lot longer. We were comparatively warm and comfortable, we had company of a sort, also we were resting.

There were some disadvantages of course as we lacked food, and the aroma surrounding us belonged to the farmyard. I am not sure that the farm animals were entirely responsible for the latter situation, as we ourselves had been on the road for six days. Despite our willingness to stay longer, we only remained there for approximately forty hours before we were once again on the road. I personally was thankful for the rest we had been given as I now felt better able to face the coming day.

This particular day started at four o'clock in the morning, which seemed to be a favourite time for the Germans. There may well have been a good reason for these early starts, but as it was still dark at that hour of the morning, assembling us was difficult. Obviously lights could not be used, which gave rise to the possibility of overlooking prisoners who had stayed behind, either by choice or because of illness. We experienced difficulty as well, trying to locate our kit before finding our way to our assembly point. It was apparent that the majority of us managed, as there always seemed to be a large crowd of prisoners streaming along the road.

The weather was no better than that which we had been subjected to earlier, it was still snowing heavily, still bitterly cold and everywhere was blanketed in white. We made very slow progress in our journeying, in fact it took us nine and a half hours to travel the sixteen miles to our next resting place.

At one stage, I thought we were in trouble and might never reach our intended destination, as in the distance, we could see a column of marching men. I say they were marching, but owing to the distance and the poor visibility, I could not be sure what they were doing except that they were approaching us. Directly they had been noticed, a strange feeling of tension developed, the sort of feeling I imagine wild animals would experience on meeting each other unexpectedly. We watched for quite some time, as they converged on us from another road and wondered who they were, seemingly not Russians, as they were all on foot and would have taken up an attacking formation on seeing us. There were too many to be a German patrol, so who were they? As they came close, they did not appear to be a threat to us, all the same, we were relieved and very pleased to be greeted in English. They were British prisoners like ourselves, although they had come from Lamsdorf. There was a similarity between their case and ours as they had no idea where they were heading for either.

We were able to converse briefly as they walked alongside us for a while, before continuing on their own line of march. We learned from them that during our march towards the Oder, the Russian Panzer had, on two occasions, been within five miles of us. On the second of these occasions, they had actually been ahead, so it would seem that we had been very close to capture. How these strangers had known where the Russians were, I have no idea, perhaps their guards were a little more communicative than ours.

Not long after the Lamsdorf prisoners left us, we discovered that our next stopping place was a large farm in the village of Heidersdorf [(now Łagiewniki)]. It was quite a surprise to me, as from the little I was able to see, the farmyard appeared to be very well stocked and apparently untouched by the war that was going on around it. On reflection, I think that numerous places of a similar remote location, would never know that a war was in progress.

True, they would have had friends and relatives in the forces perhaps, but the farms and villages would remain unscathed. I may have been misled, but to me, life was carrying on in the farm in a way that it had been for generations. Except for the presence of our guards, it would have been a peaceful haven for us to remain in, for a little while at least.

Whatever the farmer's experience had been, I don't doubt that he was quite unprepared to see such a large body of men come to take his place over. He had a lot of valuable stock on the farm and he wasn't to know how we or our guards would act. It was quite possible that together we would wreck the place. We did our best to do just that, although the guards restricted our activities considerably.

When we first arrived, we were taken into the farmyard and detailed to occupy the various sheds, barns and buildings surrounding the yard. As I remember, the yard was a large cobbled area. Except for a small entrance in one corner, it was closed in on all four sides by buildings. This made it a relatively easy place to guard.

Once again I found myself billeted with the medical staff, ready to give what little assistance I could. The accommodation we occupied was reasonably well suited to be used as a sickbay, as it was clean, airy and free of the smells associated with cowsheds. Windows framed in thick stone walls looked out onto the yard, so making the place quite light. The floor was solidly built of tiles, strong enough to withstand the stores piled upon it. In the middle, was a great stock of potatoes estimated to weigh about eleven tons and at one end stood a small stove. I presumed it was there to keep the frost from the potatoes as it was burning continuously, maintained from a stock of coke behind it.

The stove may have kept the frost from the potatoes, but there was nothing to keep the prisoners from them. Once word got around, we had endless numbers of people reporting sick. Nearly everyone who came in pocketed one or two to take out to their friends. Some, were so hungry, they couldn't wait and would grab a potato, put it under the stove, then rejoin the sick parade. There was often barely time for the potato to be heated, let alone properly cooked, before it was retrieved by the person laying claim to it.

Once having done this, some would wait to see the doctor for treatment or advice, while others simply walked out again. Those who didn't stay, were perhaps the more honest as I am certain that the majority were not suffering from anything that the doctor could cure.

I was lucky, as I didn't even have to make the pretence of standing in the queue and I am sure that the potatoes that I consumed, helped build me up for our further travels.

We were to stay in this farm for forty six hours, which was fine for us but not so good for the farmer or his stocks of food. The guards were not very happy either as they still had the task of keeping us under control and so prevent trouble breaking out. While we were actually marching, our prime concern was survival, but resting as we were, gave a chance for prisoners to devise disruptive schemes. It was a fact, sometimes over looked, but it was still our duty to hinder the German war effort as much as possible in any way we could.

We had not been there very long before there was trouble. Darkness had fallen and most prisoners were settling down to get as much rest as possible. Guards who were patrolling the farmyard looked hopefully for a quiet night. Not only did they have prisoners to consider, there was the ever present threat from the Russians. Being so isolated, the general feeling was one of peace and quiet, then without warning the noise started.

I was lying down attempting to sleep, when I heard the sound of many pounding feet. I couldn't really identify the noise, but it could have been made by a large body of men running about. I could hear guards shouting at, or to each other, shots being fired, then more sounds of running feet. I thought that the Russians had arrived in a surprise attack and were battling with the Germans. I got up to the window and peered out, but all I could see, were large black shapes rushing backwards and forwards, Added to the pandemonium in progress, I could hear the noise of someone hammering on the door of a barn, possibly with a rifle butt. This was followed by some very angry shouting in German, to be answered by equally irate English voices. If it wasn't the Russians as now seemed likely, I was anxious to know what was happening and I wasn't alone.

At last lanterns were brought and the situation revealed, it was the British prisoners, not the Russian army who had caused all the trouble. Not being satisfied with the billets allocated to them, they decided to make a stealthy change after dark. On discovering a barn full of heifers, turned them out into the darkened yard, then barricaded themselves in. The Germans panicked when they heard large bodies charging about as they must have thought that a breakout was under way. Their excitement further upset the already frightened animals, which resulted in a general melee between stampeding heifers and startled Germans. Someone in authority must have guessed at the truth and approached the barn where the cattle had come from. This resulted in the banging and shouting which I had been hearing.

It took a long time to sort that one out as the prisoners were not prepared to give up what they had won, neither would they let the cattle back in. This posed a real problem for the guards as it was difficult to try to manage unruly prisoners while the yard was full of frightened animals.

Finally the difficulty regarding the prisoners' accommodation was resolved, which then left the cattle to be dealt with, this was a bigger problem. How do you round up several frightened animals in the dark, without showing too much light and using troops inexperienced in such matters?

No further incidents occurred that night, at least if they did, I wasn't aware of it as I slept very well. Morning came, and with it daylight, which showed that the weather had not improved very much if at all. I don't think it was snowing then, although it was still very cold. This did not trouble me too much as I had a feeling that we were to remain there for another day at least. This meant of course that we would remain in our sheltered places longer, which would help us further in regaining our strength. It also meant of course that there might be more incidents to annoy the Germans, and there were.

I witnessed one such incident that could have meant real trouble. It started with the Germans suspecting that prisoners were helping themselves to the farmer's food stocks. No mention was made about potatoes, but they seemed to think that the chicken population was decreasing. In view of this, it was decided that the guards would wander about amongst us to see what we were eating. It was not a very difficult task as so few of us were occupied in this manner. One prisoner was making a great show of cooking something, in a manner which made me believe he wanted to attract the guard's attention.

The fire had been built in the open and was quite obvious to all. In time, a guard appeared on the scene and made some attempt to determine what the prisoner was cooking. The prisoner was just as determined that he wouldn't find out. Eventually an argument developed with the prisoner pretending not to understand what the fuss was about. With the argument that developed, it was a little while before the guard realised that the prisoner had built his fire against a large wooden barn door. He claimed that it was the only place out of the wind. In a very short while, the door itself started to burn.

What a performance started then. The guard accused the prisoner of arson, the prisoner accused the farmer of his stupidity in using wood for his doors and the guard of interrupting his meal. Eventually peace was restored, the barn door doused with water and the prisoner agreed to move his fire to a safer place. I am not absolutely certain, but I think it was chicken he was cooking.

All ideas of disruptive action stopped when we were given orders to pack up and move. Not a very welcome proposition, as before each march started, was the thought that this could be a long one. We were never to know how long until we arrived. Our departure was slightly unusual in that we didn't leave until eleven o'clock in the morning.

There was no explanation for this, but then there never was an explanation for anything we were told to do. We were becoming nomads, continuous wanderers with no homes, or at least, that is how it seemed to me. This was the twenty seventh of January, which meant that we had only been on our travels for nine days, but to me, our departure from Luft 7 was in the distant past.

In one sense, it could have been a dream that we were ever there, this wandering life was the only reality. I have come to the conclusion that time is not measurable by clocks but rather by events. Sometimes, a few hours can seem like days, especially during a very serious or dangerous period.

Often the question has been asked, 'Did that only happen yesterday?'. On another occasion, a year may seem to pass in weeks. To me, this whole venture, from the time of being shot down was just over seven months and yet it seemed like a life time.

Regardless of how I felt, or how my thoughts were running, I still had to do as I was told and get out on the road, ready to march. To use the term, to march, was once again an exaggeration, we were really only ploughing our way along in deep snow. The snow made very heavy going for us at times, in fact it took six hours to travel the thirteen miles to Pfaffendorf [(now Książnica)] and we were travelling light. If we had problems, what of the civilians who were attempting to escape westwards, loaded down with their most valued possessions.

Some families tried the impossible, loading carts and wagons beyond normal capacity, only to discover that road conditions would only permit virtually bare essentials. At this stage of the march, we were beginning to meet up with more and more civilian refugees. In the first stages, we had met almost nobody, which tends to support my theory that we were probably the last to leave the area. Due to the relentless pace being set for us, we were now catching up with those, who had naturally been very reluctant to abandon their homes. I remember, that whenever we met such groups, someone would call us to attention and tired as we were, we would try to march as though we were not really affected. We didn't want the German civilians to realise how miserable we really felt. Even if this action didn't demoralise the onlookers, it lifted our spirits for a while, as we remembered who we were and why we were there. I am afraid it was not an easy thing to do and as soon as we could, we would revert to our usual dragging progress.

I think it would be true to say that very few prisoners rejoiced to see the civilians in retreat. To my mind, it was most depressing to see families with all the possessions they could carry, leaving their homes. In some cases, people simply walked out and didn't even bother to close their doors. There was little point as the place would soon be occupied by Russian troops. In one village where we arrived at the onset of dusk, people appeared at their doors to see what was happening.

They were informed that we were moving westwards and that the Russians were right behind us. I saw the reactions of several of them. Some could not believe what was happening and seemed stunned by the news. Others were fully prepared and started to move out suitably equipped. A few panicked and began rushing in and out of their houses completely at a loss as to what action to take.

We had been held up in this particular village for a short while, which enabled me to observe these various attitudes and reactions. It was not customary for us to halt for a rest in the middle of a village, so the delay was most likely caused by the actions of would be refugees.

To leave a house and take to the road presents many problems. The first one to meet must be the necessity to leave at all, as it could be a panic decision regretted later. Other problems would then crowd in. What sort of food should be taken, would blankets be required, how about the old and infirm and the babies? Should bedridden grandparents be deserted to protect the young? These are all questions which would have to be considered and to do so at a moments notice must be frightening. It is no wonder that those unprepared villagers were in a state of panic, particularly as they were facing the unknown.

When we had left our camp, we had vacated buildings which had meant little to us, what is more, we had nothing of great value worth taking. We had no birth certificates, insurance policies, bank books or other important papers to protect, we only had the essentials for immediate survival. Another great difference between ourselves and the refugees, we hopefully were getting closer to our arrival home, they were in the first stages of leaving theirs.

Another thing, their decision to stay or leave depended entirely on them, a decision which was to affect their whole future. A few days earlier, I had been in a house, a farmhouse, where a middle aged woman was living apparently on her own. The guards with me were trying to persuade her to leave as the Russians were just down the road, but she ignored their advice and refused to move. Later when there were no guards present, I with two or three other prisoners tried our powers of persuasion. I wish we hadn't as the abuse heaped upon us and the world in general was quite shattering. Although our knowledge of the German language was minimal, our understanding of her attitude was crystal clear. I am sure we would have understood her in any language.

She told us that she welcomed the Russians and if they killed her they would be doing her a favour. She hated the Germans, the British, in fact just about everything and everyone, but most of all, she hated Hitler and the State.

She had lost her son in the fighting, she didn't know where her husband was and didn't seem to care as he also belonged to the State. She no longer owned her house or even her furniture, it all belonged to the State. With this, she then spat on the floor saying; "Now even that belongs to the State, so let the Russians come, I am not moving".

Her hatred and anger was extremely powerful and very disturbing, so it was a great relief to us to leave her. I had never met anyone so aggressive before, certainly not a woman. Where the house was or at what stage of our march, I have no idea, although I do remember her very well and I daresay the Russians would also have occasion to remember her.

We were far more fortunate than those who voted to stay, and even more so than our fellow travellers. We believed that if captured by Russians, we would not be ill treated once they realised we were allies. Our one fear was being captured and treated as Germans. A further advantage we had, we were given shelter every time we stopped, which was more than the civilians could claim.

The question of shelter was always uppermost in our minds. The state of our various billets was becoming less important than the necessity to be able to rest, wherever it was. Each time we started on a journey we had no idea how many hours it would last. We did not have to wait long on this occasion, as about an hour after meeting the refugees, we arrived at Pfaffendorf where we were put into a farmhouse.

Once settled in to my accommodation, I gave little thought to those civilians outside and may never have concerned myself with them again, but fate plays strange tricks. I have discovered this fact and one such trick concerned these refugees. As far as we were concerned, they were people who had no past and no future, we only saw their present state. Some we felt sorry for and some had no effect on us, but however we felt, we soon forgot them in our own troubles. To many of us, they were refugees, a class apart and would have stayed that way for me, had I not met one, although that was later.

At about the time we arrived in Pfaffendorf, a woman in her mid fifties left the town of Liegnitz [(now Legnica)] on her travels Westward. She was only a few miles north of us, experiencing the same sort of weather, the same sort of conditions. She was a very small frail woman and a very determined one. Her husband had been captured by the Russians and was in hospital, her son was with the Luftwaffe somewhere in France. She had no idea where she was going but hoped that one day she would find her family safe and well.

At the end of the war in Europe, thousands of families were scattered far and wide. Some families never met up again, but the lady from Liegnitz was more fortunate. Through continual enquiries, and very many months of waiting, she was eventually reunited with her son and husband.

Some twelve years later, while I was stationed just outside Cologne, I met and became friends with her son and daughter-in-law. Soon I was taken into their home and introduced to the parents. When I met his mother and heard of her experience, I marvelled that such a fragile woman could have survived such a journey. Later when my own family joined me in Germany, we all became very firm friends. For me, one refugee had become a real person.

Unfortunately, this was all in the future, I still had to face the present and the prospect was not very encouraging. We were destined to remain in Pfaffendorf for a mere eleven hours as by four o'clock in the morning, we were once more ordered to prepare for another day's march. The date was the twenty eighth of January, which meant we were starting on our tenth day of our travels and I wondered how many more we would have to face.

There is little I can remember of this day as so many of the days seemed the same, we had snow, ice and bitter cold. It may have been on this day when I saw a most encouraging sight. We had stopped for a few minutes rest period and a group of prisoners were standing quite near me. Just at that time, the Medical Officer was walking past, most likely scanning the groups for casualties. Suddenly he stopped and said to one prisoner,
"So you are still alive are you?", the prisoner replied "See for yourself!"
"How are you feeling?" enquired the Medical Officer.
"Very well indeed, I am cured now thank you."

As the Medical Officer went on his way, I wondered why he should pick on that one man, when so many others were failing. The question had been one of more than idle curiosity. This caused me to look closer at the man, then through his disguise of pulled down cap and turned up coat collar, I recognised him. He was the prisoner who, while at Bankau had been suffering from jaundice and had been advised not to travel with us. It was a happy story and a contrast to so many unhappy situations I had witnessed in the last few days. I felt that not everything was bad about this march. To me, he looked a lot fitter and more prepared to march than I considered myself to be, as I was feeling ready to drop. I was very thankful when not long after midday, perhaps about one o'clock, we were halted in the village of Standorf [(now Stanowice)].

Previous experience had shown me that normally we only halted in villages when we were to be given accommodation for a period. This time was no exception, but as usual we had no idea how long the stay would be. I hoped that as we had stopped early it did not mean we would be moving on again that day. There would have been many who could not have made it. If it may be considered good fortune to share sleeping quarters with farm animals because of the added warmth, then we were fortunate, as this is what we did. It was not an unusual occurrence, even so, familiarity did not make it any more pleasant. If we found the smell too overpowering, there was a choice, the farmyard. No one to my knowledge, took up that option, as the cold outside was harder to bear than the smell inside. This particular farm was no worse than usual, so it was up to us to pick the least offensive place to settle for the night. The sick and lame had no choice, they were given the most comfortable and convenient place that could be found for them. They in their state, were unable to do anything else, but trust in the care of the medical orderlies.

A few of us, although unable to give medical aid, did what we could to make sure they were comfortable. It was nothing very much, just ensuring their blankets were wrapped around them, or perhaps simply locating their belongings. When this was done, we then had to look for our own places to sleep.

Passing through a door, I came to a stable with several horses in it. They were separated from me by a fence of planks which, running parallel to the wall, made an alleyway the length of the stable. It was obvious that I couldn't sleep there so intended to investigate the rest of the building. I had just turned round and there to my horror, lying almost at my feet, was the biggest bull in the world. As I have mentioned earlier, I am extremely wary of large beasts and to come across this thing which was so close to me, really stopped me in my tracks. He was lying with his head away from me, so I didn't realise immediately that he was not chained up. When I did discover the fact, I almost chose the farmyard for my bedroom. I decided not to act too hastily, so stood a while to consider the position. While I was doing so, the bull looked round at me, decided that he didn't want to eat or gore me, so went back to sleep.

While I was still wondering what to do, others came in looking for bed spaces, but the only place remotely possible, was in the feeding trough. One brave character decided he was going into the pen as horses didn't worry him. This was despite the fact that one horse was extremely bad tempered and kept kicking the others. As they were tethered up, he decided it was safe. He reached his objective as planned, then with his blankets wrapped round him, settled down at the back of the manger where it was much warmer.

He may have been there two minutes, I am not sure, but with a sudden shout of alarm, he was out of his blankets and cowering against the wall. Fortunately, the horse who was attacking with teeth bared, could not quite reach our friend who was cornered and could not move. I believe it was Tom who shouted to him to stay where he was, as he would be rescued unhurt if he obeyed instructions.

At the start of the rescue attempt, things went smoothly until Tom, who was in the pen working his way carefully along the wall, was noticed by the violent horse. At first, I didn't realise what was happening, except that the horse was edging slowly towards Tom. Something nasty was about to happen as Tom was watching the animal very carefully and the horse was very tense. With a sudden movement, the horse fell sideways against the wall in an attempt to crush the intruder. Tom was just as fast because he knew what was about to happen and had dropped to the ground. Diving between the legs of the horse, he scrambled over the feeding trough to comparative safety. Once there, he worked his way along to the trapped man, avoiding the other horses, who strangely enough, were taking little notice of the proceedings. After several worrying minutes, the mad horse was diverted just long enough to allow the two of them to escape.

Following this alarming display, those who had come looking for bed spaces, decided to look elsewhere, leaving me alone. Well I was not quite alone, as the bull was still there, lying in the alleyway at the side of the pen. During all this upset, the bull hadn't moved and neither had I found a place to sleep. I was feeling very tired and very cold, so with great courage I decided to experiment. I reached out with my hand, placed it on the bull's rump, then awaited his reaction. I knew what mine would be if he moved, his action was the unknown factor. Slowly turning his head, he stared at me, then just as slowly did as before and settled down to sleep again. Very carefully, I wrapped myself in my blankets and laid down alongside his flank where I was as warm as toast. I waited tensely, but he gave no sign of displeasure, so after a few minutes, I relaxed enough to go off to sleep.

I had been asleep about two hours, when I was disturbed by a guard who indicated that I should follow him. As I did so, I was joined by others who had been sleeping in a passageway. We wondered what was happening, as it was obviously not an assembly for departure. We were even more concerned when we discovered that our destination was the German guard room next door. Once inside, we stood around puzzled as to what was coming next. A guard who spoke English, explained that they felt sorry for us stuck out in the cold stables, so had invited us in to get warm. Not only did they have a fire going, there was plenty of room on the floor for us. We were extremely grateful for their offer and settled down in an atmosphere far more comfortable than anything we had known for a long time. I must admit, I was not sorry to have left the bull, even though I had become quite attached to him, I felt a lot safer with the Germans.

Morning came and with it the realisation that we had been allowed to sleep undisturbed, at least until daylight. When I saw the weather, I considered we were very lucky to be under cover, as the snow was coming down quite fast and forming huge snow drifts. I knew we would have to leave sometime, although I hoped it would not be for quite a while.

The guards seemed to have settled down in a manner suggesting we were to remain for a period, so we were able to relax.

Wandering out to the stable I had shared with the bull, I saw one or two prisoners leaning on the fence looking at the horses. One leaned over too far, so causing his hat to fall into the pen. Without another thought he jumped in to retrieve it. Unknown to us, a ram was lurking around the corner, who on seeing the prisoner, started a charge. We saw it coming just in time and shouted to alert him. With a mighty leap, he just cleared the fence as the ram hit it. The planks of the fence were more than an inch thick, but they were struck with such force, I thought the ram would come through. It was fortunate for our friend that the beast's horns had been cut off at some time, otherwise he certainly would have been injured.

Just as we were discussing what had happened, our New Zealand colleague came in and was told what excitement he had been missing. Not to disappoint him, another prisoner jumped into the pen, to persuade the ram to charge. We decided this was enough as we were convinced that the fence would eventually break. The New Zealander didn't seem too impressed and explained that as a boy, he and his friends had a way of stopping a charge. He offered to demonstrate this skill, which made me wonder how it was to be done.

Waiting until the ram had moved away, he then jumped into the pen and moved to the middle. At the instant the ram saw him he charged, then when only feet away, our friend dropped to his hands and knees with his head down. The effect was miraculous, out went the ram's front legs in a desperate attempt to stop. He managed it but only just, as his head was only a foot from the New Zealander's. Gradually our friend advanced slowly on all fours, moving his head from side to side in a menacing fashion. The ram started to retreat, seemingly wanting to run, but afraid to take his eyes from the mop of flaming red hair in front of him. At last, when close to the fence, man and animal parted company.

Thrill seekers demanded that he repeat the performance which he did, but when asked to do it a third time declined. He said that the ram now knew what he was up against and next time, would not stop. We had found the demonstration very fascinating and exciting, although our time would have been better spent resting, as unknown to us, we were to be turned out later that day.

As darkness fell, I began to think that we were to be fortunate and spend another night in the warm by the guardroom fire. It was not to be, as by half past five in the afternoon, we were ready to move. We were to discover that for most of us, this was to be the worst march we were to experience. It was worse than the night of the Oder crossing and I had considered that to be a severe test. To add to our troubles, we were by now suffering even more from lack of food and our strength was being sapped by our continual exertions.

As we moved off, it was quite apparent that this was going to be extremely hard for us. The air was bitterly cold, the snow had turned into a blizzard and of course it was very dark. At a time when people at home were sitting down to tea, we were facing a night which was to be tragic for a few and memorable for the survivors. It was not long before we were faced with snow drifts over a foot deep in places and pulling a sled through that was extremely difficult. It was bad enough just trying to keep our footing. Our small group was quite near the front of the column which meant we were churning up the snow for those following which may or may not have helped them. It didn't do us much good as breaking through the fresh snow was very tiring.

Despite the fact that the snow was getting deeper, we continued our march. To my mind, to have turned out at all was a desperate move, as the weather was so severe and showed no signs of abating. Having gone so far, we had little choice as the only alternatives were turning back or stopping. Turning back meant the possibility of meeting Russian troops and stopping would result in us being snowed in apparently miles from anywhere out on the open road.

We forged on for several hours to nowhere, or so it seemed. The howling wind didn't change, the swirling snow didn't change and if I was on a different road to the one I had been on two hours earlier, I wouldn't have known. Gradually I became aware that there was an unusual disturbance occurring behind me and it was getting nearer. Other prisoners were also becoming restless and kept looking behind to see what was approaching. Suddenly out of the darkness and swirling snow, emerged the first vehicle in what proved to be a military convoy.

I thought we were the only living creatures left on earth, or at least that is what it had seemed like. For over eight hours we had been struggling along in our own small world, unaware of anything else. To us, nothing existed, only the snow, the cold and more snow. There were no people, no houses, nothing. This came as quite a surprise to me as it jolted me back to my senses. I am not sure it was what I wanted as I was better off in the stunned dull state of mind which normally overcame me on the march. In this manner, I could just keep going mechanically, until told to stop.

At the time of the encounter, we were passing through a cutting where the snow had drifted quite severely. It was so deep in places that most vehicles were brought to a grinding halt. Crews were turned out to clear the snow, while others pushed and pulled in a desperate attempt to become mobile again. Quite often they were baulked by a bunch of straggling prisoners who were in their way. We had our own mobility problems, and cared little for theirs, so we only cleared the way if we were in personal danger of being knocked down. Finally the order got through to us that we were to stop and move aside so as not to hinder the convoy further.

Moving had been bad enough, standing still was even worse, which made me wonder how many would be lost on this night. There seemed to be nothing we could do except stand and suffer until told to move. I was getting a little desperate and wondered how long I could stand it. Tom who was with me, felt the same, then just as the blizzard seemed to increase in intensity, I noticed a field kitchen just ahead of us. What it was doing there, I neither knew or cared, all I was interested in was the shelter it might give us.

In case the expression Field Kitchen conjures up a picture of a large object, I must point out that it was little more than a large cooking pot mounted on wheels. Beneath the pot was a fire box which was used to heat the contents of the pot. The whole thing was assembled in a steel slab sided box, whose measurements were approximately six feet by five and about two feet six deep.

Working our way up to it, Tom and I huddled down on the lee side to await the next move. The shelter we got was better than nothing, although the wind whipped underneath and around the sides, beating us about from time to time. Being an optimist, I looked in the fire-box to see if there was any fire in it. I was thinking that it might have just been used by the convoy and then dumped. I was disappointed as the fire was long gone out and as dead and cold as the scene around us. Crawling round to the side again, I rejoined Tom to wait for the order to move.

We waited a very long time and Tom getting rather depressed, expressed the fear that neither of us would last the night out. I must admit that I had been thinking along those lines myself, but didn't like to hear it put into words. I had realised earlier that we were in an ideal position to freeze to death, then Tom's comment confirmed it. Unable to move very much, we were getting colder and colder while our bodies stiffened up. Every so often we would be forced to stand up to stretch our legs, only to be hit by the blizzard again. I don't know how other people managed as there seemed to be no other shelter.

No one came to join us so presumably they simply stood in one spot all the time, as the only movements visible were the Germans digging their vehicles out. Situated as we were, I felt that if we both simply gave up, then it wouldn't be very long before we succumbed to the cold. In the past, I had depended on Tom for moral support, now it was my turn to help him. I had little faith in my powers of persuasion, even so, I suggested to him that we tried looking forward to the time of looking back. I told him to imagine sitting at home by a fire a few years hence, with plenty of food and cigarettes available, telling someone what it was like that night. Gradually we built up a picture of the future until somehow we felt much better and even the threat of freezing to death seemed diminished.

I wonder now, could it have been some form of self hypnosis. Having had that experience, I have tried it on other occasions when things have looked black and it has worked for me.

I don't know how long we were stuck in the snow, it seemed like hours but at half past two in the morning we were on the move again and thankful for it. Unknown to us, we were leaving behind one of our room mates. Suffering from exposure, he had collapsed in a heap, then rolled down the bank into a ditch. A German officer who was in the rear of the convoy, saw him go, so stopped his car to give aid. Apparently he climbed down, revived our friend, then took him back to the car. In a little while, when the prisoner was sufficiently recovered, the officer drove alongside the column to hand the casualty over to someone who could look after him.

I was amazed to think that anyone would have stopped a vehicle in these circumstances as it might not have been able to move again. It was a very risky thing to do, as apart from the convoy which had gone ahead and the prisoners leaving the area, there was no other traffic, it was a lonely isolated place.

The prisoners were not the only casualties that night, as we came across two people who had been frozen to death. The first was a man who had either been dumped by the roadside, or had collapsed, the second was a girl. There was little doubt she had been dumped, as she was frozen in a sitting position. I assumed that she had been a passenger in a cart of some sort and had simply frozen to death where she sat. Whatever the circumstances which had led to their deaths, there had been nobody with perhaps the strength or interest to bury them. I wondered how many casualties there were, not apparent to us.

The mention of the frozen bodies, recalled a situation that I had experienced at one stage of the march. An experience which could have resulted in me being dumped by the roadside had I not been among friends. I had just been relieved from my spell of pulling the sled, when my legs felt quite strange. It seemed as if I was walking on a feather bed about a foot above the snow. The fact that I couldn't maintain any direction didn't bother me as I felt so warm and happy. Vaguely I heard Tom shouting at me and wished he would stop. Next thing I knew was a stinging blow in the face as he hit me. I came to reluctantly, as if from a dream, to discover Tom holding me up as I walked. After a few paces, I gained my equilibrium when I was left once again to my own devices. Later on, Tom confided to me that he thought I was on my way out, which may have been the case, although I was lucky, I had friends to help me. I hope that the two frozen people we had seen, died feeling as warm and comfortable as I had been on that day.

Despite all the hazards of the weather, the majority arrived at our next stopping place of Peterwitz [(now Piotrowice)]. The time was five o'clock in the morning, which meant we had been exposed to the blizzard for twelve hours. According to reports, we had also covered a distance of fifteen miles during the night, which was something of a miracle. This the thirtieth day of January, was the start of our twelfth day of the journey. I was not sure if it meant we were nearer our undisclosed goal or simply twelve days distant from our departure point.

CHAPTER 22

This we had been told, was our last stopping place before boarding a train for the next stage of our journey. It would have been nice to believe, but I don't think many did so. We had been built up before by false hopes, only to be let down again with a bang, so it was not surprising if we were cynical. At that stage I was not very interested in trains or promises of trains, all I wanted was somewhere to lay my head. As far as I was concerned, the world could come to an end, provided it waited until next day, as I had to sleep first.

What a surprise I got, as instead of a barn full of wild horses and large bulls, I was to be billeted in a mansion. Obviously I was not to be alone, I had to share it with hundreds of others. I have little recollection of the place, due partly to the passage of time. It is also likely that few things registered as I was too fatigued in mind and body from the previous night's march. The official report makes no reference to the nature of our accommodation and the note in my diary simply states that we stayed in a mansion. I believe that it was in this place we were given the soup. Although I am not sure of the location of the event, I remember the soup very well indeed. For many, the issue of soup was a highlight, as the food supplied to us had been very meagre indeed. We were really starving and suffered as much from lack of food as we did from the rigours of the weather on the march. The Germans must have realised that we could not possibly carry on as we were, so made a very determined effort to obtain some food for us.

I have no idea what may have happened behind the scenes, but I feel confident that our own authorities, that is, the Camp Leader and the Medical Officer had exerted some pressure. How it was achieved, I am not absolutely certain but the Germans did obtain food. At the time of the event, I was given to understand that they simply commandeered it for our use. One thing was almost certain that if we hadn't taken it, the Russians following us would have done so.

It was decided that the best way to feed so many was by making a great big soup, or meat stew. This was to be done by some local ladies who had been ordered to do so. Due to the size of the order and the need to produce it quickly, some prisoners were asked to volunteer their services. I don't know why I was so lucky, but I found myself included in the working party. I was pleased to be able to help, as it gave me something positive to do. There proved to be other benefits which were not apparent at the time.

We had no idea what was expected of us, but reported for duty as directed. Our place of work was a room , probably a kitchen, where we were told to sit at a big wooden table. Large pieces of pork fat were produced and our job was to cut it up into small portions. These were then gathered up and placed into a boiler. The actual cooking and general management of the soup preparation was being conducted by three or four German women. I wondered who they were and thought that they might be farm girls, or perhaps house servants. To us they all seemed quite strong and well fed, in a far better condition than we were. They were not exactly unfriendly or hostile towards us, even so, there was a distinct barrier.

I felt that they did not appreciate being ordered to help feed us. The preparation took a very long time, as this was meant to feed something like fifteen hundred people, which was no mean task. I don't think that any of us minded being there as it was quite a change to be seated at a civilised table in a clean room. What is more, these people were not in rags as we were, neither did they smell of cowsheds and barns as we did, Endless chunks of pork fat were placed on the table and as quickly as possible, we reduced them to the required size to go into the pot. I am afraid to say that not all of the pieces got that far but I suppose that was to be expected.

One of my co-workers was concentrating on his task, when one of the younger women came up behind him and pushed a piece of pork fat into his mouth. This happened several times and I was puzzled by her action, as it didn't seem to be a friendly one. When I made comment, he explained to me that she had realised he was Jewish and thought she would upset him with the forbidden meat. This was a long way from the truth, as he was in fact delighted. He was quite prepared to eat anything, as long as he lived to carry on with his orthodox religion in easier times.

We worked very hard indeed, as we appreciated that the people outside were desperate for something to eat, as we had been. Our hunger was temporarily blunted by the illicit pieces of fat we had eaten; they were still waiting. As fast as the soup was made, it was loaded into field kitchens and taken to the yard outside for distribution to a grateful crowd. Although we remained at Peterwitz [(now Piotrowice)]for two days, we had no more than one issue of soup. Nobody was really disappointed as nobody had expected it, in fact, nobody had expected the soup we did get. We were very thankful for the two day's rest, as it was much needed. I am not sure it was consideration for us, but the fact that the guards didn't know themselves what the next move would be.

It was believed by some, that the German High Command had lost track of us for a while. This would not have been too surprising as in addition to the German forces in retreat, there were thousands of other prisoners on the roads beside our group. The lines of communication must have been overworked, as Germany was being threatened not only from the East, but the West as well. Under these circumstances, the loss of a few hundred prisoners would have been of little immediate concern to them.

On the first day of February, we departed on foot from Peterwitz, despite the promise we would go by train. As we hadn't believed it in the first place, it didn't make too much difference. It was quite a surprise to see that a thaw had set in and was not a welcome sight for those of us pulling sleds, as it was very heavy going indeed. What did affect us all, was the raw damp atmosphere and the wet snow. Although this was very unpleasant, there was little risk of casualties because of the cold, which was a very different situation to the previous march when over two hundred prisoners had suffered from frostbite.

I was present when one victim learned that he suffered from it. He had not reported sick, but was just chatting idly, commenting that his foot hurt. The Medical Officer overhearing the conversation wanted to know what was wrong. The sufferer had no idea, as he had not removed his boots for three days. The Medical Officer suggested that he do so, in order that the foot could be examined. One look was enough, he had frost bite in his big toe. To prove the point, the Medical Officer quite simply pulled away part of the toe. When the prisoner saw what had happened he was quite taken aback and became rather concerned, whereas previous to the diagnosis, he had only been rather inconvenienced by the pain. Hopefully, no one would suffer so on this day.

The weather may have relented, but we still had other problems as we were compelled to march uphill for the entire journey. It is true we only travelled for approximately eight miles, even so, it took us four and a half hours to do so. Not very far perhaps for fit men, but still very fatiguing for us and disastrous for a few.

We did have a little mild excitement to break the monotony of our journey and an opportunity to be a nuisance to the Germans. Because we had come across little traffic in our travels, we tended to spread across the deserted roads. On this occasion, we were spread out as usual when a commotion started somewhere ahead. Guards were shouting, prisoners were milling about, and above all, was the sound of something mechanical approaching. The thing was a tank, which fortunately for us was German. It was not immediately apparent that it was on its own, which made me wonder if we had run into something nasty and were in fact in a battle zone.

The guards were trying to get the prisoners moved to one side of the road, but the prisoners being dim, didn't know left from right. As a result of this we were snaking and weaving all over the road. The tank commander seemed to be getting rather desperate and was gesticulating wildly at prisoners and guards alike. By now he was down to a crawl and as the tank passed me, I could see he was very angry. While standing to one side to let the tank pass, I was overawed by its proximity. It was within about four feet of me and looked distinctly menacing. Maybe the fact that it was painted white , made it look much more sinister. At this stage, the guards were being ordered to clear the prisoners from the road with some urgency.

The prisoners were still being awkward by crowding all over the road which made me think that there would very soon be trouble for us. I turned to look at a German standing alongside me who seemed to be nothing more than an observer of this spectacle. He was nothing to do with us as he was in German army uniform, while our guards were all Luftwaffe. My attention was suddenly caught by the insignia he was wearing, which indicated he was a member of the SS. These as I understood, were members of Hitler's chosen few, really dedicated Nazis, as well as professional soldiers. On his arm was a badge, which on closer inspection proved to be a map of Czechoslovakia. This convinced me that he was someone to be avoided and as quickly as possible removed myself from his presence. While I was observing the SS man, the tank commander had made very slow progress. It must have been galling to find he was being challenged by a few hundred scruffy people on foot, particularly as his tank was such a big one.

I think that if I had been in the Commander's shoes, I would have fired a few shots over the prisoners' heads, as I believed he was just taking his tank into action. Maybe he didn't know that we were prisoners. It wasn't so very long after the tank had left us, that we heard some firing and I don't think it was practice.

The remainder of our journey to Prausnitz [(now Prusice)] was unremarkable as far as I recall, even so we were pleased to be able to stop and rest. No mansions for us this time, as once again we were housed in a farm. My particular billet appeared to be a silage shed and I could find very little clean straw to lie on. I was not too worried about it, as this was reputed to be the last stopping place before boarding a train. It had been said before, although this time, the majority of us believed it, maybe because we wanted to.

The following day arrived but no suggestion that we were to move, the same again the next day and the next, in fact we were to remain there for four days. I would have welcomed the rest had my billet been a little more comfortable and clean. I would have also welcomed it, had I and my companions not been starving. According to the official report, we did get some food while waiting, although I really can't recall it. It is not surprising that my memory lets me down as the quantities issued were ridiculous. Spread over four days, we were each given two thirds of a loaf of bread, two ounces of sugar, three ounces of margarine, four ounces of flour and three ounces of barley. In total this would not have made even one good meal.

We were faced with the inescapable fact, that until we were under control of an official organisation again, our plight was desperate. No matter what the organisation might be whether it was enemy or ally, we needed an authority in control. Until this time there would be no food, no proper clothing or shelter, no hygiene and above all, no medical assistance.

I am quite certain that there were several among us, who, although not officially sick, were suffering. The exposure and malnutrition was bound to be undermining the prisoners' health and in some cases, laying foundations for long term illness. The only hope was immediate care. I am afraid that the desired immediate care seemed to be a long way off, isolated as we were.

We had been travelling for days over open country where our only contact with civilisation was the occasional lonely village and we had seen practically no one. I considered it would take a miracle to put right all our ills. It would have helped a little had we known how things were in the outside world, but as it stood, we had no news at all. We had no idea where the Russians were, or how the Allies were progressing on the Western Front.

We did know that we had been in retreat but as far as we were concerned, everything had come to a halt. During our prolonged stay, life became very unpleasant for me, as I witnessed things I would rather not have seen. There was no violence, merely scenes of degradation. Despite the so called rations we were issued with, we were still starving and desperate for food. A few of the local population got to hear of our plight so decided to take advantage of it.

They must have been well fed, as they had food to spare. Arriving at our farm, they started to barter for prisoners' valuables, offering loaves of bread and other foods. The exchange rates were severely out of proportion and it would be no exaggeration to say that I saw a loaf exchange hands for an item worth at least one hundred times its value. This in itself was bad enough, but when I saw food being taken away because the price wasn't right, I thought that was torture. It would not have surprised me if a hungry prisoner had simply grabbed the food and run away.

To my mind, the activities of those civilians was a greater menace to our morale than anything the uniformed troops had done. To be treated severely by guards was one thing, to be tantalised and taunted by civilians was another. In our own way, we could retaliate against the troops, whereas the civilians knew they were a protected species. Fortunately this was not permitted to continue for long as soon the civilians were sent away and not before time. I am sure that if nothing else, they were presenting our guards with a security risk.

Another degrading situation developed, although this time, of our own making. It started when the farmer entered the yard and dumped food for his cattle to eat. The food as such seemed to consist of carrot tops, turnip tops or any vegetables considered unfit for human consumption. Not all that was dumped was in a bad state as every so often a carrot or turnip would appear to be quite sound. This treasure was not to be passed by, so it would be picked out and scrubbed clean under the tap.

Very soon, several more prisoners were scanning the food pile looking for decent vegetables. Inevitably there were scuffles to get the best. I had been quite prepared to pick up the odd good vegetable which had fallen from the pile, but not prepared to scrabble with others to get it. More observant prisoners had noted the time that the food was delivered and would be waiting for the farmer to turn up. On his arrival, he would back his truck into the yard, then tip the food onto the ground in front of the cows. The animals stood little chance as the prisoners were much quicker to get at the food and even pushed the animals aside to do so. This was bad enough to see, although not so bad as watching people fight each other to get into the truck before the food was even dumped. Equally revolting was the sight of food being eaten straight from the pile, unwashed.

I did wonder, just how low we would all have to sink. At last the order was given, we were to move out at six o'clock next morning, ready to board the train. The time could not come quickly enough for some, while others were most reluctant to leave. This became apparent at the actual time of departure. Getting people out of their billets was more difficult than usual as several had mentally relaxed and decided they could walk no more.

Guards became quite aggressive and it was anticipated that force might be used. Just as I was leaving the shed, a guard came in and saw a group of prisoners sitting on the floor. He demanded to know what they were doing, as they should have been assembling outside. A spokesman explained that their feet were so swollen, they couldn't get their boots on and wanted to stay behind. The guard appeared very reasonable and suggested that all who wanted to stay should line up against the wall. I felt very tempted to join them, but as I had my boots on, I couldn't use that as an excuse. The thing that really stopped me was the guard's manner, it seemed much too easy going.

I couldn't honestly believe that he would just walk away and leave us to our own devices. The five or six prisoners concerned, lined up as told, then waited, obviously very pleased with their decision. I watched fascinated as the guard raised his rifle, loaded it and fired. Nobody dropped dead, in fact nobody moved, the bullet had hit the wall above their heads. The prisoners stood there petrified awaiting the next move. Without lowering his rifle, he gave them two minutes to clear the building and anyone defying him would be shot. I thought it best to leave the vicinity quickly, although I was still in time to see those threatened prisoners miraculously scrambling into their boots, while the guard stood over them.

Thankful to be clear of the menace, I stepped out into the yard to look for my assembly point. Suddenly I was stopped in my tracks by the sound of a revolver being fired repeatedly, but couldn't see where it was coming from. My first thought was that other prisoners having revolted, had paid the price. Two more shots rang out and this time I located the action. Our German Warrant officer, Ober Feldwebel Frank, was standing in the middle of the yard, simply firing into the air to scare people. Turning round and walking towards me he gave a boyish grin, then swaggered off, returning his revolver to its holster. His whole attitude was saying 'That will shake them up a bit'.

By the time we had sorted ourselves out and got under way, it was late, not that it mattered to us. We didn't think that the train would go without us. I wish it had, but it didn't, in fact we had to wait an hour before it arrived. I am not sure what I expected to travel in, although common sense should have told me not to expect to ride in a coach. I did however have a surprise when the train turned out to be one of cattle trucks. It was certainly not going to be a comfortable ride, as we had nothing to sit on except the floor, and the springing was not of the best. Better perhaps than an open truck as we did have protection from the elements. Once on board, I realised just how uncomfortable it was to be, as with an average of fifty five men to a truck, it gave us little room to move.

As each truck was loaded, the door was slammed shut and locked, where we were to stay for an unknown period. It was very gloomy inside and the only view out was through narrow cracks. Bad as it was for us, we were much better off than the many thousands of Jewish people and other nationals who were transported in a similar manner. They were probably far more crowded and what was more, they were on a one way journey to extermination or slave labour. I don't think that I realised this terrible fact at the time, otherwise I would have been more thankful at our better conditions, or frightened at the fate that awaited us.

Once aboard, we set off on our journey. True, we had been issued with supposedly enough food for two days, which meant very little. That is how we had started out from Luft 7 eighteen days earlier, with two days rations. This time, the issue consisted of one third of a loaf of bread, some margarine and a third of a tin of meat. The journey started, as all my train journeys had done so far, with a violent jolt. If we hadn't been packed so tightly, we could have been injured. Once having started, we seemed to rattle along for hours, until I wondered when we would stop for a break.

We were fortunate that we had a latrine bucket in our truck, while others were denied such luxury. At the first stop, our door was opened to let us get out, empty the bucket and answer the call of nature. As soon as possible, we would be ordered back in to allow others to get out. We were to learn that this was not permitted every time we stopped, even if we were held in a siding for some time. This could be particularly galling, especially when others could be heard outside.

Whatever control the guards thought they had over us, it was not absolute, as I heard of at least one prisoner who made his escape from the train and there may have been more. I knew the prisoner quite well and the story of his departure was told to me by an eyewitness. At the time, he was suffering rather a lot with dysentry and at every opportunity, he would get out of the truck, then crouch down beside the railway line to ease his discomfort. On one occasion when he was allowed out, there was an empty train standing on the lines next to us.

Getting as close as he could to it, he carried on as usual in a crouching position, In the instant that no guards were actually looking his way, he rolled over sideways beneath the train, then apparently crawled out the other side. Unless the guards had searched beneath the train, or gone to the other side of it, they had no chance of seeing him. I hope he survived, as in that cold unfriendly climate and suffering from dysentery, his chances were very limited. It is possible that his attacks of illness were an act, so that the guards would be so used to seeing him by the trackside, that they would eventually ignore him.

It is only a possibility of course, but some prisoners became very cunning and devious, while others already having those traits, refined them. Our journey consisted of a series of movements from one goods yard to another, where we were often shunted into sidings. The engine drivers shunting us were not exactly gentle, not too surprising perhaps, although they could have given more consideration to their own rolling stock. There is little to be said about the journey except that it was cold, uncomfortable and unhygienic. In addition to these discomforts we were very hungry and thirsty. The rations we had been issued with, were quite inadequate for the three days we spent on the train. The length of the journey did surprise me as on several occasions I thought we had reached our destination.

Quite often we would be in a siding for so long, I was sure we had to go no further. Many times, this idea was instantly dispelled, when without warning our trucks would be coupled up to the engine with a violent crash, to be carried off on another stretch. At half past two in the morning of the third day, we came to a halt in a goods yard. Because of the hour, it was too dark to see what the place was like, so I settled down to sleep again. Daylight came to light the scene and still we hadn't moved. I thought this rather strange until I heard the sound of doors being opened. It was obvious that the prisoners were being taken off the train, which could only mean one thing, journey's end.

The sight which met my eyes did not inspire me, as a railway goods yard is not the most attractive place in the world. In the light of dawn and on a cold bleak winter's morning, the view was positively depressing. There was no time for sightseeing as immediately we left the train, we were shepherded by guards into our marching order. I hoped we would not be forced to travel far, as after three days cooped up in a confined space, my legs were not operating very well. I am sure I was not alone in my wish as others had additional problems to contend with. There were cases of frostbite, dysentry and other illnesses, also general debility through malnutrition. However we felt about it, providing we could stay upright, we were going to march. With great reluctance, I moved out of the station yard with the rest, heading for heaven knows where.

As we were leaving, I saw a sign stating that we were at Luckenwalde, a name that meant nothing to me then, as I had no idea where it was located. I was to find out soon. If this had been fiction, it is likely that we would now have come to the end of our troubles and been on our way to freedom. I am afraid this is not fiction and we were in fact heading for more troubles.

CHAPTER 23

I was right in my assumption that this was to be our destination, although I was not prepared for the large prison camp which came into sight. I had hoped never to see barbed wire again, yet here it was ahead of us, great long stretches of it. Although this new camp was in one sense a resting place, it filled me with dread as it looked a very harsh unwelcoming sight.

We had arrived at Stalag III A which was to be our new home for a while at least. Once I was settled in, by that I mean, once I had claimed my space on the floor, I reflected on what had happened on our journey here. We had travelled for twenty two days and covered a distance of roughly one hundred and sixty miles on foot, in extremely severe weather.

We had started from a point East of the town of Breslau (Wroclaw) and finished up about three hundred miles further West. This our present resting place, was on the outskirts of Luckenwalde, a town about thirty miles south of Berlin. Of the fifteen hundred prisoners who had left Luft 7 in Bankau, it was reputed that two hundred and seventy five were either in hospital or missing.

After a reasonable rest period, I was able to take stock of my new surroundings and didn't like what I saw. We were in a large International camp containing several thousand prisoners of many nationalities. Apart from ourselves, there were American, Russian, French, Belgian and Norwegian prisoners, in fact any nationality opposed to Germany. Each national group was in its own compound and not allowed to mix with others.

The huts that we were living in were brick built single storey and contained three hundred prisoners each. Basically ours was a large empty hut with nothing in it except for one small room in a corner. Initially, this room was Sick Quarters and consulting room for the Medical Officer. The whole of the floor was covered in straw and that is where we lived, if it could be called living. Prisoners formed themselves into small groups rather like families and reserved an area of floor for themselves.

There was little we could do in the way of entertainment, as the compound which contained our few huts was so small. As I recall, the only thing we could do, was walk round and round the boundary wire. Apart from this activity, the majority seemed to spend a lot of time just sitting about.

Next door to us were a group of Russians who appeared to be in a far worse state than ourselves. Any time we came into contact with them, which was rarely, they would beg for food, but as we were also starving, we couldn't help them.

Not far from our huts, were a group of seven hundred Americans whose plight was quite different to the Russians, as their major drawback was accommodation. This was much worse than ours as they lived in two large tents. The tents which were fairly low, had been erected over a big hole in the ground. This gave the inmates reasonable head room and to a certain extent, protected them from the cold winds. How they survived it I don't know, as we were cold enough in our brick huts.

The general appearance of the camp was one of permanence and something which had been in existence for a long time. It was an old camp, not like Luft 7 which we had occupied from its first day. This place was a series of camps, surrounded by one all embracing perimeter wire. Despite its apparent permanence, I felt that quite a number of prisoners, ourselves included, were lodgers brought in from the cold, we were refugees from the Russian advance.

There were some prisoners who seemed to consider themselves permanent staff, as they had been in the camp since their capture some time before. Most of these so called permanent types were generally French, with a few Belgians scattered about and although technically prisoners attached to the camp, actually lived in town. Junior ranks could expect to work and live outside, but not all of these were in that category.

We had no such benefits even if we had wanted them, we were confined to our small compound. I am afraid that as well as our compound being limited, so was our view. At Bankau I had thought the view was devoid of interest to a degree, but this was quite different. Where I had looked out on to areas which represented freedom, I now felt blocked in and isolated. This attitude probably arose because of the layout of the camp. Now we were surrounded on three sides by foreign nationals and on the fourth side, by a large sterile area. The area, which was about one hundred yards wide, formed a sort of no-man's land between the compounds and the outer wire. Normally this outer boundary was guarded in the usual manner, but during air raids, dogs were brought in to patrol the so called no-man's land.

A feature of the camp worthy of mention was the toilet block. It was rumoured that it had been built for the Jewish prisoners and constructed to create maximum discomfort for them. Whoever it was built for, it certainly was one of the worst I have come across and obviously designed by a sadist.

It was a forty seater toilet arranged in two rows of twenty, with no divisions for privacy. The seats themselves, were so high off the ground that only a minority were able to rest their feet. As if this wasn't difficult enough, the seats were tilted forward by roughly ten degress. It was a struggle to get on to the toilet and a greater struggle to stay on. Inevitably some users would start to slide forward then find there was nothing to hang on to, nothing unless a neighbour was present although using a neighbour as an anchor was a procedure not really approved as it was considered to be impolite.

It was obvious that someone had put a lot of thought into the design of the toilets and it was a pity that a similar amount of thought had not been applied to our welfare. It is possible of course that a great deal of thought had been used and we were meant to live in the conditions we were in. In addition to being in very poor accommodation without beds or heating, we also had to put up with low rations. A note in my diary records a day's rations at Stalag III A as follows:

- 1 cup German tea or coffee
- 3/4 Pint of soup
- 300g Bread
- 50g Margarine
- 1 Spoon of sugar

This diet was luxury compared to the food received on the march, as in twenty one days we each received:

- 2 1/2 Loaves of bread
- 24 Rye biscuits
- 1/8 Packet of honey
- 13/30 tin of meat

In addition to the above, we were given a small amount of sugar, margarine and barley.

Everyone suffered from the lack of food, but a few were particularly affected. This became apparent in the morning sick parade which grew longer and longer as more and more prisoners succumbed to malnutrition. In the first days, the parade was held in our hut and it was nothing unusual to see a patient in the queue suddenly fold up in a heap on the floor. These were normally taken into the hospital block where they were given rest, but little else.

The Germans became rather concerned about our physical state and told us they were doing their best to obtain some Red Cross parcels. Due to the pattern of the allied offensive, we were being isolated in the North of Germany, so making it difficult for the Red Cross supplies to reach us. More and more people collapsed, so putting severe strain on the hospital which was becoming overcrowded. We prayed that we would soon be given adequate food. I began to think that food was a myth and I would never eat properly again.

During this period of waiting for parcels, Tom had gone to the hospital block to help with the sick prisoners. One day he came in with a slab of concentrated sugar which he asked me to look after. This was meant to be kept in reserve in case we were forced to march again. The temptation to sample it was so great, that I took it from its hiding place one day, with the intention of simply biting off a small corner. I am afraid my hunger was so severe that it got the better of me as I started eating just a little each day. My conscience was troubling me as I knew that I was letting Tom down and each time I took some, I swore to myself that it would be the last time. To my horror I realised that it was finally all gone and I prayed that it would never be necessary to tell him what I had done. Each time I saw him I wondered if he would mention the sugar or would he perhaps give me something else to look after. I hoped he wouldn't do either of those things as I know that given more food, it was likely to have the same fate as the sugar.

Fortunately it was not required, as we never went on foot again. After a month on the starvation diet, we received the news that a quantity of Red Cross parcels had arrived in the local railway yard. This was wonderful to hear and the issue could not be made quickly enough for us. There were insufficient parcels for one each, which came as no surprise, but we were grateful for what we did get. Our share was something like one parcel between four, whereas those in hospital had a much bigger share. No one complained about this, particularly when it was borne in mind that anyone of us could well finish up there ourselves.

Once things had become better organised, the sick parades were no longer held in our hut and the orderlies had also moved out. Three or four of us decided to move into the room which they had vacated, as it gave us a little more privacy. At about four o'clock one morning, someone came to our room in great distress.

He told us that his friend was very ill with stomach pains, and was needing the doctor. We explained that this was no longer occupied by medical staff and directed him to go elsewhere for help. Apparently he didn't find the doctor but saw a medical orderly instead. The orderly, without visiting the sufferer suggested that he should be brought to the sick parade later in the day. It was pointed out that the stomach pains were being experienced by many people, so this was not an exceptional case. Unfortunately, the sick prisoner didn't last until the parade time, he died at seven o'clock. We didn't find out what the trouble was and didn't pursue the enquiry as the situation was no surprise to us, bearing in mind the general suffering.

Shortly after our arrival at Stalag III A, our Luftwaffe guards informed us that they had to leave and in future we would be guarded by soldiers from the German army. They said they were sorry about it but there was nothing that could be done. They expressed the hope that we would be treated reasonably well. Strangely enough, I think that quite a number of us were sorry to see them leave as we had suffered a great hardship on the march with them.

Once they left, we were to be guarded by strangers who had nothing in common with us and might treat us more severely. Just prior to their departure, the Russians had made another breakthrough and were supposedly heading in our direction. Because of this, a notice was posted stating that nobody was to leave camp under any circumstances. Should anyone be caught outside, they would be shot. This didn't affect us personally, but it did stop working parties and guards from leaving camp.

We knew that an Austrian Corporal had planned to visit a girl in Berlin, so thought to remind him of the notice. He told us that it probably didn't apply to him and in any case, he knew an easy way out of camp. He was a remarkably confident person and one who seemed to have far more power than his rank warranted, even so, we considered him fool hardy. When we suggested that he didn't go, he replied that he would see us in the morning. Next morning came and there he was full of smiles. He had just got off the train from Berlin and had obviously got back into camp safely.

We asked how he had managed to avoid detection, and got no answer as he was giving nothing away, but he did tell us a remarkable story. It concerned his train journey into Berlin. Sitting opposite him on the train was a man in civilian clothes. There was something strange about him as he didn't appear to fit in with the local people. After studying the man for a while, the Austrian asked him who he was, as he didn't appear to be German.
'No' said the man 'I am a British soldier on my way for a night out, just as you are!
'Do you realise who I am?' asked the Austrian. Back came the reply;
'Yes, you are a guard in the prison camp and have no more right to be out than I have.
I will see you in the morning.' True to his word, he was on the train in the morning. How he managed to get back inside the wire puzzled the Austrian, but he managed it.

Eventually when our Luftwaffe guards left us, the Army guards moved in and we were rather concerned how they would treat us. Life could become much more unpleasant if they chose to treat us badly, so we just hoped that everything would be alright. There was one big change which we didn't appreciate, whereas the Luftwaffe seldom came into our quarters, the Army appointed a permanent guard to each block. This guard spent all of his time in or around the block and virtually only left us at night.

Our barrack Fuhrer, was a middle aged man, who had been a prisoner of the French during the 1914-18 War and did not have a kind word for them. He sympathised with our plight as he knew how we were feeling, all the same he didn't completely relax his vigilance over us. His general attitude was quite different to our previous captors, where they had been severe and professional, he was fairly easy going. It became obvious that we would be able to get him to bring food into us, providing we put a little pressure on him.

By this time, we were enjoying the benefits of Red Cross parcels and feeling much better for it. We had also taken over the room vacated by the medical orderlies, which allowed us to live in a more civilised manner. As we were sitting down to a snack one day, he entered the room and sat on the floor with his back to the wall. He eyed us with envy as we were drinking coffee and eating cheese with biscuits. The only coffee that he could get was ersatz, made from roasted acorns. Being polite hosts, we asked him if he would like a cup and he jumped at the chance. This was not enough, so we offered him cheese and biscuits which he really enjoyed. When that was finished, we completed his happiness by offering him a cigarette.

It was then that we dropped the bombshell. He was to bring us a loaf within two days, for which we would give him the current black market rate in cigarettes. He sat back horrified and protested that he could not do it as he would be in serious trouble. We pointed out to him, that he would be in greater trouble should we report that he had been eating our rations. He decided that he was trapped and would have to do as asked. We were fair to him in our dealings as we always gave the current price in cigarettes and only asked when it was essential to our well being.

Normally we obtained our bread from working parties of Yugoslavs, who brought it in from town. They would pass the bread to a middleman, who would then pass it on to us. Every so often, there would be a purge when the Germans would search everyone going in and out of the gate. This would put a stop to their activities for a while and it was at such times we would resort to pressurising our guard.

Many guards were used in this way, although some did it voluntarily as it was a very profitable pastime for them. One guard was so proud of his prowess as a smuggler, he showed us the inside of his coat, it was more suitable as a magician's coat than a soldier's uniform greatcoat. It was so full of special pockets, he was able to carry a great many illicit items for trading.

The guards ran a great risk supplying prisoners with black market goods. The risk lay not only in being caught by their own authorities, but being reported by prisoners. I heard of cases where unpopular guards were offered cigarettes, then reported to another guard. It was the quickest way to get rid of someone considered to be a menace.

Generally speaking, we got on quite well with our particular guard and he became a sort of father figure. He himself was fairly relaxed with us and spent quite a lot of time just sitting in our room. There was no question of him being there to watch our group in particular, he simply came to the room because he felt more comfortable there. I think that he sometimes forgot that we were supposed to be enemies as he treated us in a most casual way.

One day he came in with an elderly German, who had been drafted into their equivalent of the 'Home Guard'. This poor man seemed to have no idea of military matters, least of all how to handle his own revolver. He seemed to be very worried about this, as at any time he was expecting to come face to face with invading Russian troops. I didn't think too much of his chances with or without firearms, but at least he did deserve some sort of protection.

With great patience, our guard explained to him how to strip, clean and load the revolver. During the demonstration, which was carried out in our presence, the weapon was laid on the table in front of us. This surprised us greatly as by the time the instructor was finished, we knew as much about it as he did. Our guard had shown about as much concern with us being there as he would have done had we been German soldiers.

The fact that people of advanced years were being trained to defend their homes, seemed to indicate that they were expecting a last ditch stand. Despite this there was a strange air of confidence about our guards. I found this rather disconcerting in a way, as although faced with overwhelming forces, they still thought they would win the war. They believed that a secret weapon was ready to defeat all attacking forces. This weapon was so powerful that victory for Germany was assured.

It was unlikely that they were pinning their faith on the pilotless flying bombs the V1. It also seemed unlikely that the rocket propelled missile the V2 was their salvation. There had to be something else quite devastating which would give them the miracle they required. They seemed to know little of this weapon except that it was to be used in the near future. I now believe that they were referring to an atomic bomb which Germany was working on. This really would have turned the tables on us had it been developed in time, but fortunately it wasn't.

Whatever the Germans said or believed about secret weapons, they were still unable to prevent the RAF and USAF from bombing them by night and by day. Night raids affected us mostly, as we had the inconvenience of going without lights for hours at a time. No bombing took place near us, it was mainly aimed at Berlin and surrounding towns, still we had to take precautions.

The morning after one particularly heavy raid, our guard came into the room and slumped down against the wall. It was obvious from the stunned look on his face that something serious had happened. We questioned him repeatedly in an attempt to find out the cause of his distress. Reluctantly he informed us that his house had been bombed during the night by the RAF. As a result of this, his wife and seventeen year old son were buried in the rubble. His bitterness was not against us, but against the war in general, which was a very surprising attitude under the circumstances.

When he arrived next morning, we asked him if there was news of his family but there was none. Each day we asked the same question with the same result. We felt reasonably sure that his family had been killed and that he would finally have to accept the fact. We were very sorry for him as despite his loss, he had to remain on duty guarding us. On the fifth day, he came in jubilant, his wife had been dug out of the ruins and was on her way to hospital. It was a relief to know that his loss was not a total one. With the saving of his wife, he began to be more cheerful, reporting to us on her state of health. Three days later he came on duty, a completely changed man.

Not only was his wife improving, his son had been dug out alive and unhurt. It seemed that the son had been trapped in the cellar, where he had remained for eight days before being discovered. Eventually after fourteen days in hospital, his wife was fit enough to be discharged. Our guard was so pleased at the news that he promised to bring his wife up to the camp to see us. Apparently she had heard so much about us from her husband, she wanted to see what we were like. We felt a little nervous about this, even though we would be separated by barbed wire.

We were still members of the RAF despite our status as Prisoners of War and it was the RAF who had been responsible for her sorry state. Finally we were convinced that she meant us no physical harm, as she also accepted that it was war and not a personal vendetta. Next day, true to his word, he appeared outside the wire with his wife and pointed us out to her. We were at a safe distance had she wanted to throw anything at us, but fortunately nothing like that happened. All she wanted to do, was wave and reassure herself that we were only human beings after all. I do believe that given the opportunity, both she and her husband would have welcomed us as friends instead of enemies. It is possible that as he had been a prisoner in the previous war, he thought we had a lot in common and also that he understood our plight.

Apart from the episode of the guard's family, which had come to a satisfactory conclusion, there was little else to hold our interest. We had no books, no music, no theatre, in fact no entertainment at all, at least nothing was organised. Perhaps because of this dearth of amusement, the discovery of a piano was good fortune indeed,

I don't know why it was there, but it was found just inside a deserted hut. It so happened that with us at the time, was a fellow who had been a prominent member of the Piano

Accordion band at Luft 7. One of his musical talents was as a pianist, so we persuaded him to play for us.

His playing was such that even tunes I had never liked suddenly seemed to come alive. After a while, I realised that a guard had joined the group standing round the piano and seemed to be paying particular attention to the music. During a lull, he asked the pianist if he could play other things beside dance music. The pianist admitted that his classical repertoire was limited, but he would do his best.

After one or two false starts, he succeeded with a composition by Strauss. I can't remember exactly what it was although it seemed to please the guard, as without further ado, he burst into song. He had an effortless clear voice and despite the slight imperfections of the music, he held us spellbound. I had heard plenty of tenors but none like this and when he had finished, I congratulated him on his performance. It is small wonder that he was good, as prior to his joining the service, he sang with the Berlin State Opera company. I really enjoyed that short period of entertainment but unfortunately we never again had the chance to repeat it. I suspected that such entertainments were not officially approved.

We did have some entertainment one evening, although of an entirely different nature and the audience was much larger. While out in the compound after dark, an aircraft was heard flying around overhead the camp. It seemed to be a fairly light aircraft which was either in trouble, or acting very dangerously. It started its act by descending towards the camp, until I thought it would crash into our buildings. Before it did so, it climbed away rapidly. It then repeated the performance from a different direction, once again climbing away from low level. I then got the impression that the aircraft was trying to land, but didn't know where he was. If I remember correctly, his difficulties were compounded by a very low cloud base.

Finally, to deter him from landing in amongst us, all the camp lights were put out, which really confused the pilot, he could be heard flying about aimlessly overhead. It was then that someone had a bright idea and several boundary wire searchlights were switched on, then directed towards the fields alongside the camp. It wasn't exactly the best form of illumination but better than nothing. This seemed to be what the pilot wanted as he could be heard heading towards the lights. As he started his approach, we waited anxiously, not knowing who he was, or what he was doing there. He may have been German, or even British.

This would only be revealed when he landed. Eventually the pilot closed his throttle and a dim shape could be seen descending towards the field. He touched down with a thud, then bounced wildly on the rough ground, but by a miracle, managed to keep an even keel. As he pulled up safely, the searchlights were switched off, although not before we saw that it was a Fiesler Storch. Even though it was an enemy aircraft, there was no mistaking the spontaneous applause. We were pleased to witness some very skilful flying which had saved someone's life.

There had to be more to life than waiting for such unusual spectacles, interesting though they may have been. We were in need of many more things beside entertainment. We needed food, clothing and footwear as well as medical supplies. There seemed to be no attempt by the Germans to improve our conditions, but maybe that was because they were unable to do so. In particular, food was becoming scarce again as Red Cross parcels did not reach us regularly. As a result of this particular shortage, there were fewer English and American cigarettes available.

Cigarettes were considered to be the staff of life to the prisoners, smokers and non-smokers alike. Smokers needed them because they were smokers and non-smokers also benefited from them for their black market value. A few cigarettes would purchase food, or items unobtainable in camp, so a man without cigarettes was a pauper. As mentioned earlier, most of the cigarettes received came from the Red Cross parcels, but in addition, we did have some French cigarettes. I don't remember how they arrived, I only remember that we had them. As far as I was concerned, they were a permanent feature of camp life and could be classed with the guards, the barbed wire and the searchlights.

These often maligned cigarettes were known as Elegantes, which I believe were made from French home-grown tobacco, and was a very coarse tobacco. When I first saw them at Luft 7, I tried to smoke one. To do so was a punishment as they were a very fierce hot smoke. Not only were they fierce, the taste was not in agreement with my palate. I was not alone in this, as most people found them impossible to smoke and what is more, they were worthless on the black market. Some use had to be made of them, so they became money tokens in card games. Even there they had little value as nobody seemed to mind if they won or lost them.

The shortage of cigarettes really hit us when it was realised that the good cigarettes we had, were needed in exchange for food. We had to find a substitute to smoke. This was when the Elegantes came into their own, no longer were they used for gambling, instead they were used as originally intended, to be smoked. By this time, they had become very dry and battered through being handled so often, but for those of us who were compulsive smokers, it was better than nothing. Ron the Flight Engineer who was living in the next hut, helped out considerably by giving me a few decent cigarettes to smoke. He had obtained them from his hair cutting activities and I was extremely grateful to him.

I am afraid that not everyone had Elegantes to smoke, neither did they have any of the better cigarettes. This and the lack of food as well as the uncertainty of our future, began to have quite an effect on people's tempers. Some people were sullen, while others became positively violent. There must have been many small fights and squabbles between prisoners, but none as far as I know were so violent and public as a fight between two French Canadians. It all started when one of the Canadians decided to boil some water using a home made immersion heater.

To do this, he placed the heater in a can of water, then plugged it in to the mains supply. The equipment was rather crude and faulty, as a result the circuit was overloaded and the circuit breaker jumped out. The system was quickly restored, only to fail again almost right away. Another Canadian approached and asked him to stop causing the power failures. He said that it was important that the power supply should be maintained, although did not give the reason, as that was known only to a few. He was in fact waiting to hear the BBC news on a secret radio receiver. As he was also using mains power, it upset him considerably.

The Canadian boiling the water was quite sure that the fault was not his, so continued to use the heater. In no time at all the power failed again, then there was real trouble. The Canadian who had been listening to the news, stormed into our hut in a rage. He walked up to the other man and hit him hard enough to knock him down, then the fighting started with a vengeance. Uninvited, a crowd gathered to witness the two who were in bitter and fierce combat. From where I stood at the edge of the crowd, I saw one man lying on his back, with the other sitting on his chest. In an attempt to dislodge his assailant, the floored man was doing his best to strangle him. The other in the meantime, while fighting for his breath, had hold of his opponent's hair and was banging his head on the floor. Despite the fact that there were several onlookers encircling the combatants, nobody dared interfere.

The fighting became so vicious that the result had to be serious injury if not murder. At the height of the fighting, a third Canadian pushed his way into the crowd and asked what was happening. When told, he then wanted to know why nobody had stopped it, as one or the other was liable to be killed. The new arrival was a mild mannered quietly spoken person who never liked to see trouble. It was suggested derisively that if he felt so strongly about it and was brave enough, why didn't he try to sort it out. It didn't seem a very fair challenge as the new arrival was of medium build, whereas the two fighting each other, were well over six foot tall.

Stepping into the circle, I saw him grab one in each hand, pull them to their feet and hold them apart. He then informed them that unless they wanted more trouble, they should go their separate ways. I could hardly believe it when I saw them respond meekly and part company. They may have had enough and welcomed the intrusion which allowed them to stop. They may have also realised what they were up against had they challenged him. I think that very few people who saw what happened, had realised just how powerful he really was. I certainly had no idea, but when he picked me up later to demonstrate a point, I was absolutely powerless against him.

It was also significant that a group of people who used to taunt him, promptly left him alone. Prior to this demonstration of his strength, these people used to amuse themselves by challenging him to fight. I think it had something to do with his Jewish religion. His reply was to walk away as he wanted no violence. It hadn't been realised then, that it was they who would have suffered most, only he knew that.

Another incident which I witnessed, did not have a violent outcome, although it could well have done so. The provocation in this case was probably greater. If we had not been starving the situation would never have arisen, or had such potentially serious effects. A prisoner who I believe was a Polish airman, came up to the group I was with, holding a piece of bread. He was almost beside himself with anger and disbelief. He told us that another prisoner, unseen, had taken a slice from it. It had happened in the minute or so that the bread was left unattended. We found it difficult to accept that another prisoner would do such a thing, even though our plight was desperate. The Pole was adamant that he had been robbed and started searching for the missing slice. In no time he was back with a slice of bread, followed by a prisoner who wanted to know what was going on, as he himself owned the slice.

When it was demonstrated that if fitted exactly to the larger piece of bread, the offender admitted the theft. If the Pole had hammered him into the ground, he would have got what he deserved and no one would have gone to his aid. Instead of doing this, the Pole demanded that on our return to England, the man should be court-martialled. I hope he was but I doubt it. Before we were finished, there were many more things which should have gone before a court-martial.

I wondered what our chances were of getting back to England in the near future. We had been full of hope before we left Luft 7 and our hopes were dashed. We had been full of hope again when we ended our march, as many had believed. we might be marching to freedom, but again we were disappointed. Where was our next hope to come from and if it came, would it last?

This of course was always a big question in our minds, but recently everything seemed to have gone quiet again and we were despondent. It seemed strange to think that only a short time previously, we had been fleeing from the Russians who not only had been at our heels, but had also been ahead of us. At a time when we expected things to happen quickly, there was suddenly nothing, the news had ceased for us. I don't know how long this lasted, maybe four or five weeks until we heard that both East and West Fronts were very active. This was very heartening indeed and it seemed that it was going to be a race as to who reached us first. The closer they came the greater the activity, then the doubts came creeping in, what was to be the final outcome?

We were in a sandwich, our allies were approaching from either side, while we with the Germans, were in the middle. It was to be hoped that the Germans would suddenly give in and we would be freed, although it was beginning to look as though they might fight to the bitter end. Although we could not see the war on the ground, the war in the air was very apparent. Bombing raids in the area became frequent and for night after night, we sat in darkened billets while attacks were taking place around us.

One night there was a terrific explosion, it didn't make a lot of noise as it was muffled, but the ground shook severely. Next morning, I was told that the RAF had dropped a ten ton bomb on Juterborg airfield a few miles south of us. Whatever it was, I had never experienced an explosion like that before. It was now becoming apparent that a big onslaught was taking place, as apart from the night raids, there were endless day raids. We watched as hundreds of bombers appeared in huge formations, a really formidable sight.

As the Western Front got closer, so did the bombing and I was under the impression that softening up operations were in progress. Most of the day bombers we saw, were American Flying Fortresses and their technique was for the formation to drop all of their bombs together. This was unlike the RAF system of individual aircraft bombing. With the RAF, the target was subjected to a steady flow of bombs for about fifteen minutes, with the Americans, the bombs came all at once. I don't know which was the more demoralising.

During this period, there were wave after wave of aircraft. They were coming so close to us, I thought that had we been a few feet higher we would have been able to see the bombs actually land. This massive group bombing had a peculiar effect that none of us had seen before. Shortly after the bombs had burst, shock waves could be seen travelling across the cirrus clouds six miles up.

The bombing continued for days and the tension mounted for us as we started calculating the hours to freedom. It seemed that it would be the Americans or British who would get to us first. Then came the bitter blow, the Germans announced that we were going to be removed from our camp and taken to Bavaria.

To be withdrawn from the chance of imminent freedom, was very hard to bear. The only conclusion that could be made, was that we were to be held as hostages. It was fairly obvious by this time that the Germans were almost finished and would have to surrender. Any continuation of the conflict would only be in small pockets of resistance. We didn't want to be in one of those small pockets.

Another aspect not relished, was the danger involved in such a move. There was heavy fighting in the area, particularly in the South, where Russian and American forces were rapidly closing the gap. It was through this gap that we would have to be taken. Our chances seemed minimal. If it was to be supposed that we did get through to Bavaria, what of the future for us?

It was planned that the move was to take place in batches. Huts would be emptied in rotation and parties formed ready for transportation by train from the local station. As trains became available, further parties would be moved. This gave our particular group a breathing space as not only would we be among the last to leave, we hoped that the supply of trains might cease before it was our turn. I heard an unconfirmed report that one or two British officers of senior rank, were taken by car in an attempt to reach Bavaria. It seems that they were to be our advance party but were unable to get through, neither did they return to camp.

Even if the story of the officers was merely hearsay, I do know that on the 12th April 1945 the first batch of prisoners were assembled and marched out of camp for the local railway station. Once there, they were loaded into cattle trucks, with the intention of heading south. They did move a short distance from Luckenwalde but were unable to continue. The route had been cut by a joining up of American and Russian forces. After some delay, the trucks were brought back to the station to await developments. On arrival, the prisoners remained locked in, until the protestations reached such a level that they were allowed out. Then apparently they took charge of the station. I heard of one prisoner who went up to the ticket office and broke off the wooden shelf at the ticket window. When chased by the ticket collector who wanted to know what he was doing, replied that he wanted it to light a cooking fire on the platform.

During this time, we in camp knew very little of what was happening to those on the train, all we heard were rumours. Eventually word got around that they were returning, which we fervently hoped was the truth. What a relief when they actually appeared coming in through the gate. As may be imagined, they received a very noisy welcome from all who waited to see them as it had been thought that we would never meet them again. Not only did it mean that they were back in the fold and comparatively safe, there was now a chance for the rest of us to remain where we were. None imagined that the camp was really secure, as it was gradually becoming hemmed in from either side. It seemed we were almost certain to be in the middle of the final battle ground. Despite this, we were better off than being scattered about Germany locked in cattle trucks.

I am afraid that the rejoicing over the return of our colleagues was marred by the news of an attempted escape. This occurred the night before the party were brought back into camp and involved three RAF prisoners who were unaware that the others were returning. I can only assume that they did so to avoid being taken hostage which at the time seemed likely.

If there had been any planning, it wasn't apparent, but simply a straightforward breakout. During an air raid alert when the boundary lights were put out, the three of them climbed the inner compound wire and got into the darkened sterile area. They then headed for the outside wire intending to climb it. They must have been desperate, because they would have known as we did, that extra dog patrols were mounted during these blackout periods. The dogs picked up their scent which alerted the guards. Immediately they opened fire on the escaping trio. Two of them were hit, while the third ran for his life. He was a very lucky man, as he ran in the right direction and managed to get back over the wire into our compound undetected. The other two were not so lucky, one was killed and the other injured, a disastrous result to what proved to be an unnecessary escape attempt. The third man who got back, was very shaken indeed, and when I spoke to him two days later, he still appeared rather stunned by it all.

It is easy to criticise their attempt, but had they been successful in their escape, while we were taken hostage, it is they who could have criticised us for just sitting and waiting. We did not have long to wait as on the following weekend, the Russian assault commenced.

CHAPTER 24

The week following the attempted evacuation to Bavaria was a long one, as we had no idea what to expect. The Germans seemed very anxious to retain their hold on us in the face of all opposition. This was not a comforting thought because people as determined as they appeared to be, were capable of doing anything. I had heard a rumour that we could all be shot, which at the time seemed a bizarre idea. I did not attach too much importance to this as there were many more factual things to worry about.

Morale received a boost when we heard that American troops advancing rapidly, had overrun the city of Magdeburg. This put them less than fifty miles away, so it was only days for them to reach us. By our calculations it would be five at the most. Then came the most bitter shock of all, they had stopped their advance. Not only had they stopped it, they were actually withdrawing back across the river Elbe. This was extremely difficult for us to accept as the opposition was crumbling fast. The only conclusion that we could reach was that politics were involved. We felt deserted.

Bombing in the area continued as before, although the troop movements we were interested in seemed to have stopped. Before we could be extricated from this potential hornet's nest, we needed either a German surrender, or friendly troops to recapture us. At the time, neither possibility seemed imminent. I did however see German troops active, they were working on the grass verge outside the boundary wire. They were laying a cable and every so often I saw them stop and bury something. It was a bit too far away to see exactly what it was they were doing.

Because of the rumours I had heard, my imagination led me to believe that instead of shooting us, they were mining the area outside the camp. I never did find the explanation although it was most likely a telephone or power cable they were burying.

Friday started as any other day, simply routine despondency, and looked as though it would continue that way, but it was not to be. By eight o'clock that evening on the twentieth of April 1945, Russian artillery opened fire on Luckenwalde. We had often looked forward to their arrival, now they were on our doorstep. The fanciful dreams we had nurtured, were liable to mature into a nightmare of reality. I doubt if many prisoners had ever given serious thought to the possibility of being on the wrong end of an artillery barrage as we now were.

There was nothing we could do and nowhere we could go, we just had to hope that they would not shell us. Our billets were no protection from any projectile larger than a rifle bullet, so if anything did come our way, we would be in trouble. In the past I had experienced several heavy bombing raids, but this was quite different. For those of us on the edge of town, it was a continual rumble of heavy guns which went on and on. What it must have been like in the town, I could only imagine.

I stood in the compound with others, looking towards the action, but all we could see, were gun flashes. At that time, the shells were not coming near us despite the fact we were right on the edge of the town. We hoped it would stay that way. After a while, as there was nothing to be done, I went to bed where I finally settled down to sleep to the lullaby of the artillery. I woke up once or twice during the night and heard the guns still hammering away. This continued all night long until sometime about seven o'clock in the morning, the gunfire ceased. Even when the shelling had stopped, there was still cause for concern as we didn't know what the next move was likely to be. A sense of waiting for something to happen was perhaps heightened by the sudden quiet.

It was very strange that no guards were around, I had expected to see them in a state of concern or excitement. Then the news came through that they had deserted us. This was quite amazing considering the lengths they had been prepared to go to in order to keep us as prisoners.

My first reaction was disbelief that they really had left us completely. I expected to see them return at any time. Later when it was quite apparent that they had gone, I felt very concerned at the situation. Although it was known that the Russians were in the area, none had actually put in an appearance. In addition to the Russians, I believed that there were German troops all around us, either in hiding or in defensive positions. This placed us in a very vulnerable situation indeed, as we could be attacked by either side and we were still locked in. Apart from this aspect, there was no law or order any more, prisoners of all types and nationalities were wandering around aimlessly, or doing as they thought fit.

We were in the midst of an ungoverned rabble. It was strange to think that technically we were free, but free with nowhere to go. To leave camp would have been dangerous as we were in an area of belligerent forces, and to stay where we were, made us sitting ducks. If we had known where the opposing forces were, it would have helped us assess the situation a little better. I did not think that the camp would be attacked unless we were mistaken for Germans, but we could be overrun by either side should we be in the way, as consideration for us would be minimal or even non-existent.

While this new found freedom was going to our heads, a few of the more sensible people decided to enter the German records office to retrieve the documents of as many prisoners as they could. They felt that it was advisable to keep these records out of other peoples' hands, I was extremely relieved to receive my own, which I have kept safely ever since.

I was a little alarmed when later in the day I saw one of our guards walking through the camp. I thought it strange that nobody seemed concerned and mentioned this fact to a colleague. He explained that the guard had surrendered to us and was only one of several. I couldn't quite understand why they should do such a thing unless they were deserters. Alternatively it could have been that they themselves were deserted by their own people so had come to us for safety.

Whenever they arrived and for whatever reason, they were put into cells and locked in, to await further developments. Not all that came in wished to be locked up. During the afternoon, I was walking down through the main camp road, wondering what was going to happen next. I very soon found out as striding towards me, was a very smartly dressed German Officer. I wasn't quite sure what action to take as my training had not equipped me for accepting a formal surrender, so I hoped that he knew the drill.

Stopping me, he demanded to know where the Senior British Officer was located. Before giving him directions, I asked if he had come in to surrender himself. I thought for a minute he was about to have a fit. In an arrogant and outraged manner, he sharply informed me that he had no such intention. He was in command of a fighting unit in the woods just outside the camp gate. His was an anti-tank unit and he had come in to see why we were wandering about. We were obviously no longer under armed guard which made him suspect that an uprising was in progress. This could make his present situation precarious.

He also informed me that if the camp roads weren't clear of prisoners in fifteen minutes, he would turn his guns on us and blow the place apart. Providing we obeyed his instructions he would hold his fire, but would come into the camp at six o'clock next morning, to search for hidden weapons. He then went on to tell me that for every weapon found, he would shoot one hundred prisoners. Should he find four weapons in a block containing three hundred prisoners, then he would shoot everyone in that block and take one hundred from the next hut and so on.

As soon as he had stormed off in search of the SBO, I passed the information to as many people as I could before disappearing into my own billet. The next few hours were anxious ones as I knew that the German had not been talking for talking's sake and fully intended carrying out every thing that he said he would do. When he returned in the morning, he was bound to find something which he could have classed as a weapon. I lay in my blankets that night wondering if this was to be my last. I could understand being fired at while I had been on bombing raids and I could understand being fired on if I was attempting to escape, that after all was to be expected as we were at war. What I couldn't accept was being executed by a firing squad for someone else's bravado in hiding a weapon.

As I mentioned earlier, I had doubted that our guards intended to shoot us, but this was a different matter. The commander of the anti-tank unit had every reason to carry out his threat as he was fighting for his life and those of his companions. Despite all of these worries, I fell asleep with the hope that the morning would not be as bad as I feared it could be.

Just about first light, I was disturbed by a lot of activity outside in the compound, people were hurrying past and calling to each other. At first I thought that the anti-tank commander had turned up, although I would have expected the prisoners to be rather more subdued at his appearance. Having decided that it was not so, I wondered what it could be, so got up to investigate. As I arrived outside I saw prisoners running towards the wire which separated us from the main camp road. There was no doubt now about the excitement being generated. This was obviously something big which was happening, so with others, I also hurried to the wire. I heard a comment about Russians several times but could not really understand what people were talking about.

What puzzled me even more, everyone was looking down the road towards the main gate. When I asked what was happening, I was told that the Russians had arrived, but I still didn't understand as I could see no masses of troops or armoured vehicles. All I could see was one of our RAF prisoners talking to someone, then I realised they were two Russian soldiers on a motorcycle and sidecar. The RAF man who could speak Russian, had approached these two when they had ridden up a few minutes earlier and had explained who we were and that we were prisoners. This surprised the Russians as they had not known of our existence, but promised that their authorities would be informed right away.

When they finally left us, there was a great deal of excitement among the prisoners, as it was now only a short time to our release. I did think about the anti-tank commander and wondered if he would turn up later. He could have done a great deal of damage to us if he had felt so inclined, as we remained unprotected. A promise made by two Russian soldiers may have been well meant, but unless it was backed up by troops, we were still in danger.

We waited anxiously for hours, wondering what was happening as everything had gone remarkably quiet. It was possible of course that the Russian authorities were simply not interested in us. This would have been understandable considering they had only just captured Luckenwalde and were probably very busy. During this period, prisoners became uneasy as the Russians had not appeared as expected and doubts started to creep in.

When least expected, we were rewarded by the sound of tanks approaching. They might have been Germans, but I didn't think so. To our great joy, it was Russian tanks that appeared on the scene. Immediately this happened, the RAF man who could speak Russian started to open the main gates. Before he could complete his task, I saw him called forward to the leading tank where he was engaged in brief conversation with its Commander. Reluctantly he returned to the gates and closed them which made me wonder what was behind this move. I was not left in doubt long as with a burst of power the tank surged forward and smashed the heavy gates aside. It was awesome seeing the destructive force at close quarters which made me hope that they did not intend smashing the camp completely.

Fortunately, the leader, followed by others, moved on down the main camp road. Amid all the jubilation, a Russian prisoner, beside himself with relief, rushed to greet his comrades. Just before he got to the first tank, he slipped on the cobbles. I watched horrified as the tank driver neither slowed nor swerved but just drove on unchecked. In desperation the Russian rolled into the gutter on the side furthest from me, but I knew he would be crushed. After the tank had passed, I expected to see a few mangled remains, but to my surprise, the body got up and threw himself clear before the next tank arrived. He had survived the ordeal untouched, although only just, as the tank track could not have been more than a foot from him.

After the first few tanks had passed through the camp, more arrived. One decided to start demolition in his own way. By attaching a cable round a post, he commenced pulling down the barbed wire fencing. This was very dangerous for the spectators as barbed wire under tension was breaking and whipping about all over the place. Very soon, they were asked to cease this activity as apart from the danger, it was more spectacular than useful.

More and more tanks followed which if my memory is correct, numbered over one hundred. At various intervals during the day, they entered camp by the east gate and left by the west gate, probably the shortest route. I couldn't see where they were going, except that they headed towards the woods which had contained the anti-tank unit. They may have gone into action although I doubt it, as we heard nothing.

Visiting the spot later, there was no evidence of a battle but it was obvious that German troops had been in the woods. A lot of equipment was lying around abandoned and surprisingly, a dead horse which someone had started cutting up. I assumed from this that whoever had occupied the place had been hungry.

At one stage, while the tanks were still in camp, I saw several Frenchmen jumping up and hanging on to them, which seemed a very strange thing to do. I was informed that the Russians had expected all of us to join them in the final assault on Berlin and only the French had responded.

When we refused, because of the Geneva Convention, they were most displeased with us as they did not accept the Convention or its guidelines. It prevented us from fighting in any theatre of war in which we had been taken prisoner. This didn't seem to bother the French, who were in fact bound by the same rules.

Even had we wished to join them, we were unfit, underfed and poorly clothed. In addition to these factors, those of us who were aircrew were not trained to fight on the ground. I don't know if the Frenchmen did go off to fight or even wanted to do so, but they certainly made a big show at the time.

Following the arrival of the Russians, the sequence of things became rather confused in my mind, although many facts remain clear. The Russians who arrived first were front line troops, the actual spearhead. They did not stay long but continued to pursue the enemy, which resulted in some fighting in the area. These were followed by garrison troops, whose main duty seemed to be security and consolidation. Any pockets of resistance were mopped up by them.

As things became very quiet, we were allowed out of camp, providing we remained within a mile of the boundary wire. This was a great pleasure to be able to wander around almost at our ease, I say almost as we were still under the surveillance of Russian patrols who were covering the area.

It was always a little disconcerting to meet up with these Russians on a quiet road, as they didn't understand who we were. There was always the possibility that we could be mistaken for Germans, as to a Russian, the German and English languages would sound very similar. Another thing was the likeness between the RAF blue uniforms and the German grey. A further problem was the language difficulty, as they could not speak English and refused to speak German. As we were unable to speak Russian we were forced at times to use the language that they hated, German. This was always risky as then they would start waving their guns about and get terribly excited.

On one occasion when I went walking on my own, I approached the camp main entrance and stepped into the road to pass through the large gateway. As I did so, the Russian sentry lowered his bayonet to the on-guard position and ordered me back. I thought I had done something wrong by attempting to go out, so turned disappointedly to re-enter camp. This was not right as the Russian shouted at me and waved his rifle violently. Now I knew I was in trouble as he was directing me towards the guard room. I was about to step inside when more shouting stopped me. The sentry now quite cross, came over and prodding his bayonet dangerously close to me, guided me out through a small side gate. I had no idea what had prompted this action, but did as directed. I really wondered where I was being taken and for what reason.

After I had left the gate several yards behind me, I realised I was no longer being followed, so turned around apprehensively to see why. The sentry was back at his post and was taking no more notice, except to wave me on my way. I then concluded that they had some funny rules and all that they had intended was that I should have used the side gate.

I walked for an hour but decided it was not very safe on my own, so returned to camp. This time I was not going to make the same mistake and boldly walked up to enter by the gate by which I had left earlier, I was in for a surprise, as quite suddenly, I was stopped by another bayonet being levelled at me. It may have been the same sentry but as they all had very similar Asiatic features, I couldn't tell. This time I thought it meant I was being refused entry and considered how I was going to prove my identity. At last all was revealed as after a similar performance to that which attended my departure, I was directed through the main gateway. I could have understood this one way traffic system if there had been any traffic, but I was the only moving thing in sight. I never did fathom how their minds worked.

On another occasion I went out, but this time with Tom and was a much more interesting walk, he was taking me to meet a local German parson. Apparently Tom had been out walking aimlessly on his own, just as I had, when he came across a church in a nearby village. As he wandered through the churchyard, he was met by the parson who introduced himself. After a brief conversation, Tom promised that he would return another day for a further talk and would probably bring a friend along. I was a little concerned at this meeting, as even if he was a man of the church, he was still a German. Another thing which bothered me was the fact that the Russians might object to our association with the Germans.

Fortunately we did not meet up with any Russians, or even see any once we had left the camp, which made me feel a little easier. After walking for about fifteen minutes, we came across the church in the village. It was a quiet, restful place and I felt more relaxed there. As we entered the churchyard, we were greeted warmly by the parson and as soon as I had been introduced, we were invited into the house to meet his family.

They were very interested to hear of our life as prisoners and seemed genuinely sorry that we were so poorly fed. Just to prove the point, they asked if we could go for a meal with them on the following day. When we expressed doubts that they could afford the food, they assured us that they had plenty. It seemed that only city dwellers went short. The thing they really lacked was soap and when we told them that we could bring some, they were very pleased to hear it.

Next day, we made ourselves as neat and tidy as we could and presented ourselves at the parson's house in good time for the promised meal. I can't remember what it was except that it did us more good than they knew how. There was a drawback of course which was nobody's fault. For a short space of time, we were living in a civilised atmosphere, quite a change from our normal primitive method of existence. Unfortunately an existence we were going to have to return to. Just sitting around a properly laid table, among a family, made us realise what we were missing. It did more than this, it made us wonder if we were to ever experience this manner of living again. Somehow there seemed to be no tomorrow, at least, the future seemed extremely vague and if things were to improve for us, it was going to take a long time. It may have been the environment we were in which caused this feeling as I got the impression that once again we were in a village among people who were apparently untouched by war. Their life was completely alien to ours or so it seemed. If we were going to exchange our present life style for a more civilised one, then a lot of adjustment would have to be made.

I knew in my mind that due to our experiences, we would never again be able to accept life as it had been before. Despite my earlier misgivings regarding meeting these people and the disturbing thoughts which were aroused, I was very pleased to have met them. The meal was excellent as I remember and we were truly thankful that they had fed us so well. Before departing, we offered them the soap we had promised. If we had been pleased with our meal, it was nothing compared to the excitement that they displayed on seeing our gift. In their eyes, our offering to them was so generous, they insisted on giving us food to take back to camp. We received some eggs and a small joint of bacon, plus a few items we had not seen for a very long time. This certainly was our lucky day, but eventually we had to depart and return once more to our normal way of living behind the wire.

As we passed through the village on our return to camp, we came across a most interesting sight, a Russian tank. This was the first Russian vehicle of any type which we had come across. All the tanks, trucks and vehicles we had previously seen, were supplied by the Americans to help the Russian war effort. I don't know what it was, except that it was big, at least, it seemed so to me. By the state of its paintwork, I didn't think that it had seen any action. Strangely enough, despite the purpose it was intended for, it looked quite peaceful, parked by the roadside unattended.

Maybe because it had not been in action, it had no real atmosphere about it. This was the only thing of note we saw on our short walk back to camp.

Once back in my own living space, I compared it with what we had just experienced. This perhaps made things worse as what I was looking at was the real world. The family in the village were living in the dream world. The real world was fighting, murder, looting and rape, not to mention the sickness and starvation that was around us. How long we would have to tolerate this was a completely unknown factor. Already it was quite apparent that our liberation was not of prime importance to the Russians. After the excitement of their arrival, this attitude of theirs was quite depressing. Then came the registration and the start of another phase in our life, this time under Russian control.

CHAPTER 25

Our registration by the Russians was a long drawn out affair which seemed to take hours. We had been informed that we were to report to a certain building one afternoon to have our Name, Rank and Number recorded. I joined the queue and waited for my turn, but nothing seemed to be happening. There were something like four hundred prisoners in front of me and as far as I could see, they were not moving. Then came some light relief in the form of a Russian soldier with a piano accordion.

He started to play a tune, unrecognisable to us, but he performed it quite well. He was perched near the entrance to the compound where everyone could hear him. In case people didn't appreciate it the first time, he played it again. After the third time we could recognise the tune. By the tenth repeat, we were becoming a trifle uneasy and by the twentieth time we were seething. The comments made about him, proved that our Russian musician could not possibly understand a word of English. It also seemed to prove that he only knew one tune.

Completely oblivious to our reactions, he played on and on, his features impassive. After a while, it took on a sinister aspect, as we began to wonder why he was there, was it some form of torture as there was no way of escaping the noise? I don't know how long I was in the queue, maybe two hours, but until I had registered and cleared the compound, that persistent accordion player haunted me. The registration was a simple affair although made farcical by some who thought it amusing to register as Lord Nelson or Donald Duck.

Whatever the purpose was for registering our names, I could see no point in giving a false one as it made little difference to our fate. If the Russians had meant to take us back to Russia for example, being named Napoleon instead of say, Stanley Brown, would not have altered the decision in the slightest. It was obvious that the Russians would want to know who they had in their charge although I suspected that it would only be to their benefit, not ours.

The perpetual performance by the Russian accordionist, was the second example I had seen of single minded apparently pointless actions. Just previous to our registration parade, I saw a group of Russian soldiers drive into the middle of a compound, in a car they had found somewhere. They were Asiatic types, similar to some of the tank crews we had seen. Once in the compound, they put the steering wheel on full lock then started driving round and round in circles. At first I thought it was a joke and that they were simply showing off. It became less than a joke it became pointless as they continued on the same circle for time after time. I am not sure, but I believe there was an accordionist in with them then. What I really couldn't understand was why they were doing such a thing, it was certainly not for our benefit and didn't seem to be doing them much good either. Eventually the inevitable happened, they simply ran out of fuel. Without more ado, they promptly got out of the car and left it where it was.

There was another side to the Russian way of life, one I had not suspected and it was brought to my notice by a friend. He directed me to a compound which had been vacated by Russian prisoners. I went, simply to see what was to be an unusual sight in all this squalor. Some Russian prisoners with religious beliefs, had constructed a small church at the end of one of the barrack blocks. It was not very big but beautifully painted and decorated. It was a haven of peace inside a grim exterior and the coloured walls were like a splash of light.

There was a powerful atmosphere about the place and I thought of the stories it could tell. I wondered how many Russians had gone there for a few minutes' rest and to offer up their final prayer. I am certain it was well used, as the Russians seemed to be the most persecuted of all. Most of the Russian prisoners I had seen, were dying of starvation or had been worked to the point of exhaustion. Because of this I think it was likely that the church, or shrine had been constructed much earlier by long serving prisoners. What surprised me most was the fact that they were able to obtain the necessary tools and materials. Some Germans must have been sympathetic towards their cause, otherwise it could never have been done.

Just before I left the Russian compound, I decided to investigate a curious looking brick building. I had noticed it when I first entered, but that had not been the prime purpose of my visit. The building was not very big, about sixteen feet by eight feet and only one storey high. In the long wall were two steel doors. In the end walls were small windows covered by bars. The place appeared to be a form of confinement, so full of curiosity, I opened one of the steel doors. This revealed a very narrow cell, containing two bunk beds. Another prisoner who was examining the place with me, opened the second door to reveal a similar cell. This was very strange as we couldn't understand why they were so far apart, yet not wide enough to accept a third cell.

While I was pondering this, my inquisitive colleague, had wandered to the other side of the building. I heard him shout to me to come and look, puzzled by his tone, I hurried round. He had opened a door and was staring into a big brick oven or fireplace, which occupied the space between the cells. The fire, when alight, would have heated both cells, as the walls of the oven, were their inner walls. There was little doubt that it was a torture chamber in the form of a sweat box, as the size of the fireplace indicated that a big fire could be lit there. This was a grim sight indeed and quite a violent contrast to the place of worship we had just been viewing. We had no inclination to stay, but hurried back to our own compound.

Thinking of this later, I recalled stories I had heard. They were stories we all had heard, of Russian prisoners being confined on short rations for two days, then sent straight back to work. Was this the place they had been confined in? Although I never spoke to any Russians who were subjected to this treatment, I had no doubt it had been used. This could have explained why I had seen so many Russian prisoners in the last stages of collapse begging food from us.

The Russians were not alone in their suffering as we also had our quota of starving people, although not to the same extent. It was hoped that the liberating forces might rectify this situation, but we were disappointed. The Russian policy was to live off the land, in other words, get what food they could from the local area. By the amount of food they gave us, it must have been a very poor area indeed. We were supplied from time to time, with bread of a sort, baked by people who may have done their best under the circumstances, but it was hardly ever cooked properly. Quite frequently, the outside looked good but the inside was a soggy mess which did not help my digestion one little bit. There was obviously a special technique to baking the German black bread.

To make the bread more palatable, we were issued with some metal tubes said to contain cheese. There were no labels to indicate what the tubes contained, but we were assured it was cheese. They looked like toothpaste tubes and when squeezed, a substance which resembled toothpaste oozed out. I regarded my first issue with grave suspicion but being so very hungry, decided to try some. To my surprise, it did resemble cheese, even though it was in paste form. I can't say that I enjoyed either the cheese or the bread, but as I had nothing else, I was compelled to eat them or go without. After a while I developed such violent indigestion that even a drink of water caused me severe pain.

The bacon and eggs we had received from the parson, didn't last long, so we thought we might look for vegetables next time we ventured out. Suddenly our hopes were dashed, as fighting had broken out around us and we were told that it was no longer safe to go outside camp. I am not quite sure how it all started, but it seemed that there was a much larger force of Germans in the area than had been believed. Not only did this mean restrictions for us, it also put us into the danger zone once more.

None of us imagined that the war was over as even though things had quietened down, there was still air activity. This was not unusual of course as there had been many aircraft in the area during the past few weeks. Despite this, I was quite concerned when I heard the drone of aircraft approaching. It was an unusual noise coming from a southerly direction, whereas most aircraft approached us from the West. Many heads turned towards the sound and to our surprise, we saw several Russian bombers at quite low level. In attendance were small fighters, which seemed to be cavorting all over the place doing aerobatics. This was quite a contrast to any other flying we had seen and was fascinating to watch. It may have been a special Russian technique, but the way the fighters were behaving, they were likely to run out of fuel if they had far to go. The bombers which were medium sized aircraft, plodded steadily on, apparently ignoring their more exuberant escort. They seemed so slow and the fighters inattentive, I felt that they were extremely vulnerable to air or ground attack. Although I did not see it, I read a report which stated that three of the Russians were shot down by German fighters.

The group or formation was heading towards Berlin, possibly to back up their troops who were preparing to enter the capital. That was the only time I actually saw Russian aircraft, although they had bombed us when we were at Bankau on the Polish border, but that was at night.

The real danger to us came during one night when ground forces engaged in a fierce battle just outside the camp. They were reported to have been right up against the boundary wire. I heard nothing of this, so I must have been sleeping soundly. A second battle took place one or two nights later, but again I heard nothing. It was this action which made us realise the risk we had been running walking about outside the camp. The Germans were very active in their resistance and it seemed that they intended to go down fighting.

Not all fighting was confined to night attacks as we witnessed skirmishes on at least two evenings. As we were not allowed out, we amused ourselves by walking around the compounds or by simply standing and staring at the outside world. One particular evening, I caught sight of a Russian tank emerging from the woods just outside the camp. As it crossed the field in front of me, it started to fire shells into the woods opposite. I couldn't see what it was firing at and as far as I could tell, it was not being fired at. It continued firing at intervals and eventually disappeared into the furthest woods.

I expected it to reappear, but for a while nothing happened, then to my surprise a German tank emerged. This repeated the Russian tank's performance, but in reverse. As it came closer, it started firing into the woods nearest to us and continued to fire until it also disappeared into the woods. No one who was watching could really understand what was happening, it all seemed like a combined forces exercise.

I am sure it was much more desperate than what it appeared to us. We waited a while to see any developments but there was nothing. This had been the only activity which took place, there had been no anti-tank guns, no rifle or machine-gun fire, nothing, just the two tanks firing into the woods. Somehow it didn't seem real, but rather like remotely controlled toys making intermittent popping noises. Strangely enough, although we were fairly close to the action none of us showed any more concern than idle curiosity. It was nothing to do with us, it was not part of our war, only a game being played by two teams.

On a second occasion, another strange incident occurred. This also happened during the evening and started when a machine-gun in one woods, opened fire on the other woods. After a short period another machine-gun opened up in reply and maintained a short duel with the first. As before, there was no sign of anything or anybody, except the two guns firing at each other without any apparent conclusion. Again just another simple exercise. The woods played quite an important role in much of the fighting in the area as it seemed they were occupied by various fighting groups. The anti-tank unit had occupied the woods to the West, at least until the Russians arrived. Now the woods to the North West contained Russians and those to our North Eastern boundary sheltered the Germans.

Just to casually look at the woods, there was no indication that they were concealing troops, in fact it was a picture of serenity and peace. Even when I had walked through them a few days earlier, there had been that same feeling. Apart from the pieces of discarded equipment, there was no evidence of occupation, although I was to receive visual proof that troops were still in hiding, at least, proof enough for me.

A day or so following the restrictions on our movements, I was feeling a trifle disconsolate, as nothing seemed to be happening as far as we were concerned. Anxious to have a fresh view of the outside world, I wandered casually along to one of the gates which was nearest to the woods on the North East corner. I stood for a while, just looking and thinking that it would be nice to roam through those trees once again. As I stood there, my attention was drawn towards a private car coming from the direction of the town. This was the first non-military vehicle I had seen for quite a while, apart from the Russian joy riders in the compound.

Just before it reached me, it pulled up on the grass verge and three or four soldiers got out. My first impression led me to think that they were part of our camp organisation who had borrowed a car to return to duty. Then I noticed that they were all carrying rifles or sub-machine guns and in addition had hand grenades in their belts. As I watched to see what they were about to do, three or four more saloon cars drew up.

These also disgorged armed soldiers who joined up with the first arrivals. I was still wondering why they had used civilian cars, when the newly assembled group, crossed the road at a jog trot and disappeared into the woods. If they were going on patrol instead of returning to camp, why the unorthodox form of transport? I didn't have time to find out. Having waited for a few minutes to see if they would reappear again, I heard unusual noises.

Because the trees muffled the sound, it took a few seconds to realise that they were coming from rifles and automatic weapons. It was very apparent that there was quite a skirmish taking place not so far from where I was standing and that I would be better off elsewhere. As I turned to retreat further into camp, I discovered that I would have something like fifty yards to traverse before I could gain cover of the nearest building. I wanted to run, but didn't do so, as that would have been giving way to panic, after all they weren't actually firing at me. Even so, there was a strange creepy feeling in my back as I walked away as quickly as dignity would allow.

A short while after this incident, I was visiting our newly established RAF Headquarters, which was not very far from the gate where I had witnessed the patrol entering the woods. Idly, I noted a group of maybe ten or more Russians being assembled on the opposite side of the road. By their manner and dress, they did not appear to be a regular fighting group, despite the fact that they were all armed with sub-machine guns. The person in charge, was having some difficulty in getting them into the order he desired. Although I did not pay particular attention to them, I did notice that they were quite disorganised and rather nondescript. There were so many people wandering around that a few more were hardly worthy of note.

Having dismissed them from my mind, I had turned and was talking to a companion. Quite suddenly, there was a burst of fire from an automatic weapon and my instant reaction was to drop to the ground. I knew without being told that the Germans had broken out of the nearby woods and we were under attack. I expected to hear a reply from the many people and soldiers who were carrying weapons, but nothing happened, there was not another shot fired. I was completely at a loss as to what was happening, so looked up to see where the Germans were. I was in for a big surprise, I was the only one lying on the ground. Other people were carrying on as normal, except perhaps for the one or two who were looking down at me in utter amazement. I glanced across at the armed group to see what action if any they had taken, They were still in the same place, but the leader was shouting at one member. Sheepishly I got to my feet, to be immediately questioned by my colleague. I explained the reason I had dropped to the ground, but instead of being understanding, he laughed at me.

He then told me what had happened as he had seen it all. As the group across the road were preparing to march off, one of them decided to move his sub-machine gun into a more comfortable position on his shoulder. Whether by accident or design, the safety catch was off and the gun ready to fire. As he hoisted the weapon, his finger caught the trigger, which fired off several rounds into the air. It was fortunate that he hadn't blown anyone's head off, although I cursed him for scaring me and making me look a fool. I wasn't really sure who the group were except that I was told that they were a firing squad brought in to carry out any executions deemed necessary.

It must not be imagined that life was one big horror day after day. Certainly I felt as others did, that life could be a great deal better, as some days were good and some bad. If they had all been bad, then I might have been reduced to a gibbering wreck cowering in my billet. I am sure if I had done so, I would have received little sympathy from my fellows. If I had been in such a state of nerves, I would certainly have stayed away from the boundary wire for safety.

As it was, I often went there to bask in the warm sunshine and at the same time gaze out over the fields and woods. There was often something different to see, maybe a few soldiers passing, or perhaps military vehicles on the road outside. One such day, standing by the wire, I saw a Jeep containing Russian officers driving towards me. They slowed down as if expecting something, then finally pulled up within a few feet of me.

They were not at all interested in my presence, but something that was coming towards them. I first felt, rather than heard the hoof beats on the grass and it wasn't until they were quite close, I could actually hear them. I was a little anxious as to what was about to happen as it seemed rather unusual. At last the horseman came into view and thankfully he was a Russian, so there was to be no violence. The thought had crossed my mind that it was an escaping German, then there would have been real trouble.

When the horseman was within feet of the Jeep, the driver held up his hand to command the horseman to stop. I was amazed at the reaction, the rider leaned on the reins and pulled the horse up from full gallop. The sheer power of the horse could be seen as well as felt as it started its deceleration. The rider had absolute control and sat on the horse as though glued to it. As the horse came to a standstill, the rider pulled him upright until he was standing on his hind legs and pawing the air. With a sharp pull on the reins, he twisted the horse round so that when it landed on all four feet again, it was pointing back towards the Jeep.

I had read about the cavalry, I had seen films depicting them and even seen stunt riders in fairgrounds, but this was a real cavalry officer in action. The incident in itself was of no great importance as it seemed that the officers in the Jeep had only stopped him to discuss something. What did impress me was seeing this rider at such close quarters as he had passed within six feet of me. I could well imagine foot soldiers facing a charge of such horsemen. I am sure it would have required a lot of courage and discipline to stay in place. Perhaps the thing that impressed me more was the control that the man had over the animal. This was quite a different aspect of life to me, as I had been brought up among ships, aircraft and things mechanical, whereas he probably lived on horseback.

As the horse and man went back in the direction they had arrived from, I envied him his skill and co-operation with such a powerful animal. I also knew now, that there were such things as Russian cavalry, I had actually seen one and this turned them into real people. The incident of the Cavalry officer, was a story book character come to life, and a new experience to store in my memory.

What I was to experience next had become very common place in recent times, Once again I was at the Headquarters office carrying out a minor duty. During a short break, I decided to walk down the road to the gate I had visited previously. There was nothing special about the road, except that it was the only direction I could walk without coming up against barbed wire. Another prisoner, also on duty, decided to accompany me. It was not our intention to stay away long and it was certainly not our intention to return as quickly as we did.

As we approached the gate, we saw several fighters diving, turning and climbing over a collection of buildings not far from the wire. My heart sank as I thought that the Germans had scored a victory somewhere and were doing their version of a 'Victory Roll'. It was very disturbing as the sight of German aircraft had been extremely rare of late. I couldn't understand though, why they were so low, as the local Russian forces could have shot them down fairly easily. To my mind it meant only one thing, German troops were again in the vicinity in force. I didn't really think that we personally were in immediate danger, all I felt was a sick feeling that the recent gains our allies had made were lost. I made some such comment to my companion, who was no moral help to me, as he readily agreed with my views.

We watched the aircraft for a minute or so, taking no pleasure from seeing them. Then I heard a strange intermittent noise, partly drowned by the aircraft engines. It was the sort of noise we had heard before and sounded very much like firing. Then we realised it was firing. Obviously the Russians had objected to their behaviour and were shooting at them using small arms. Strangely enough, the fighters continued as before and ignored the guns, or so it seemed. We watched, puzzled at this behaviour, until my companion said;
"They are not being fired at, they are doing the firing, but why?"
We pondered this a few seconds, as the situation seemed to become more and more confusing. Suddenly, he shouted in alarm;

"They are not Germans, they are RAF, run for cover, they may come this way!"
Without further ado, we ran as fast as we could, to put any sort of building between ourselves and the aircraft. No dignified retreat for me this time, no walking away as before, I wanted to run and did.

What we had mistaken for German FW 190s were RAF Typhoons carrying out a ground attack. They were completely unexpected, as in this sector we had seen only Russians or Germans. As a matter of fact, these were the first RAF aircraft I had seen at close quarters since being shot down, normally they were at twenty thousand feet or thereabouts.

Having regained our breath, we looked out to see if they were coming our way, but fortunately for us, they had completed their attack and departed. As it turned out, we had been in no immediate danger, even if we had stayed to watch as they did not get too close to where we had been standing. We were not to know that at the time of course, so had taken the wisest action. It was not always possible to avoid such an attack as normally they came without warning, in fact the element of surprise was essential for their own safety.

One such attack occurred one night while I was asleep. It all started with a dream, a dream so vivid that I can still recall the main features. In the dream, I was overlooking a very large city which I knew to be Berlin. It was night time, but the size of the city was defined by several small patches of light spread over a large area. The illumination could have come from street lighting or burning buildings, that wasn't too clear. Just then I became aware of the noise of an aircraft overhead. I looked up into the blackness but could see nothing, this bothered me, as I thought I should be able to. Suddenly the engine noise rose to a scream, so it was obviously in a very steep dive. The defenders whoever they were, switched on a searchlight and to distract the attacking fighter pilot, waved their hands in the beam so causing it to flicker. The fighter pilot was not put off, but continued his dive straight down the beam, firing at the searchlight. The aircraft now became visible and turned out to be an old biplane.

There was something amiss though as it was making too much noise for its type. The searchlight operators did not seem perturbed by his firing but continued their actions despite the risk to themselves. I was only an interested observer in all this and wondered if he would manage to hit the searchlight. I was not to find out, as without warning I received a violent jolt and felt myself being dragged sideways. I was awake in the instant to discover that I was being pulled from my blankets and then thrust roughly against the opposite wall. Someone held me down and ordered me to stay there. Something dangerous was happening, so I didn't argue but obeyed instructions.

I was thoroughly confused for the instant, although able to recover enough to see the shape of a night fighter hurtling past the window. He was not very far above our roof and the flashes from his guns reflected on the wall inside our room. Once the danger was past, I realised it was Tom who had dragged me out of bed and ordered me to stay still. Whereas I was only confused, he was very badly shaken. He had been awake and had heard the attack develop from the start, which made him realise the danger we were in, I was more fortunate, as I only heard the build up in my sleep, so to me it was only a dream. By the time I had realised what had happened, it was all over. I learned later that it was a JU 88 which had made the attack that night. I don't know what he was after, but no damage was done except to our nerves.

Another similar attack was made another night, but again there were no casualties. I did hear that a cannon shell blew a hole in the wall of the house once occupied by the German Camp Commandant, but that was about all. Such events as this became news for a while, but only to people directly affected, others were thinking about things they had seen or been involved in. I heard many stories, which to the person concerned, may have assumed major proportions, but to the listener, it was just one more story to be soon forgotten.

It was a strange life we were leading, as we listened to tales of robberies, murder, execution, looting, desertions and many more things, without being greatly troubled, unless of course it was likely to directly affect us. It was a way of life, not one of our choosing perhaps, but it was one which we were forced to make the best of. Some of the stories told, showed that the situation was becoming lawless, it also meant that we were very insecure and the sooner we were away from it the better.

Even though there were differing matters of importance to the individual, I think it fair to say that we all had two interests in common. The first of these was the urgent need of food, the second, the desire to be clear of this place and back into the civilised atmosphere of home. Nothing else mattered, unless it was one of survival. All other considerations took their place lower down the list of priorities and would be satisfied providing the first two aims were achieved.

In this frame of mind, the news that the Americans had arrived, spread like wildfire. This was a piece of news that anybody and everybody was prepared to listen to, The Americans were not a great force, only two war correspondents who had discovered us by accident. If they could get here, others were bound to follow, so we were as good as saved. To make certain of this, they promised that they would return to their own lines with the information as soon as possible. This was virtually a repeat of the Russian despatch rider's promise twelve days earlier. It was hoped that the Americans would be as quick to respond as the Russians had been. Excitement ran high, as something was moving at last. It was hoped very sincerely that they returned safely and did not get caught up with any fighting on the way.

The following day the fourth of May 1945 came the big news of an American convoy which was on its way and would arrive that evening. The following morning we were to climb aboard and be on our way to freedom. Some prisoners had not waited for this event, they had already started walking West. We were to be transported, while they had to proceed on foot, that was their misfortune for being impatient.

The day was a long one waiting for that convoy, then suddenly it appeared. What a sight it was, as I recall, there were something like one hundred and twenty trucks. They drove past the camp in a never ending stream to the wonder of the watching prisoners, I had never seen such a large convoy.

Next morning we were to wait for the trucks to reverse direction and drive up outside the camp on the main road. It was to be an early start which mattered little to us, all we wanted to do was leave. Most happy occasions are marked by a celebration and if I remember correctly, we celebrated this one by cooking the chicken. The way in which we came by the unfortunate bird was a story of daring and adventure, at least it was under the existing conditions. To describe the thing as a chicken would conjure up a false picture, as this one turned out to be a very mature hen.

A day or so earlier, someone had approached Tom and asked him the proper method to kill a chicken. As Tom had been a professional butcher in civil life, he was able to give this information. Naturally we were very curious, as we hadn't seen such a thing for a very long time, and asked the fellow if he had one. The answer was in the negative, but he was quite determined to go and look for one, now that he knew how to handle it.

He was feeling particularly hungry at the time and was anxious to keep his strength up. The man seeking the information was Dave the Canadian, the strong man who had separated the fighting French Canadians. We tried very hard to dissuade him from going on such a venture as it was still quite dangerous outside the wire. The Russians were not actually keeping us in, but there were still marauding German troops in the area as well as touchy Russian patrols, not to mention prisoners of various nationalities all out looking for food. As he was not to be deterred, he set out, fully briefed on the way to kill a chicken. He had promised that on his return, he would come to let us know how he had fared. He also promised that if he caught anything, he would share it with us.

We didn't care so much about the chicken, in fact we doubted very much that he would be able to catch one. We were more concerned about the state of his health, wandering about in the hostile outside world. We hoped that he would get back safely. We waited for an hour or so, but no sign of Dave, then another hour went by and still no sign. There was little we could do, except wait a bit longer then make a decision. After four hours, we became rather worried about him, as we were convinced that he had run foul of one or more of the dangers we had spoken of. At last we decided that we should report him missing, although we weren't sure what good it would do. People were frequently going missing whenever they decided to walk westwards and there were several already doing so.

Just when we had given up hope, our door burst open to reveal an extremely dishevelled but triumphant Dave carrying a chicken. He explained that he had borrowed a bicycle from an unsuspecting German civilian and had set off on his quest. He cycled for a while before he saw a chicken ahead of him which he was determined to catch. He set off in pursuit and chased it down the road at high speed, then as the hen attempted to get through the hedge, he had jumped off the bicycle and grabbed it. He then tucked it under his arm and prepared to kill it in the approved manner.

He was surprised when he heard angry German voices on the other side of the hedge, so in haste, he leaped onto the bicycle. Riding as fast as he could, he tore down the road, with the chicken squawking like mad. Not wishing to attract too much attention, he realised he had to silence the bird. He didn't want to stop in case the owners caught up with him, so did the next best thing. Letting go of the handlebars, he grabbed the chicken by the neck and silenced it. Due to his initial meandering round the country roads, then his final wild flight, he lost his way completely. This accounted for his protracted outing as it had taken him a very long time to find his way back to camp.

We were very pleased to see him, chicken or no chicken, even so we were interested in his escapade. Tom looked at the chicken and asked how it had been killed. He was assured it had been done in the approved manner with two fingers either side of the neck and thumb at the base of the skull. Tom was very puzzled and looked at the bedraggled thing Dave was carrying.
"Where has the head gone?" he asked.
"Oh," said Dave. "I was in such a hurry I pulled it completely off. If you want it, I've got it in my pocket."
I was startled by this statement and even Tom was a bit shocked, despite his experience as a butcher.

By the time Dave had returned with the chicken, it was too late to eat it that day, so it was put aside for another time. I felt that now we had the thing, it was going to create a problem cooking it because no one seemed particularly anxious to do so. When it became obvious that we were about to leave the camp, it meant that the bird had to be cooked, or ditched. No one was prepared to waste food, so that is how I finished up cooking it, someone had to.

Was this prize of a day or so before to be our final prison camp meal, it seemed so, although it was almost too good to be true. I had agreed that I would do my best with the cooking, but knew it was not going to be an easy task , through lack of the proper facilities. All our cooking equipment had either been destroyed or left behind at Luft 7 which presented me with my first problem. After hunting around, I found or borrowed a baking dish of sorts, certainly not up to the standard I was used to. The second problem was the construction of a cooking fire, which I solved by placing two house bricks about six inches apart, then building a fire between them. The baking dish rested insecurely on the bricks as it was in constant danger of being blown off by the wind. I wished I could have done the cooking under shelter, but there was no place to do so.

Having built my fire and greased the pan, I wondered how I was to cook a large bird in such a shallow dish, as the sides were only one inch high. Not only was the dish shallow, it was badly made and I discovered, it also leaked. The only answer was to break the chicken up into small pieces, then pile them all into the dish. Having done this and made sure the fire was burning well, I settled down to my appointed task, then it rained. I was not going to be beaten, so leaned over the cooking, to keep the rain off. This was not a particularly comfortable attitude, as it meant kneeling down in the dirt. Anyone watching me, must have thought I was insane, I certainly thought I was. My main concern was to prevent the chicken being ruined. I needn't have worried, I had already done just that. After a while, my attitude which I had adopted in leaning over the fire, plus the inclement weather, made me decide to speed up the cooking process. Just to make sure that I killed any bugs which may have collected on the meat, I baked the pieces until they were black all over. That was when I called it a day and pronounced the meal ready.

The inside was almost raw, as I knew it had to be, although those who helped me eat it, were kind enough to declare that it was very good. Somehow it was not as I remembered chicken served up for Christmas dinner at home. I don't think that it mattered what we had to eat that last evening, as we knew that very soon, we would be eating as much as we wanted once we were freed.

We were so full of confidence, that when fate dealt the next blow, we were stunned into disbelief. The Russians had decided that we were not leaving on the American convoy. This was something we simply could not understand. We were no use to the Russians as far as we could see, in fact we were more of a nuisance to them. Whatever we thought, the Russians had control over us and we were not leaving in the morning. According to the story that we were given, the Russians were not satisfied with the credentials of the American Colonel in charge of the convoy. Before we could be released, proper authorisation would have to be obtained from Supreme Allied Headquarters. The Colonel was to remove his men and equipment from Russian territory within twenty four hours. If he failed to do so, then he and his men would be imprisoned and his vehicles impounded.

This story may have been embellished a little by those who conveyed the message, although there was a ring of truth in the statement. There was no doubt that the convoy was to return without us, but as for arresting the Americans, this may have been more of a threat than an intention. Whether the last part of the statement was true or not, it certainly caused a lot of concern, as had it been carried out, we could have become involved in a nasty political or possibly military confrontation.

Having resigned ourselves to this serious set-back, our interest was re-awakened by the whisper that we might leave after all. Before the Americans left in the morning, they were intending to make a big detour, so that the convoy was pointing in the right direction for their return journey. By doing this, they would be able to drive along past the camp again. Once there, they would halt briefly to enable those who wanted, to take the chance to climb aboard. Tom and I discussed it a while, then decided that we would go, as the situation in camp was becoming intolerable.

When morning came, with our kit packed, we waited for the appointed time that the convoy was to appear. To our great relief, the trucks drove up and halted as promised. This was a great moment as we headed for the convoy, one we had waited so long for. I must admit I was a little apprehensive, as I wondered if there was anything which could stop us now. We had suffered so many setbacks in the past, I was beginning to accept them as being quite natural. This may have been rather a pessimistic view perhaps, but one born of bitter experience.

There was something else to consider, as what we were doing was completely opposed to the order given by the Russians. We were not alone in this flagrant disobedience as other prisoners were flocking out in droves through a gap in the wire. The two hundred yards that we had to walk to the trucks seemed a very long way. I was afraid they would leave before Tom and I got there, I wanted to run I was so anxious, but restrained myself to a fast walk. At last we arrived at a partly filled truck and proceeded to climb aboard, helped by those already there. In no time at all, our vehicle was full and so were the others in front of us.

Strangely enough no one was moving yet, despite the fact that it was only supposed to be a brief stop. Then I realised that a disturbance was taking place somewhere further down the line. Then I saw it, a cordon of armed Russian soldiers moving into place. Their object was very plain indeed, they were there to stop the convoy moving. Then came the order to disembark as we were not going anywhere. Seeing that some prisoners were reluctant to leave, a few rounds were fired over our heads, as a form of encouragement to do as we were told.

The sight of several soldiers pointing guns at us, was spur enough and we left our vehicle much quicker than we had got into it. We needed no further prompting to return to our old billets as it seemed much safer there than with the convoy. Finally, after a delay while the vehicles were searched, the convoy moved off, watched by many prisoners whose hearts were very heavy indeed.

Some time later, I met a prisoner who had remained hidden in one truck, underneath the driver's seat. He managed to avoid being caught and finally arrived at the American lines. I considered that he had risked a lot, bearing in mind the mood of the Russians at the time. Now that the Americans had gone, what hope was there for the future, there was nothing for us to look forward to. I personally felt that whatever happened, the Russians would not permit the Americans to enter their territory again. Thus started a new era in our lives, with a mood of despair and despondency.

CHAPTER 26

Had anyone asked me what I thought life would be like should I be taken prisoner at any time, I would have said that it would be humdrum. I imagined I would sit in a wired off compound until hostilities ceased, then I would return home. Life would have been simple and boring. How little did I know what it would really be like. Since being shot down, my life seemed to have moved along in quite definite stages, each stage starting with hope and ending in disappointment. Perhaps disappointment was too mild a work for the black despair I had been plunged into from time to time.

The first stage had been the actual event of being shot down and surviving, only to realise that I was trapped on a roof. Then the escape from the roof and the days of evasion which ended in eventual capture. This was followed by our time in prison camp, buoyed up by the thought that the Russians were bound to catch up with us soon. To our despair, we were removed from that risk at the last minute. Our march westwards started off in hope, as I knew we would end up by being released, or at least I hoped so, but it finished in another prison camp. The arrival of the Russians a few weeks later and the realisation that we were not being freed.

The most recent stage, the arrival of the Americans who were going to take us home but had to go back without us. Now the latest stage, this was quite different to other stages, it had started badly, so how would it end? This was a most depressing period for the majority of us as we no longer had any hope. Hope was a factor which helped so many to survive the march, the hope that we would finally be saved. Now we were deserted by everyone, as both the Russians and the Americans had failed to come up to expectations and we remained captive.

It was very difficult to imagine that there was anything which could help us in any way. The Americans were unlikely to return for various reasons and the Russians were either too busy, or too disinterested to arrange our release. Whereas in the past we had attempted to organise our lives to make things more comfortable and interesting, now, there was no sense in attempting to arrange anything. It was mainly a case of survival, until something was done to improve our situation.

We obviously couldn't stay long as we were, the Russians would have to do something. There was the possibility of course that we could be moved East into Russia, although that seemed unlikely. In fairness, it was difficult to imagine that we had much of a priority in the Russians' plans. They were attempting to look after their own forces and at the same time run a war. German troops were still fighting them and they also had to control the civilian population in the captured towns.

Another thing to add to their problems, a large number of Displaced Persons, or DPs as they were known, were roaming westwards. These people were civilians of many different types, who had been transported from their homes by the Germans and forced to work wherever they were needed. Others had been made homeless by the war and had nowhere to go. Large numbers were beginning to congregate in our camp, but whether they came of their own accord, or were directed, I don't know. They were of various nationalities collected from all over Europe, adults and children, even babes in arms. These may have been families although it was difficult to tell. Some undoubtedly were rogues and vagabonds, while others were genuine workers, skilled and unskilled, but to me, they all looked the same. I didn't understand them at all and felt that it was better not to become involved with any of them. Many of these people suffered greatly and led very unnatural lives in the recent years, as a result they had become extremely hardened in their outlook on life. They seemed to regard us with as much suspicion as we regarded them, as in all probability they didn't know who we were and what is more, most likely didn't care.

My attitude toward them was more instinctive than fair as they were after all, still human beings, who were generally lost and bewildered. They were mainly a collection of individuals who had been forced to live together by circumstance. We in our turn were better off as at least we belonged to an official organisation and were treated as such.

As they arrived, they were allocated the billets which we had originally occupied, where it seemed they were all humped in together for a communal form of living. It was difficult to imagine what was to become of them, as in many cases, they had no home to go to, they really were displaced persons. Although it seemed unlikely at the time, we could have been sent home, as this would have relieved the increasing problem of hungry hordes, but we remained.

The billets we had moved into were more civilised than the original places, as now I had a bunk to sleep in. It was little compensation for remaining where we were, but at least it was more comfortable. The food however didn't improve and we were still as hungry as ever. It is true that there were not so many to feed as there had been, but there was still not enough for those who remained. Some of those who had left us, did so because of sickness and were removed to hospital, others did so by choice. When it became apparent that we were not being officially evacuated, many prisoners decided to take matters into their own hands and just walked out through the wire. The Russians made no apparent attempt to stop them, but our own RAF authorities did. I was told, as were others, that no one was to leave camp in an attempt to walk home. Those who did so, were liable to be court martialled.

I gathered that one reason for the order was the danger that the prisoners were running, through being unprotected in any way. Fighting was still taking place, also there were many roving bands of people, who had no allegiance to anybody. The whole place had turned into a chaotic state without any laws, except by those imposed by guns or some other means of force.

I did meet up with at least one prisoner who had decided to make his own way home, his experience was quite a novel one. According to his story, once out on the road, he waved down an approaching truck which stopped to pick him up. On board were two or three Russian soldiers who were very pleased to meet him. As well as he could, he explained by sign language that he was aiming to get back to England and apparently in agreement, they started off westwards. He was treated like a friend and given food to eat, as well as being liberally supplied with vodka.

He in his turn, was very pleased with his new found companions and attempted to find out where they were taking him, but without success. He realised that it was not possible to travel too far West without coming across American troops and was very surprised when he saw none. This state of affairs lasted for two days, with the Russians remaining as friendly as ever. However much he tried he was unable to find out where he was. By this time he started to get very worried with the situation and wished that he had never become involved, then to his surprise, they stopped the truck and indicated that he was to get out.

As soon as he had done so, the truck drove off with the happy Russians, leaving him completely bewildered. Having no idea of his position, he decided to keep on walking westwards to see what would happen. The further he walked, the more confused he became, as he had the feeling that the surroundings were familiar. Then the awful truth dawned on him, the Russians had dropped him off at the spot they had picked him up two days earlier, he was just outside the camp.

I know that not all those who walked had such strange experiences, at least a friend of mine, a glider pilot by the name of Steve Garrett made it safely. He managed to get back and then inform my family that last time he had seen me I was fit and well. If he had said safe, he would not have been telling the truth, as I thought that we were far from safe. Shortly after the departure of the Americans, news was passed around that the Russians were intending to evacuate us. The information was rather vague and not really reliable enough to build hopes on. So often in the past had our hopes been dashed that we were now becoming very wary. It was rather difficult to imagine that the Russians would be prepared to transport us when they had refused to let the Americans do so.

It would have saved them a lot of time and effort, but now they would have to assemble a similar convoy. To me it seemed impractical and unlikely, which I believe was an opinion shared by others. There was no time given for our supposed departure, which was little help to us and our morale. It may seem that we were being impatient, I am sure we were, but in our position, a day was a month long and we wanted everything to be done immediately. There was little appreciation of what was happening in the outside world, just a few rumours, or what ever it was that we could actually witness. The Americans may have been trying to arrange authorisation to move us and the Russians might have been attempting to assemble a convoy, it just wasn't apparent from our limited viewpoint.

Although things had gone against us, it did no good to stand by the wire and will a relieving convoy to appear, some other way of occupying our minds had to be found. It was very fortunate that quite near to the camp, was a deep water filled quarry, surrounded by grassy banks and shrubs. It was only a few minutes walk from our billet and we discovered a very pleasant spot in which to spend an hour or so. By this time the weather had turned very warm indeed, so warm in fact, that people were swimming in the quarry. No one had reported it to be safe or even clean, but it seemed alright, so we decided to try it. It was not really a place for a non swimmer as the water was something like one hundred feet deep, fine providing you didn't attempt to touch the bottom.

This became a favourite spot for us and quite often, a small group would gather for a swim. We would find a quiet place where we could undress and enter the water without being disturbed or disturbing other nationals who had similar ideas. As I recall, there was little if any communication between us. Frenchmen and Dutchmen kept to themselves, so did the English. In fact we virtually remained in isolation from one another. It could have been that the language was a barrier, as sign language was hardly the thing to use for a social gathering, it was too big a strain. In my experience, it was only ever used when it became essential to exchange information.

It may sound cynical, but as so often happens, our pleasant visits became rather spoiled, partly due to some of the Displaced Persons. There was no reason why they shouldn't visit the place, they were quite entitled to do so. It was the women who spoiled it, as they would sometimes stroll round the quarry quite unexpectedly. As we had no swimming costumes, we had to keep a constant look out for them. Should they appear while we were in the water, we would be forced to stay where we were until they had gone. If we were sunbathing, we would have to grab for our clothes. It may not have bothered some nationals but it certainly did us, we were not so uninhibited as they were. I got the impression that at times the women did it just to annoy us. It may well have been very amusing for them to see our reactions particularly bearing in mind the sort of communal life they were forced to live.

The women were a bit of a nuisance who could be avoided with care, but the real disturbance came from the Russians. At first it was not apparent what was happening, except that a couple of Russian soldiers walked down to the water's edge and threw something in. It seemed a very strange thing to do, particularly as they stood and stared at the spot where the object had entered the water. Within seconds it became quite apparent what it was, as with a bang, a hand grenade exploded under water. I didn't know what effect this would have had on us should we have been swimming and I certainly wasn't prepared to find out.

True to say, no one was in there at the time, but later, when ever the Russians appeared, the swimmers disappeared. They did not visit the place often, which was just as well because of the possible danger. It did mean however that we had to keep a look out for them as well. I could not make up my mind if the soldiers had a purpose in using grenades, or whether it was just idle amusement. If it was the former then the purpose wasn't obvious and if the latter, then it displayed an irresponsible attitude.

If they were being irresponsible, I would have expected disciplinary action to be taken against them, although the more I saw of these troops, I realised that their form of discipline was totally different to ours. There seemed to be little or no formality between the ranks, in fact it was all very easy going. Despite this attitude, I felt that those in charge, would when necessary, impose rigid control on their junior ranks. From what I had observed, it seemed that a Russian soldier had few restrictions to contend with. Providing his actions did not meet with disapproval from his superiors, all was well. Should he do something wrong, then his punishment was quick and severe.

I saw one example of the attitude between the ranks, which surprised me considerably. It happened while I was on duty at the RAF Headquarters office. On this occasion, a Jeep drove up with three Russians on board, two were officers and the third, an ordinary soldier acting as an armed escort. The officer who was passenger, climbed out of his seat and walked towards the office. We were quite taken by surprise and failed to salute him as he passed, we had not realised until too late, that he held a very high rank. If he had been British, we would have received a swift rebuke for failing to recognise him.

The driver who was a junior officer had not bothered to move, but had remained in his driving seat. The armed escort watched the senior officer depart, then climbed from the Jeep in a leisurely manner. With apparent lack of concern, he removed his rifle from his shoulder and propped it against the wall. Having done this, he took out his cigarettes, lit one, then relaxed against the wall next to his rifle. I could visualise the scene had this been a British trio who had arrived, there would have been plenty of stamping and saluting, while everyone else stood to attention. This was quite a big contrast and we were amazed at the casual display we had witnessed. It may be that when in an operational theatre, our troops are more relaxed with each other, although I doubt if it would happen to the same extent.

As the driver had nothing to do but wait, two of us decided to see if we could communicate with him. We were pleasantly surprised to discover that he spoke quite good English and was willing to talk. To open the conversation we asked him what he thought of the Jeep he was driving. He remarked that it was quite a good vehicle and did what was required of it. We then asked if he was grateful that the Americans had supplied them with such good equipment. This took the smile off his face as he promptly told us it was Russian. We tried again thinking that he had misunderstood, but there was no misunderstanding, it was a Russian vehicle, built in Russia, for Russian use. It was our turn to be astounded and pointed to a plate printed in English, which quite clearly stated the place of manufacture in the United States. Not to be outdone, he explained that it was very simple, the plate engraved in English meant that the particular vehicle had been built for export to America.

Nothing could persuade him that the majority of tanks or trucks they were using in that sector were American, so we dropped the subject. This did not end our conversation, far from it as he continued to speak to us about their tactics. We found this quite interesting, as we had little knowledge of fighting on the ground. Our conversation was terminated quite abruptly, when the senior officer appeared. He climbed into the passenger seat without any ceremony and waited to be driven off. The armed escort, not particularly disturbed by the appearance of his superior, quite casually put out his cigarette, then just as casually, climbed into the back of the Jeep. Once aboard, they shot off, and that was that.

Not everyone had such agreeable meetings with the Russians, the Germans would vouch for that, although I was rather thinking of those like ourselves, who were their allies. One such person felt that he had been rather harshly treated by them and was so incensed, he came to us for sympathy. He was a Belgian soldier who had been living in town with a German girl. On that particular day, the Russians had come into the house, discovered who he was, kicked him out then moved in themselves. We asked him how it was that he lived in town, as wasn't he supposed to be a prisoner, or had he left the Belgian army? He replied that he was still a soldier, but preferred living in town to staying in camp. He divulged that not only had he been living there for three years, he had also been working for the Germans. He couldn't understand why we agreed with what the Russians had done as he had deserved all that he got. It was felt that his values had become rather distorted since being captured.

By this time, there were many people gathered together, all receiving some sort of shelter and protection within our camp boundaries. They differed widely in their sympathies, as well as in their nationalities. There were a few like the Belgian who were unable to decide whether they were prisoners or civilians. Then there were collaborators who had been left behind by the Germans and felt rather insecure. The majority however were genuine prisoners of war who intended to remain as such, until returned to their own countries. Finally mixed in with everyone else, were the Displaced Persons. These people could have been anybody, as unlike those in uniform, they could not be classified. As suggested earlier, not all of these people were from forced labour camps, some were of doubtful origin, but who would know what they were, once they had mixed in with the genuine DPs.

This hotchpotch of humanity, was an unhappy and dissatisfied group, whose main aim was to return to a normal life as soon as possible. Normal life meant food, clothing, houses, jobs, in fact many of the things taken for granted, that is until they are no longer available. Many were without hope, but fortunately we did not fall into that category as there was a slight possibility that we would be repatriated eventually.

Then came the end of the war in Europe, so that was it finished, now we could go home, but how? Things hadn't changed one little bit as far as we were concerned, we were still living behind wire, we were still being guarded by the Russians and we were still hungry. The day that the announcement was made, should have been one of great rejoicing as we had been waiting for it a long time. It had been nearly six years since the outbreak of war, which had developed into a very harsh and disastrous struggle, but now it was over.

My reaction was a feeling of depression and anti-climax. I don't know why, but in the past I had imagined that the announcement that the war had ceased, would have been a real day to remember, a day when everything would suddenly be put right. Of course, common sense should have told me that it wouldn't be at all like that. The day was so flat and miserable, that after dark a few of us decided that we had to have a small celebration. We had no music, no drink, no food or fireworks, in fact none of the things that people would normally celebrate with, although we could have a bonfire. In no time at all, pieces of derelict hut were blazing away in a little heap on the ground, while we stood round, wondering what we were doing there.

Our celebration did not last very long as it was rapidly terminated by two Russian soldiers who were on patrol. At first, we saw them waving and shouting, but ignored them, as we didn't understand what they wanted. When they loosed off a few rounds we understood and put the fire out very quickly, which seemed to be the right thing to do. We discovered it was no good us celebrating Victory in Europe, that was only for the politicians, the Russians were still fighting. The Germans hanging on with grim determination, had retained a few pockets of resistance in the area.

Feeling even more depressed, we broke up the gathering and retired to our billets, sunk in our own private thoughts. There is little that can be said about the days that followed, except that we waited to see if the Russians were going to move us. There was little to do and no inclination to look for anything to do. We simply waited.

Finally approximately five weeks after the Russians had first taken over, we were given the order to prepare for departure. They had assembled a convoy and were ready to transport us to the Americans. There seemed to be a condition however, that we would only be taken as far as the river Elbe and no further. On arrival at the meeting place, we would be handed over to the Americans providing that there were a specified number of Russian prisoners to be given in exchange. I am not sure where these prisoners were coming from, but our Russian caretakers required a very high exchange rate in bodies.

From this information, I got the impression that we were in fact being used as a basis for bargaining, in other words we were hostages. I don't know how true or official the information was, I only know the depressing effect it had on me. Although I had been told we were leaving, it was difficult to appreciate or even believe. There had been so many setbacks, that it would have caused no surprise to me if we had arrived at the Elbe and even then been turned back.

I began to feel in a way that it didn't matter anymore, we weren't going home and that was the end of it. Home and country were becoming remote and the whole affair had taken on an air of fantasy. Our main concern was the lack of food and clothing, there was nothing unreal about that.

A secondary requirement was to leave the camp as soon as possible and never return to it, almost anywhere would do as long as we didn't stay where we were. To me, this camp had been a harsh place, quite unlike Luft 7 at Bankau. That had not been a holiday camp, far from it, although there were some pleasant and some amusing memories as well as unpleasant ones. The most important feature was the law and order we had been governed by. Not all of this was imposed by the Germans, as we originated much of it ourselves. Some of the rules were made from necessity, while others just developed naturally as the requirement became apparent. It had become very obvious, that where no laws existed they had to be created, as life was very difficult if not impossible without them.

Our stay at Luckenwalde had deteriorated into an existence where there were few if any laws, unless they were those of the jungle. The appearance of the Russian convoy was proof that they now intended to move us out of Luckenwalde. As far as I was concerned, it couldn't happen quickly enough. As I climbed into the truck which was supposedly taking me to freedom, I felt little emotion, in fact it was not much better than the feeling I had experienced on the day that hostilities officially ceased.

There was a vague feeling that perhaps this was something different and we really were going somewhere. Where this was to end, no one could say, but as long as it didn't finish up back at camp again, it wasn't too important.

I remember that in our particular truck, there were thirty souls packed into a twenty-five man capacity. True, we had little or no kit, which was just as well and as it was a nice warm day, it didn't matter that there was no cover on the back, in fact it was a good thing, as we were able to view the passing scenery. When at last we started moving out, my thoughts were on what lay ahead of us, was the future to be better or worse? I hoped it would be for the better.

Once away from the camp, we found ourselves driving through open country on a rather bumpy road. This was not very comfortable for those sitting down and even less so for those standing up, as the springing was not up to limousine standards. Things could have been a lot better had we not been so hungry. As I recall, no rations were issued, neither was there a promise of any. To add to my personal discomfort, I soon became very thirsty, but unfortunately we carried no water or any other liquid with which I could slake my thirst.

After driving for some time, I noticed that we were approaching a village and that the vehicles immediately ahead of us had stopped. I was curious about this, particularly as several women were standing by the roadside, apparently passing things up to the prisoners in the trucks. As we got closer, it all became clear, as then I could see that they had milk churns from which they were serving out refreshing drinks. There was no food unfortunately, simply the drinks, but even that would be very welcome.

Finally the truck ahead of us pulled away and it was our turn to be served. The women seemed very anxious to please us, although we had no idea what they were saying. I suspected that they were Russian workers imported to carry out domestic duties. They were all very strong looking women and seemed more suited to being behind a plough than doing fancy needlework, or playing with children. Despite their rugged appearance, there was no doubting their pleasure at being able to help us.

As soon as we had stopped, cups were passed up to us, filled with a cool white liquid. Gratefully I accepted mine and was about to take a drink, when I noticed that others were hesitating. I could see nothing wrong as it looked quite fresh, then I tasted it. What a shock I received, as instead of cool fresh milk, it was buttermilk. I had never seen it before and didn't even know that it could be drunk. I don't quite know how to describe the taste, as I thought it to be among other things, sour, bitter and watery. A poor description perhaps, but I do know it made me feel sick. I still had a cupful of the stuff and I considered how I could get rid of it. I looked over the side of the truck at the serving woman, in the hope that when their attention was directed elsewhere I would be able to pour it away. No such luck, several of them were gazing up at us, pleased to think that we were enjoying their offerings. I tried to pass my cup onto anyone who would take it, but their reaction was the same as mine, they had suffered the torture, now it was my turn.

I then noticed that one of the women, by using sign language, was urging me to drink up quickly, then hold up her hand, ready to receive the cup when I had emptied it. I gathered from this that there was a shortage of drinking utensils and not wishing to deny anyone refreshment, I attempted to oblige. Steeling myself against the taste of the liquid, I swallowed it as quickly is possible. Thankfully I leaned down and handed my empty cup to the waiting woman. In an instant, she handed me another full one, then stood back to watch me enjoy that one as well.

Even if I had been able to speak fluent Russian, I would not have dared to explain how I felt about the drink as they were all so obviously pleased to be doing something for us. I would not have upset their feelings for anything as I felt that this was a little oasis of friendliness in an unfriendly world. How I managed that second cup I just don't know and no one was more pleased than I, when our driver started his engine and we moved off. As we left, the woman who had done their best for us, unable to communicate by word of mouth, grinned broadly and waved until we were out of sight. They must have had a busy morning as there were several hundred to be served.

After several miles of hot, dusty and bumpy roads, I wished that we could find a good road surface to drive on. Then I had my wish as we turned onto an autobahn and I began to regret that we had done so. This was a real joy to the driver, as foot down, he hurtled along the road, at what seemed like full throttle. It wasn't only the speed which bothered me, it was also the debris spread over the road surface. This caused our driver to swerve from side to side so as to avoid some of the larger pieces. At high speed, I didn't think it was quite the thing to do.

Every so often, the convoy was halted for no apparent reason and we just waited on the road until told to move again. The stops were not of long duration, maybe ten minutes or so, but every time they occurred, our Russian driver left his vehicle, laid down on the roadside and went to sleep. We couldn't make up our minds if he was very tired or very drunk, but tended to believe he was drunk by the way he was driving. It was as well for us that the roads were deserted apart from our convoy, otherwise we might never have made it, as I am sure we would have had an accident.

I have described the collection of vehicles as a convoy, but that was not quite the right description for them. They were quite widely spaced and I got the impression that each driver was acting independently, intent on getting to the rendezvous at his own speed. The stops we made, were essential to enable the road ahead to be checked for booby traps or surface damage as there were numerous holes in the road. The irregular spacing between vehicles, may have been done to minimise the risk of ambush as without doubt, anyone attempting to predict the arrival of a particular vehicle would have been presented with difficulties.

The journey along the autobahn was a very strange one and proved to be quite eventful. The first thing that affected me was the uncanny atmosphere of driving down a major highway and finding it empty. As just mentioned, our convoy was the only thing on the road and because of the way it was spread out, quite often we were completely on our own. I knew there were vehicles ahead and behind but not being able to see them, meant they weren't there. I had the same feeling then as I had experienced on occasions during the march, we were the only living things left on earth. There was no other sign of life, except ourselves, there were no birds, animals or humans and if it hadn't been for the debris left by humans, they may have never existed. Everything was silent and still, an atmosphere which became slightly oppressive whenever we made our stops.

After travelling several miles, we approached a bridge which was carrying a minor road over the autobahn. There was something very odd about it as it didn't look the same as the others we had passed under. When we got closer, it was realised that the bridge had been made unsafe, by the simple method of blowing a gap about a foot wide, across each end. This was definitely a trap for the unwary, particularly anyone using the road in the dark. It would have appeared safe even from a short distance, as it had not collapsed onto the road below, but remained balanced on a central pier. As we drew nearer I expected our driver to slow down, on the contrary, he decided to proceed as usual and thundered on under the bridge fairly close to the vehicle in front. I was sure I would see it topple at any time, but it remained where it was. Presumably it stayed there until the whole convoy got through, as no one made any comment afterwards, except to say that they had seen it. If the Germans had left such things as this, I thought of others they could have left for our benefit and hoped that we would not be caught by them. There was nothing that I could do personally, except make sure I was careful.

For some time we had been travelling through pine forests and noticed huge palls of smoke in the distance, billowing up from the trees. I know the weather was quite hot, but not so hot as to cause forest fire. Because of the distance, it was not possible to determine how they may have started. It could have meant that military action was taking place, or had just recently done so. If that was the case, I hoped that we would not become involved.

Before long, our interest was taken by the sight of craters in the road which we were forced to negotiate. Some reasonably small ones caused by shells were little hindrance, but the bigger bomb craters made our vehicle leave the road and drive past on the grass verge. One part of the road we came to presented quite a problem as a huge section had been blown away. This had not been caused by bombs, but by demolition teams, who had destroyed the section which crossed a deep gully. It seemed that the only way to overcome the difficulty was to turn back, which could have meant a lengthy diversion. A discussion took place amongst the drivers, who decided that they would attempt to cross by means of a very steep rough track alongside the demolished roadway. When I saw the inclines that were to be tackled, I considered that there was little chance of success.

As our vehicle moved into position at the top of the downward slope, we were ordered out and told to follow it down. Once at the bottom, it would require every man from the truck, to help push it up the other side. I don't know exactly how deep the gully was, probably about one hundred feet and the distance across something like two hundred yards. However deep or wide it was, it was going to be a very difficult and risky task.

I watched as our truck left the road and entered the downward track which was so steep, I expected to see it slide down out of control. From the driver's viewpoint, it must have been even more alarming, as he was in it. Very carefully he edged his way down until he reached the bottom, then after crossing the rough but comparatively level ground, he faced the upward slope. This was even more dangerous, as not only was the driver at risk should be slip backwards, so were we now, as we had the job of crowding around the truck and pushing.

After many arduous minutes and a great deal of exertion on our part, we once again reached level ground. The most credit though should be given to the driver, whose skill had made it possible. I looked back to see the next truck start its descent, thankful that we at least had made it safely and hoped that they would. Having traversed that difficult patch, we climbed aboard and once more hurtled off down the autobahn in pursuit of the others. If we thought then that our troubles were over we were mistaken, as there was more to come of a similar nature. On reflection, I doubt if many prisoners really thought that we had nothing else to face, as we had been so conditioned by troubles in the past, we began to assume it was the normal thing. In the back of my mind, was the thought of the biggest obstacle of all, the actual exchange of prisoners at the river Elbe, or the refusal by the Russians to do so. The first requirement of course was to get to the appointed place of meeting, although even that was beginning to appear as though it could be anything but plain sailing.

The further we progressed through the pine forests, the more apparent it became that we were getting very close to the fires we had sighted earlier. Soon I was to discover just how close, as rounding a bend, I could see that the trees bordering the right hand side of the road were well alight. It was not a very comforting sight to be faced with, partly because of the danger it presented and partly because it was burning unchecked with no one to fight it. Almost as soon as we reached the first of the fires we came across a huge bomb crater, so large that it filled the road. This was another major problem, as to our right was the burning forest and on the other side of the road, densely packed trees. I was really puzzled by the fact that there were no other vehicles in sight, they had all disappeared somewhere. While I was contemplating this fact, a Russian soldier stepped out into the road and directed us to turn onto a track which led into the forest. This was crazy, as didn't he know it was burning? Our dutiful driver turned as directed as though it was the most natural thing in the world and drove in amongst the trees along the forest track.

We had not gone far, before we turned parallel to the road along another track, where we continued for maybe two or three hundred yards. As I had been brought up in a city, the thought of seeing a forest fire had never entered my head, yet now I was getting my experience at very close quarters.

The atmosphere was decidedly unhealthy, as trees all around us were smouldering and here and there flames could be seen as bushes and undergrowth caught fire. On the ground, large areas blackened by ash, produced a lot of heat and smoke. I was very pleased when we had passed the crater without incident and were able to regain the road where we could breathe slightly less smoke laden air.

From then on, we seemed to be in the middle of one of the fire zones, and at times were hemmed in, as trees on both sides of the road were burning. I can't remember now how I heard it but I was told that the fires had been started, not by shells or bombs but by Russians with flame throwers trying to flush the Germans out of hiding.

Whatever the truth, it was giving us cause for concern as we didn't know what else to expect if we carried on in the same direction. We didn't have to wait long for the next difficulty, as another massive crater was seen in the road ahead. This one was even bigger than the last which again gave us the choice of entering the forest or turn back. Following the procedure we had adopted before, we turned off the road and drove down a comparatively wide track, presumably a fire break.

After driving into the forest for roughly two hundred yards, we were all getting a little concerned that we had been misdirected as things were becoming decidedly uncomfortable. It was at this stage, that someone reminded us that we were riding above a tank of petrol, not a healthy situation under the circumstances. Our driver seemed unconcerned and pressed on as though he did this sort of thing every day, maybe he did, but we weren't used to it.

By the time we had reached a point four hundred yards into the fire, things had become almost intolerable for us, but there was very little we could do, except to hope to come out of it soon. Just then, we came to a track which enabled us to head back towards the road and not before time for most of us. Just as we were negotiating the corner, one of our party exclaimed loudly in disbelief. We wondered what he had seen and crowded to his side of the truck to share in his startling discovery.

There on the ground, amid all the smouldering and burning trees, sat two Russian soldiers, contentedly puffing away on cigarettes. Somehow, the sight of those two, made me feel that perhaps things weren't quite a bad as I imagined and we weren't all going to suffocate or burn to death. Even so, I was extremely thankful when we finally reached the road again. Fortunately that was the last of the forest fires we were to encounter although it was a little while before we realised it.

The most disturbing thing that I had seen through that particular stretch of forest, was the sight of a charred corpse, bloated to an outlandish size. I thought that possibly he was the victim of a flame thrower although without experience of these weapons I couldn't be sure, The nationality was not readily apparent although I thought he was German. Why, I wondered, had he been dumped by the roadside and was he the only one, or were there more like him in the forest?

After several hours driving, we pulled into a large open area and joined the vehicles of the convoy which had preceded us. This apparently was as far as the Russians were to take us, which seemed strange, as we were in the middle of nowhere. In time other trucks arrived and we were all assembled. During this period, we had to remain in the trucks and wait, although what we were waiting for remained a mystery. I did notice that we were parked quite near a river, which I assumed was the Elbe. I had expected something much bigger and more imposing. On the other side of the river was another large convoy and the insignia on their vehicles denoted that they were Americans.

Nothing happened for a while, until some Americans left their convoy and approached the Russians. To do this, they had to cross the river on floating pontoons, which to me looked rather insecure, I could see no sign of a bridge or any evidence that there had been one, so this presumably had been a ferry crossing point. I had the feeling that something was wrong, as there was no sign of the three or four thousand Russian prisoners which were supposedly to be offered in exchange. I thought there was a feeling of mistrust in the air and a rather sullen atmosphere. I may have imagined this, although I don't think so. The lack of exchange prisoners bothered me, but I couldn't really believe that the Russians would take us back at this late stage.

At last the Americans broke off from the conference they were having and waved to their vehicles to cross the river. When the whole of the convoy had driven across to the East side, they were directed on to a loop road. This brought them round until they were heading towards the river again. This couldn't be right, they weren't leaving without us, although it certainly seemed like it.

We hadn't moved, but were still in the Russian trucks during this procedure. Just as the leading American truck reached the river again, the convoy was halted and the order given for us to disembark, then board the American vehicles. This was done under the watchful eye of armed Russian guards. The atmosphere remained tense and our American driver seemed quite edgy. I don't know if he was expecting trouble as he gave no sign of pleasure at seeing us. As each vehicle was loaded, it was allowed back across the river by the pontoons, then told to wait until the rest had completed the crossing.

While waiting on the West bank, we asked about the Russian prisoners who were supposed to have arrived with the Americans, but our driver knew nothing of such an arrangement. We then requested that the canvas cover be removed from the back of the truck as we wanted to be able to see where we were going. This was refused, as we were told we had to remain under cover. I don't know if this was a general order, but no amount of argument would make our driver change his mind. He told us that we weren't really safe yet, as we were still well inside Russian held territory. The covers could and would be removed on arrival in American territory and not before.

I had often tried to imagine what our release would be like, quite a noisy, happy occasion. Allied troops would enter camp, the guards would surrender quietly, there would be cheering, smiles and handshakes all round, followed by our rapid transportation home. This was proving to be nothing like it. The process was a long drawn out affair, attended by a great deal of uncertainty. There was no jubilation of any kind and very few smiles, in fact many prisoners faces showed concern.

Finally, our truck started up and we moved on for yet another stage in our long journey. This time I hoped to freedom and home, although I still wasn't convinced and felt no elation. As there was little that we could see, there is nothing to say about that section of the journey, except that I suffered a feeling of insecurity. When eventually the covers were removed, we were able to breathe more freely, not only because we had more air, but we assumed that we were then in American held territory.

With the ability to see what was going on in the outside world, it came as something of a shock to discover evidence of recent fighting in the area. Several times I saw graves of soldiers, buried where they had fallen, with their steel helmets resting on the burial mound and a simple cross to identify them. Possibly a common enough sight to a soldier, but to those of us who fought our war in the air, we seldom if ever, saw such things.

After driving for approximately two hours since leaving the river Elbe, we entered the town of Halle early in the evening. This was to be our stopping place and thankfully we disembarked from the convoy. It seemed that at last we were on our way home. Once clear of the vehicles, we were led into the yard of what appeared to be a large warehouse. An American who was responsible for our welfare, climbed onto some stone steps where we could all see him, and bid us welcome to the American lines. I wasn't so concerned with the welcome, I wanted food first, the welcome could come later. Pointing to brick buildings which looked like storage places, he told us that we could bed down there, as there was plenty of space for us all. Nobody made a move towards the billets, but waited for the American to continue talking.

He seemed rather puzzled and after a short pause, informed us that we would meet him again in the morning. There was a stunned silence until someone shouted,
'When do we eat?'
'Sorry' came the reply 'the cookhouse is closed.'
'Right' shouted another, 'if you don't open it we will'.
For just a little while, things became very tense and I could see that there was about to be serious trouble. The American's attitude was quite aggressive, which made me believe that they were possibly no more friendly towards us than the Russians had been.

Faced with the threat of revolt, he backed down a little and asked us when we had last eaten.
'Yesterday' was the answer from most of us.
'Four years ago ' shouted one prisoner.
Such a clamour was set up by our demands for food, that he began to realise just how desperate we were. Calling for a chance to speak, he promised us that if we found ourselves a place to bed down for the night, then he would organise some food as soon as possible.

Doing as we were asked, we dispersed to find a bed space. The building I entered was quite old and consisted of three floors which were now empty of stock. The place which I chose to sleep, was a space on the wooden floor. The lack of comfort, didn't bother me at all, as food was the main consideration. I will say, that once the Americans got the message, it didn't take too long for the food to be produced. Apologies were made for the nature of the meal, but they had not expected to feed so many right away, in fact no preparations had been made. They needn't have apologised, as what we received was very good indeed. Maybe it was not a meal that a well fed person would have appreciated, but to us there was more than enough. Each prisoner received a small tin of meat, slices of white bread and some butter, followed by coffee. This was real coffee, not the German ersatz type made from acorns.

The coffee was very good and the meat even better, but what really impressed me most was the bread. It was proper white bread which tasted really marvellous, in fact it was so good to eat, I didn't even want any butter on it. I did try spreading some at first but considered it a sheer waste, so carried on eating slice after slice of plain bread. The strangest experience of all, was knowing that I could eat all that was in front of me, with no thought of saving any for another time as there would be more when required.

We had often discussed what we would do if presented with unlimited food and it was agreed that we would just keep on eating and eating. Our fantasies concerning food, involved really massive steaks, eggs, bacon, potatoes, in fact, all sorts of food in huge quantities. To match this, we imagined appetites of giants. Now we were facing the true facts, as one small tin of meat and the few slices of bread were proving too much for us. I saw many unfinished tins of meat, left by prisoners who were unable to cope. We were the group who not so long before, were so hungry that we were prepared to take the American cookhouse by storm if necessary.

That night was a disturbed one, as all night long prisoners were suffering stomach pains through overeating and being compelled to leave their beds to go outside. I felt a little uncomfortable I admit, but I had not been a long term prisoner as some of these were, my stomach had not shrunk quite so much.

The following morning, I felt more rested and relaxed, helped a lot by the knowledge that food and cigarettes were readily available. Now for the next stage of the journey wherever that might lead, and naturally enough I wanted it to happen immediately. We had been fed, watered and rested, what else was there to do, but climb on to a transport and get moving. There was only one problem, no transport was available. I wanted instant action which on consideration was quite unreasonable, as the Americans were dealing with not just a few prisoners, but hundreds.

What I felt or thought, made little difference, as we remained with the Americans for three days, a very long three days. Despite the impatience, it was appreciated that they would get us out as soon as possible, but it would take time as we were not their first concern. I had to do something to occupy my mind, so when one of the Americans asked a few of us to help in some domestic chores, I agreed to go along. If it had been washing and cleaning type chores, I would have opted out of that, but this proved to be a trip to the outskirts of town to collect logs for firewood. It was nothing very demanding and not a great contribution, but at least it was a little help in return for what they had done for us.

The following day I had a very interesting visit, one which was quite unexpected. A few of us were given permission to wander around the local German airfield, one which up to a short time before, had been operating against us. There were some damaged fighters and bombers lying around, wrecked by the departing Germans. Although unfit to fly, they were still almost intact, which enabled us to see the type of instrumentation and equipment they had used. With extreme caution, I climbed aboard one of them after being reassured that they had all been checked for booby traps. As none had been found, I was still a trifle apprehensive, in case there were some, very cleverly concealed.

It was a very eerie feeling sitting in a bomber and wondering what the crew may have been like and had they perhaps flown to England on bombing raids. The same with the fighters had they perhaps engaged us in combat from time to time, or maybe even shot us down. A trifle fanciful perhaps, although it was quite true that I had been bombed several times by such bombers and I had been in combat with the same types of fighters on more than one occasion. They looked so forlorn and powerless now, pushed to one side of the airfield. Never again were they likely to strike fear into the hearts of anybody as they may have done during their life span. If they were not to be used as museum pieces, then their likely fate was a breakers yard. Interesting as it had been, I was pleased to leave that airfield and the thoughts it conjured up.

On the third day we left for Brussels. We were loaded on to Dakota transport aircraft and sent on our way. It was a most uncomfortable journey due to the heat, the turbulence and a very uncomfortable canvas seat, also I felt air sick. Up to that stage of my short flying career, I had never experienced such a feeling and hoped that I would not disgrace myself by using the sick bag. It was not anxiety or even excitement, as I believe that at the time, my emotions were almost zero. If I felt anything at all, it was not because I was going home, it was only that I wanted to leave the area as quickly as possible, home didn't exist, but then nothing was real.

After a flight lasting approximately two hours, in which we bounced westwards across Europe, the aircraft finally landed at Brussels. On our arrival, we were met by the British authorities who were to look after us until the following day. It was then that we would be taken on the final leg to England. If nothing else, we were back with our own people, those who could understand what we were saying and even knew something about us. Very quickly we were taken into the city and billeted in hotels which had been especially set aside for the purpose.

After a meal and a chance to get cleaned up a little we were each given pocket money to do what we liked with and told to report again in the morning. Providing there were no problems due to the weather, we would then be taken back to the airfield for our flight home. I don't know how other prisoners felt, but once free to do exactly as I wished, I didn't know what to do, or even what I wanted to do. I wasn't mentally prepared for the city and felt quite out of place, I heard later that I was not alone in this.

There were several possible reasons for my frame of mind, the first was the state of my clothing. I was dressed as I had been for quite some time, an RAF battledress blouse, army trousers, wooden soled boots and a cap without a badge. My navigator's brevet, which I had given away while evading capture, was replaced by one I had made from pipe cleaners. This had not mattered much before, as my companions of recent months were in a similar state.

Anyone seeing us now, not knowing who we were, could well be forgiven for believing us to be guerilla fighters, or members of a rebel band. Everyone else we saw, who were not returning prisoners, seemed to be dressed in neat clean uniforms and shining footwear. This in itself was a complete contrast to the world we had just left, as we had been associating with troops who were either engaged in combat, or had just withdrawn from battle and were dressed accordingly. No big city life and atmosphere had been apparent in those forward areas.

Other things to contribute to the strange feeling, was seeing shops with goods in the windows, street lighting, and a general air of freedom. We had of course lived in a war time existence for several years, then suddenly been introduced to a peace time existence, while still retaining a war time mind. In one sense, I suppose we were rather like actors, who, walking on stage to take a final bow, discover that the audience has already gone home.

With some misgivings, I wandered out into Brussels in company with Tom. We had faced the problems of the march together and those during our stay at Luckenwalde, now we were to face a different experience and give each other moral support. He felt as I did but agreed we should do something and not just withdraw into our shells. I don't really know where we went as neither of us were particularly interested in Brussels, we were only passing time until our next journey. We did visit a bar, but I certainly didn't enjoy it, as we were so out of place amongst the various military personnel thronging the place. Some of them were very well dressed indeed and seemed to be wearing walking out, or special dress uniforms. They came from various countries, but none had anything in common with us, not even our own nationals. It may have been that they also had no idea who we were. This was quite a different Brussels to the one I had been imprisoned in nearly a year before, a Brussels that few of these would have known anything about. Some may have been in the battle to recapture the city, but even they would not have seen it as it was under the German occupation, a grim foreboding place. Finally, deciding that we had seen enough, we returned to the hotel to wait for morning.

Next day, with nothing to do except sit about until the transport arrived, I decided to do some shopping at a perfumery near the hotel, I wanted to buy something to take home as a present for my wife and perfume seemed to be a reasonable idea. Perhaps it was a strange thing to do under the circumstances, but I felt I had to take something back. The mere fact of using money and actually buying something with it, was still a tremendous novelty. The girl who sold me the perfume may have considered my attitude a little strange, as it took me quite a long time to decide to part with my money for what was little more than a sample size of perfume. The trouble was, I wanted it but felt reluctant to part with the money I had so recently been given. Later that day it would be little use to me, as I should be back in England where I could use proper money.

Sometime round about mid-morning, we were called to board the transport for the short trip to the airport. On arrival, we were assembled in groups to await an aircraft. These were arriving very frequently and as soon as they were loaded, took off again. Very soon it was our turn and I watched anxiously, as the Lancaster we were to board came in to land and taxied towards us. It was a strange sensation climbing into it, particularly as a passenger.

Somehow it didn't seem to be the same type of aircraft which I had left in such a hurry a few months previously. Everything was in its right place, the crew behaved in a normal manner and it was the same mark, yet somehow it felt different. The aircraft was not designed to carry passengers, only bombs, which meant that we had to sit on the floor over the bomb bay and brace ourselves for take-off. There was very little that we could see from our position, except through the very small windows in the side of the fuselage. It didn't matter to most, as all they wanted to see was England, they had seen enough of Europe to last then quite a long time. I must admit, I was just a little apprehensive as we made our take-off run, as this was to be the last stage of our journey to England. Safely airborne, I relaxed and waited until the aircraft levelled out before I moved forward to see where we were. In a very short time, the white cliffs of Dover appeared, a sight which many travellers had longed to see, the sight which meant home. One by one, the passengers were called forward to see what was to our eyes, a dramatic sight. They viewed it mostly in silence, then returned to their positions in the fuselage and waited for the next big moment, the landing. As the throttles were closed for the descent, there was some tension among us as this really was the final moment which had to go right. As the wheels touched, the tension relaxed and we waited patiently for the very last act, which was to step out onto the soil of home.

The door opened and the other passengers started to leave the aircraft, then it was my turn. I could smell the clean air, and see the green fields, it was wonderful, but then I discovered that I had a small personal ordeal to face. Standing waiting for me to get clear of the aircraft was a member of the Women's Auxiliary Air Force, in other words, a WAAF, who had come to escort me over to the reception hanger. I tried to avoid her, as I wanted to speak to no one, but she insisted on carrying my kit for me, so to avoid making a scene I allowed her to do so. I am afraid that at first I was not very communicative, until I discovered that she was one of a group of girls who had volunteered to help welcome returning prisoners. I learned that most, if not all of them, had lost husbands or boyfriends and while helping us, were asking questions in an attempt to ascertain their fate. I only wished that I had cheering news for her, but there was none.

While walking from the aircraft and talking, I didn't notice where we were going, so it came as a surprise to me, when the WAAF handed me my kitbag and wished me good luck. We had stopped near a group of men who looked like medical orderlies. One of them beckoned me over towards a stretcher and told me to lie down. This of course was a mistake, I was quite fit and told him so. Unfortunately he insisted, so wonderingly I did as I was asked. The reason soon became clear as advancing on me was an orderly armed with a great big syringe filled with delousing powder. Rather unceremoniously, he puffed powder up my arms, down my neck, then the greatest indignity of all, up my trouser legs. At last, free to go, I waddled off looking like a disgruntled flour sack, to an overwhelming committee of welcome, I really was home.

The day, 27 May 1945.

Warrant Officer Navigator Stephen Masters, R.A.F., aged 22, has arrived home at 21, Knowsley Road, Cosham, after being a prisoner of war. He is the eldest son of Mr. and Mrs. C. S. Masters who were bombed out at North End. W.O. Masters enlisted in August, 1941, and after 24 operational flights over France and Germany his plane was hit over Amiens on June 19, 1944. Four of the crew were killed, but he escaped by parachute. He was in a forced march for 21 days from Breslau, but was released by the Russians soon after.

Postscript

The homecoming was not quite as joyful as it could have been, as it was not until then that we discovered the fate of the other crew members. We three, that is Ron the Flight Engineer, Nat the Wireless Operator and myself were the only survivors. It was the outcome we had anticipated, as the chances of survival of Alan the Pilot and the Gunners Tom and Bill, had been almost nil, even ours had been slim. The one fatality we pondered on was that of Speed the Bomb Aimer, as he had baled out before me. I have since been told that he was killed on landing.

It has now become apparent that none of us had much of a chance to escape, as I estimated that the aircraft hit the ground fourteen seconds after Ron left it and he was first, Nat being fourth to jump, could have had little more than ten seconds. We were lucky, we returned but the others who failed to do so, are now interred in Arras along with many more who never made it.

They have become just another statistic to all but a few friends and relatives. Upon reflection and considering all that happened, it is quite remarkable that any of us returned, let alone all three. According to what I was told by the Germans, the survival rate for aircrew whose aircraft were shot down, was one and a half men per aircraft. If this was fact, then we had come out of it quite well, working on that average. Having survived the first calamity we then suffered the rigours of POW camps, where sickness, lack of food, enemy action, or accident could have claimed us. This was followed by the march, which in itself was a major hazard. The final stage, the Russian attack, was perhaps the most dangerous.

Because of the march, we had evaded the Russian advance on the Oder by a narrow margin, only to be placed into what became a very exposed position, just a few miles South of the main target Berlin. Any advance on the capital, would almost certainly have overrun us, whether they were Russians or Americans.

It took a few weeks for the last assault to develop, as at first the Russians, having reached the Oder, remained there a while before breaking out and turning north to Berlin. In the meantime, other Russian forces were making directly for Berlin from the East. The German troops, retreating from these advances, now found themselves trapped in the narrow segment south of Berlin, They could go no further West as the British and American forces were waiting on the other side of the Elbe. If they meant to defend the capital, they had to stand before it.

Referring to a historical analysis of that particular sector of the war, the Russians had mounted their new campaign to overrun Germany in mid January 1945. The area in Silesia where our prison camp Luft 7 had been situated, came under attack by forces led by Marshall Konev. A few weeks later on 16 April 1945, the Russians moved out from their positions on the Oder and Neisse rivers and turned towards Berlin. It is reported that they had 2.5 million men, 6250 tanks and 7500 aircraft. The Germans faced them with one million men, 1500 tanks and 3300 aircraft. It was during this period of the final assault on Berlin that we were overrun at Luckenwalde by one of the armoured spear heads.

Looking at the disposition and size of the opposing forces, it is a wonder that we came out of it virtually unscathed. It is true that not all prisoners were so lucky, although the majority survived. Being thankful to have returned, I attempted to settle down to a normal life again but fate plays very odd tricks, as within a short space of time, about three years in fact, I found myself back in Germany. I had been very anxious to leave it and had done so helped by the Russians. Now I was back, trying to break a blockade of Berlin, imposed by those same Russians. The job was to airlift food and supplies to the beleaguered city, an operation which became widely known as the 'Berlin Airlift'

I wondered at times what I was doing there as ex-prisoners like myself were given the option to withdraw but none to my knowledge did so. Perhaps I stayed because I knew what it was like to be starving as they were, or I may have stayed because I couldn't settle.

One day while standing on the airfield at Wunstorf near Hanover, I had a very strange conversation with a German, who was quite a few years older than myself. The weather was bitterly cold and in general the flying conditions were poor. Quite unexpectedly, he remarked that he and his wife felt sorry for the aircrew who were flying on the 'Airlift'. I asked him why he felt this way and he told me it was because of the conditions we were facing. I pointed out to him that not long before we had been doing our best to destroy each other, yet now he felt concern for us. He agreed, but pointed out that the war was over and now we were risking ourselves to protect his countrymen, while he and his kind were powerless to do very much to help. I keep finding that life is very strange and quite unpredictable.

About the Author

Steve Masters was born in Portsmouth in January 1923 and was educated at the Technical School (now the Portsmouth Building School). On leaving school he became an apprentice shipwright in the Naval Dockyard. During this time he became a member of the Dockyard Home Guard and was on duty at the first large scale bombing of Portsmouth on the 10th January 1941. On returning home he discovered that the local area had been severely damaged, but fortunately all the family was safe. He decided then that he wanted to join the Royal Navy, but was told that because he was serving in the naval dockyard this was not allowed, it was a reserved occupation. He discovered that he would be able to join the Royal Air Force, providing he agreed to complete his apprenticeship when the war was over.

In 1941 Steve joined the RAF as a trainee Aircrew Navigator at the age of 17½ and in October 1942 started flying training in South Africa and qualified as an Air Navigator in January 1943. After further training he joined Bomber Command 622 Squadron at RAF Mildenhall in November 1943. In April 1944 he joined No. 7 Squadron P.F.F Oakington (Path Finder Force). He was shot down in Northern France over Arras in June 1944 after 24 operations when this story starts.

Steve was repatriated after the end of the war in June 1945 and released from the RAF in 1946. He volunteered to rejoin the RAF in 1947 and joined Transport Command. In July 1948 he was flying supplies into Berlin as part of the 'Berlin Airlift' until August 1949.

Between September 1949 to 1954 Steve joined Bomber Command and eventually became a Navigation Instructor and then a Link Trainer Instructor. In September 1954 he was flying in night fighters, first from Leeming - North Yorkshire and then from Wahn near Cologne in Germany until July 1957 when he joined a Communications Flight transporting senior officers.

In July 1958 Steve joined an Air Sea Rescue squadron 275 based in Leconfield - West Yorkshire and in August 1958 moved to Aldergrove in Northern Ireland, returning to Leconfield in May 1959 and continued with the Air Sea Rescue until November 1960.

Following a short re-training period, Steve was posted to RAF Seletar Singapore in March 1961 where he flew in Twin Pioneers transporting troops and equipment into the Malayan peninsula and to Brunei and Borneo, mostly to jungle landing strips. It was during this time that the Brunei revolution took place. In August 1963, he returned to the UK first to join Officers Training School but withdrew, partly from ill health at the time and partly because he was told that he would be 'flying a desk' on completion of the course. He then joined a Communications Squadron, first at White Waltham and then at Odiham, through to June 1965 when he retired from the RAF with a heavy heart. He told his brother Doug that he thought it strange that when he was not flying he thought he ought to be and then when he did he wondered why?

On leaving the RAF Steve joined a large retailer in the role of Time and Motion study manager in their warehouse. He never particularly enjoyed this role and decided to join the Concord(e) project around 1967, where he was arranging safety procedures for pilots with the aid of a simulator, first in Toulouse and then in Filton (Bristol). This made him a great deal happier as he was working on a pioneering project with aircrew and was also able to use his Time and Motion experience.

In 1988 Steve finally retired, but became enthusiastic with fund raising for the RNLI inspired by the time he spent with Life Boat crews and the admiration he had for them when he was with the Air Sea Rescue squadrons. He also spent time woodworking which had always been a hobby. First of all he made toys for his grandchildren and once people in the local area got wind of this, he started taking orders but only ever covered his costs, but he put a great deal of time and care into these projects.

Sadly Steve died in November 1995 at the age of 72 due to cancer, leaving his wife, two children and their spouses and two grandchildren.

Steve Masters at a 7 Squadron
Reunion in May 1995

With thanks to Steve's brother Doug Masters for input to this brief history.

Printed in Great Britain
by Amazon